Two week loan

Please return on or before the last date stamped below.
Charges are made for late return.

0 3 OCT 1996 CANCELLED		
19 JAN 1998		
-4 MAY 1999 CANCELLED		
2 4 CANCELLED		
3 CANCELLED 1999		
19 MAR 2001 CANCELLED		
WITHDRAWN		

Managing Policy Change in Britain:
The Politics of Water

Managing Policy Change in Britain:
The Politics of Water

WILLIAM A. MALONEY
and JEREMY RICHARDSON

EDINBURGH UNIVERSITY PRESS

For Patricia Josephine Maloney
and
Jack Mazey-Richardson

© W. A. Maloney and J. J. Richardson, 1995

Edinburgh University Press Ltd
22 George Square, Edinburgh

Typeset in Linotron Times
by Koinonia, Bury, and
printed and bound in Great Britain

A CIP record for this book is available from
the British Library

ISBN 0 7486 0669 6

Contents

Tables, Appendices and Figures

List of Abbreviations

AONB	Areas of Outstanding Natural Beauty
AWE	Association of Water Engineers
BA	British Airways
BMA	British Medical Association
BMU	Building Maintenance Unit
BT	British Telecom
BWA	British Waterworks Association
CAWC	Central Advisory Water Committee
CBI	Confederation of British Industry
CCA	Current Cost Accounting
CCC	Consumer Consultative Committee
CIA	Chemical Industries Association
CLA	Country Landowners Association
CPPU	Central Policy Planning Unit
CPRE	Council for the Protection of Rural England
CSC	Consumer Service Committees
DGFT	Director General of Fair Trading
DGWS	Director General of Water Services
DOE	Department of the Environment
DHSS	Department of Health and Social Security
DTI	Department of Trade and Industry
DWI	Drinking Water Inspectorate
EA	Environment Agency
EC	European Community
ECJ	European Court of Justice
EEC	European Economic Community
EFL	External Financing Limit
ENDS	Environmental Data Services Report
EU	European Union
FOE	Friends of the Earth

FSB	Federation of Small Businesses
HC	House of Commons
HCA	Historic Cost Accounting
HL	House of Lords
HMIP	Her Majesty's Inspectorate of Pollution
ICE	Institution of Civil Engineers
IEEP	Institute of European Environmental Policy
IIMD	International Institute for Management Development
IMF	International Monetary Fund
IPHE	Institute of Public Health Engineers
IRBM	Integrated River Basin Management
IWE	Institute of Water Engineers
IWEM	Institution of Water and Environmental Management
IWES	Institution of Water Engineers and Scientists
IWPC	Institution of Water Pollution Control
MAC	Maximum Admissible Concentration
MAFF	Ministry of Agriculture, Fisheries and Food
MHLG	Ministry of Housing and Local Government
MMC	Monopolies and Merger Commission
MSC	Management Structure Committee
NALGO	National and Local Government Officers Association
NAO	National Audit Office
NBC	National Bus Company
NFU	National Farmers' Union
NLF	National Loans Fund
NCC	National Consumer Council
NRA	National Rivers Authority
NUPE	National Union of Public Employees
NWC	National Water Council
OFT	Office of Fair Trading
OFTEL	Office of Telecommunications
OFWAT	Office of Water Services
ONCC	OFWAT National Customer Council
PSBR	Public Sector Borrowing Requirement
RCC	Regional Consultative Council
RCEP	Royal Commission for Environmental Pollution
RRCC	Regional Recreation Conservation Committee
RSG	Rate Support Grant
RSPB	Royal Society for the Protection of Birds
RWA	Regional Water Authorities
SAS	Surfers Against Sewage
SCC	Scottish Consumer Council
SCCS	Scottish Chambers of Commerce

SLF	Scottish Landowners' Federation
SSSI	Sites of Special Scientific Interest
STUC	Scottish Trades Union Congress
SWC	Statutory Water Companies
SWCA	Statutory Water Companies Association
SWQO	Statutory Water Quality Objective
TGWU	Transport and General Workers Union
WAA	Water Authorities Association
WASC	Water and Sewerage Companies
WAC	Water Companies Association
WOC	Water only Companies
WRB	Water Resources Board
WQO	Water Quality Objective
WSA	Water Services Association
WSAC	Water and Space Amenity Commission
WSPLC	Water Service Public Limited Companies

Preface

The effective management of natural resources is one of the most important functions of a civilised society. Similarly, the supply of basic utilities, such as energy and water, is an indicator of the extent to which a society can meet the basic needs of its citizens. In advanced industrial societies, both of these functions are invariably subject to some form of public regulation. This is especially true for the utilities, as they are often natural monopolies. This regulation varies from outright public ownership to the statutory regulation of private monopolies. A study of the politics of water, therefore, should prove a fruitful analysis of the role of the state and its capacity to steer or control a policy sector of central importance to society.

Our study is concerned with a fifty year period of water policy in Britain and our hope is that our analysis will shed light on the process of policy change over time. In doing so, we have the added objective of testing the utility of one particular, rather dominant, 'model' of analysis – the so-called policy community/policy network approach to the analysis of the policy process. The model was developed at a time when the British policy process appeared to be characterised by policy stability, considerable consensus and fairly stable patterns of participation in the policy process. However, the 1980s and 1990s have seen quite rapid policy change in all western democracies – especially in Britain. Many policy sectors – including water – have been subject to a degree of turbulence hitherto unknown, and it is possible that the network 'model' is exhibiting intellectual fatigue.

In selecting water as our case-study, we have built upon our previous work with our colleagues Grant Jordan and Wolfgang Rüdig, to whom we owe a considerable debt. We also owe a considerable debt to the Anglo–German Foundation for its crucial and generous support of our research. As always we are indebted to those directly involved in the policy process. They are too numerous to list individually. However, we are especially grateful to the Water Services Association and its staff at Queen Anne's Gate for their willing assistance to us over many years. Similarly, Bill Harper and his colleagues at Thames Water, and Sir Gordon Jones and his colleagues at Yorkshire Water have been very generous with their time. Without the constant patience of people in the industry – always willing to tolerate our lack of detailed knowledge – this project would have been impossible. We owe an especial debt to Peter Hall who has done much to educate us over the years and who kindly read through an earlier draft of this manuscript. His knowledge of the industry has helped us to avoid many basic errors! Any remaining errors of fact or interpretation are, of course, the sole responsibility of the authors. We should also like to thank Marie Lucas and Linda Bromley for typing successive drafts of this manuscript and Mark McAteer for reading and commenting on the proofs. Their skill and good humour have been invaluable to us, as has the assistance of Annabel Kiernan in preparing the tables.

Finally, we have dedicated this book to two people who died as it was being completed – Patricia Josephine Maloney and Jack Mazey-Richardson.

PART 1

Managing a Backwater

1

Analysing Policy Change: Technical Problems and Political Solutions

We trained hard, but it seemed that every time we were beginning to form up into teams we would be reorganised. I was to learn later that we tend to meet any new situation by reorganising, and what a wonderful method it can be for creating the illusion of progress while producing confusion, inefficiency and demoralisation.

Petronius, AD 66

THE TECHNICAL AND POLITICAL DICHOTOMY

As John Kingdon suggests in his pioneering study of the agenda setting process, there are three kinds of processes involved in determining the political agenda – problems, policies and politics (Kingdon, 1984, p. 17). Of particular importance to this study is his observation that agendas can be influenced by the 'inexorable march of problems pressing in on the system'. Arguably, water is the most important utility service. Thus, in most industrialised societies – and in probably all developing societies – the disposal of waste and the supply of clean water have become an ever-pressing and worsening problem. As demand for water increases, and as agricultural and industrial development creates further problems of water pollution, so public policies have to be developed in order for societies to cope – indeed for them to survive. Of equal importance to the actual trajectory of the water supply problem is the increasing amount of scientific knowledge that there now is of pollution and its effects on man's health and on the natural environment. Again, as Kingdon suggests, a second contributor to governmental agendas and alternatives is the 'process of gradual accumulation of knowledge and perspectives among specialists in a given policy area, and the generation of policy proposals by such specialists' (ibid. p. 18). Thus, real world problems do not exist in isolation as some objective phenomenon. They are interpreted by specialists (who may often disagree); possible solutions are not neutral as between different sets of interests in society; and political decisions are needed to mediate between competing interests, competing ideas and competing values. This study of the formation and implementation of water policy in Britain over the period 1944–94 is, therefore, a study of the processes by which the technical problem of meeting increased demands on waste disposal and water supply systems has been mediated through the political process.

To many readers it may seem odd that there is a 'problem' for public policy to solve. Britain is a relatively wet country and would not generally be thought to have a water supply problem. Moreover, as a small island surrounded by large oceans, it has some natural advantages, in terms of waste disposal, not enjoyed by many of its European neighbours. Neither natural asset has prevented water from becoming a focus of a long period of public policy and organisational change or of intense public debate. Only Scotland has escaped the technical need for policy change largely because its natural supply of water is so plentiful compared with the situation in England and Wales. Even in Scotland, however, water has more recently achieved a very high degree of political salience and a high degree of political mobilisation – thus illustrating the argument that public policy-making is not solely 'problem driven' but is also driven by politics and ideology. For the English particularly, there have been growing problems of water supply and waste disposal caused by the pattern of urban and industrial development and the unavailability of water. Inevitably, therefore, policy change has taken place. Without it, major water supply crises would have occurred, in addition to the serious problems caused by occasional droughts. Moreover, perceptions and expectations have been changing also, often encouraged (or caused by) a significant 'Europeanisation' of the policy sector and by policy change itself.

In practice, technical problems which affect society are solved (or not) by a process of public policy-making, often involving a whole range of actors. In this study of policy-making, however, the technical problem is the starting-point of the political process. For example, actual and projected water sharing difficulties exerted a strong influence on the major reforms introduced by the Water Act 1973. Data appeared to indicate that England and Wales were likely to face water supply problems as a consequence of economic growth, changing consumption patterns, increased pollution of surface and groundwater, and the disequilibrum between supply and demand in certain regions. The basic problem with which politicians and administrators had to deal is illustrated in Table 1.1.

Table 1.1 illustrates the levels of residual rainfall across Britain and the different water sharing problems faced by different countries in Britain as well as the different problems facing the various regions in England. For example, England and Wales had an annual average rainfall (between 1941 and 1970) of 912 mm for supplying a population of some 50 million, although there is a sharp rainfall gradient across the country. In contrast, Scotland had an average rainfall of 1,431 mm and a population of only some 5 million. (However, even Scotland has experienced droughts.)

Something as simple as the distribution of rainfall can have profound policy implications, of course. Porter identifies three natural characteristics of the hydrological system which have implications for management structures. First are the flow characteristics of water. These may enable successive downstream use of water but may be insufficient to prevent upstream abstractions or discharges from having envi-

TABLE 1.1: Residual rainfall (annual averages) and abstractions.

Region	Average annual rainfall 1941–70 (mm)	Average annual residual rainfall (mm)	% residual rainfall committed to abstractions	Density of popula-ation (per km²)	Population (000)	Area (km²)
Thames	704	225	55	836	11,500	13,750
Severn-Trent	773	300	37	383	8,300	21,650
Southern	787	310	25	411	4,300	10,450
Yorkshire	818	380	23	338	4,600	13,600
Anglian	611	150	18	204	5,600	27,500
North West	1,217	750	14	471	6,800	14,445
Welsh	1,334	870	10	145	3,100	21,300
Northumbrian	879	450	9	276	2,600	9,400
Wessex	864	410	9	250	2,500	10,000
South-West	1,194	680	3	138	1,500	10,880
England and Wales	912	460	16	334	50,800	152,000
Scotland	1,431	–	–	65	5,100	77,750

SOURCE: Kinnersley, 1994, p. 40.

ronmental effects on downstream quality and quantity. Thus, depending on the flow characteristics, policy-makers may face serious problems relating to externalities – in this case upstream users imposing costs on downstream users. (Externalities are defined by Kinnersley as 'essentially unintended or indivisible, not part of any conventional market transaction, but none the less able to distort market transactions and prices' [Kinnersley, 1994, p. 17]). Second is the natural association of ground-water and river flow, both of which need to be managed in a co-ordinated and complimentary fashion. Third, as outlined above, is the uneven physical distribution of natural resources (Porter, 1978).

These three technical characteristics, taken together, almost suggest their own administrative solution – the management of the total hydrological cycle for each river basin or group of river basins. As the cycle is an interrelated process, it seems rational for administrative logic to follow technical logic. In a sense, the technical imperative is so strong that the necessary public policy almost writes itself. It is not surprising, therefore, that the concept of Integrated River Basin Management (IRBM), with its choice of the river basin as the basic water management unit, was seen as a rational means of exploiting natural hydrological and topographical features where precipitation is collected and used for its many, often conflicting, purposes. IRBM is an administrative system which seeks to reduce externality problems by making the organisation which is responsible for the supply and distribution of clean water also responsible for the collection of discharged waste. The natural flow characteristics of water mean that when the administrative boundaries are hydrologically based, problems cannot be passed on so easily to neighbours. Thus, there is a strong disincentive to allow the discharge effluent without consideration of environmental and economic impacts.

In addition to the purely technical benefits of having integrated multi-purpose organisations based upon the IRBM concept, there are also claimed to be administrative and financial benefits, as follows (McDonald and Kay, 1988, pp. 42–3):

1. Small systems generate insufficient revenues. This weak financial base constrains possible expansion and improvement.
2. Reduction of competition among utilities encourages a socially equitable allocation of resources within the region as a whole.
3. Amalgamation of utilities encourages economies of scale and allows the provision of specialist facilities and staff that could not be justified within each smaller authority.
4. Larger management units facilitate basin-wide integration of functions and encourage long-term planning.
5. Water resource fluctuations, which can be severe over a small area, are generally moderated in a regional context.

There are, of course, administrative (and political) disbenefits of a regionalised system, as follows (ibid., p. 43):

1. The excessive concentration of power within one organisation.
2. The dilemma which results from the requirement of the same organisation to both operate a resource system and enforce controls on that operation.
3. The growth in administrative bureaucracy that may slow decision-making and which separates decision-makers from the community which they serve.

Thus, a nice simple solution to a straightforward technical problem appears not so simple after all. Like many public policies, the devil is in the detail!

In this respect water is no different from other utilities. Bumstead has argued that the combination of factors which shape the development of regional or area-wide utilities, 'is based upon 70% politics, 20% engineering knowhow and 10% luck' (Bumstead, 1979, p. 708). Similarly, in commenting on the history of water policy, David Kinnersley reminds us:

> The management of water requires a large technical input for which the skills of engineers and scientists are still crucial. But the conspicuous change in the last fifteen years or so is how prominent and compelling economic, social and legislative, or regulatory, issues have become. (1994, p. xii)

In practice, therefore, water policy in Britain has not remained as a classic example of a professionalised sector of public policy. Over the past decade, particularly, water policy has been transformed from a technical policy area characterised by extremely low political salience and professional dominance, to a more politicised policy sector involving a much wider range of actors. This transformation is in part due to the fact that the supply of water in England and Wales is now wholly undertaken by private companies. This institutional arrangement contrasts with the situation in many other advanced economies where water supply and sewage disposal remain in the public sector, possibly reflecting the very special position which water holds in public perceptions. The very fact of privatisation has, therefore, become entangled in debates about the rising costs of water and the increased costs of dealing with more complex waste. These problems would have arisen in any case (as would have the major effects of Europeanisation), but questions such as high profits for privatised water companies and high earnings for their senior executives have been linked to the debate about how the basic need for clean water should be met. Moreover, rising costs have been attributed to a particular policy change – privatisation – when costs would have had to rise under any system, either public, private or a hybrid of both.

REFORM BECOMES ADDICTIVE?

The water industry in England and Wales has been subject to two *major* reorganisations in the relatively short time-span of fifteen years: *regionalisation* in 1974 and *privatisation* in 1989. Regionalisation in England and Wales created an organisational structure which radically reduced the number of administrative units and created boundaries based upon the IRBM concept discussed above, that is, the 1974 reforms were essentially a technical/rational/professional solution to possible supply shortages. Later, privatisation undermined this technical solution to a considerable degree, for example by separating environmental control from water supply and sewage disposal and by setting up a completely new regulatory regime. In short, the 1989 reorganisation was, in contrast, more economic/ideological, than technical/rational in its origins.

Following that reform, the ten former RWAS – now Water and Sewerage Companies (WASCs) – created under the Water Act 1973, supply water to approximately 75 per cent of consumers in England and Wales, and provide all the sewage and sewerage services in their areas. The remaining 25 per cent of water is supplied by twenty-one Water Only Companies (WOCS) (formerly Statutory Water Companies (SWCS) (OFWAT, 1994) which are not involved in sewage collection.[2] In fact, private water companies have been supplying water in Britain for over a century.

While the privatisation of the water industry appears to represent a radical break with the past, it is worth highlighting the fact that in Britain in the late nineteenth and early twentieth century, water was supplied by private organisations. At that time the municipalisation of water services replaced private ownership largely because of two main factors. First, parliamentary-sanctioned regulation of private concerns proved to be unsatisfactory. Secondly, private ownership appeared to be an inappropriate institutional structure because companies failed to attain the necessary profit levels required to make the industry an economically viable proposition. The municipalities saw water, as well as other utilities such as gas and electricity, as a useful source of funds to enhance their development. Thus, in the water sector the institutional structure has turned full circle: from private ownership, to predominantly municipal control and back to private ownership. Indeed, it could be argued that there was more meaningful competition at the turn of the century than is currently the case. For example, three companies (London Bridge, New River and Chelsea) operated in London. However, such competition in water markets led to 'high costs, poor quality service, and low dividends' (Foreman-Peck and Millward, 1994, pp. 30–1).

At the outset, one must also be attentive to some of the special characteristics of water. First, it is probably the most essential utility service, and has significant implications for public health. Secondly, it has certain natural properties, which, given the current level of technology, are unalterable – for example, its hydrological, geographical and topographical characteristics. Thirdly, the water industry is a natural monopoly *par excellence*. The sector comprises a capital intensive network structure through which water is distributed to comparatively large numbers of customers from a relatively small number of locations. The sunk costs involved in the provision of water services mean that one producer can supply the good at a lower aggregate cost than could two or more firms in a competitive environment. One monopolist supplier is the most efficient means through which economies of scale can be maximised. Potential competitors are discouraged from entering the market because they would find it uneconomical to replicate the high sunk costs. All of these factors have significant ramifications for the institutional structure of the water industry, and its management and regulation – and for the politics of water. No wonder, therefore, that David Kinnersley, a senior figure in the industry for many years, felt it appropriate to title one of his books on the industry *Troubled Water: Rivers, Politics and Pollution* (Kinnersley, 1988).

MODELS OF POLICY CHANGE

That water policy in Britain has seen a long period of policy change is beyond doubt. Making sense of this change process is more difficult, if only because it is impossible to *measure* change in any meaningful sense. From the outside the picture of change may appear quite different from the perception of those directly involved in the process. At first sight the 1974 reforms, for example, appear to be a major shift in the direction of public policy. Gray (1982) perceives the 1974 reorganisation as a 'radical restructuring', while Jordan et al. (1977) describe it as 'a very sudden rejection ... of the previous system' (Jordan et al., 1977, p. 318). Such labels suggest that this change represented a radical departure from exisiting public policy for water. Hence the 1974 reform of water policy in England and Wales can be presented as one of the best (and rare) examples of radical policy change seen in the British post-war polity. Viewed without any historical or longitudinal perspective, 'policy radicalism' appears to provide an appropriate description. However, if one charts the development of the industry in greater detail and over a longer period, a process of policy succession is discernible. Thus, it appears that policy development in the water sector may often have a closer relationship to the process of policy succession than policy innovation, which any one 'snap-shot' would suggest.

Policy succession can be characterised as 'the extent to which the policy actors, the process, and the substantive outcomes of the policy succession process are all shaped by the existing policies which succession is intended to replace' (Hogwood and Peters, 1983, p. 131). Policy succession involves the purposive replacement of existing policies within the same policy sector. However, while it may entail certain novel elements, governments are not becoming embroiled in a completely new area of uncharted activity when attempting policy succession. Moreover, the process of policy succession appears to be a common phenomenon in western polities. Hogwood and Peters (ibid.) and Hogwood (1987, p. 35) suggest three main reasons for this:

1. There are relatively few areas in which the Government does not already have some involvement.
2. Existing policy itself leads to the emergence of issues for resolution.
3. The pressure of commitments or resources means that new demands which require expenditure will be less likely to get serious attention.

Thus, as Lindblom points out, we find that 'policy is not made once and for all; it is re-made endlessly. Policy-making is a process of successive approximation to some desired objectives in which what is desired itself continues to change under reconsideration' (Lindblom, 1959, p. 86). Lindblom perceived policy as being the result of a series of successive steps, with each change building upon its predecessor.

The operation and outcomes of existing policies may be the catalyst for successive or, indeed, for radical policy change. New policy proposals emerge not as a consequence of an absence of policy in a sector, but usually because of difficulties inherent in current policies, or because of unforeseen or adverse consequences resulting from the interaction of diverse and sometimes incongruous policy programmes. As Aaron Wildavsky pointed out, *policy is evermore its own cause.* Wildavsky maintained that the shape and direction of past policies can be, and on many occasions are, the most significant element to which all future policies have to adapt. Thus, 'more and more public policy is about coping with the consequences of past policies' (Wildavsky, 1979, p. 4).

The development of water policy in Britain as policy succession has been implicitly identified by many observers. For example, the Association of River Authorities welcomed the publication of the Water Bill in 1972 (subsequently the Water Act 1973) by stating that the regionalisation proposals represented a 'logical development of its own members' work in water and conservation management' (*The Guardian*, 14 January 1972). Porter has also drawn our attention to the fact that the Water Act 1973, which came into effect on 1 April 1974, 'builds upon a body of water law and practice developed gradually over the last century' (Porter 1978, p. 18).

Yet policy change might be characterised as both *successive* and simultaneously *innovative*. The juxtaposition of the two concepts may initially appear quite contradictory. However, innovative or radical policy change can emerge from a series of successive steps. Lindblom noted that change tends to add up, 'often more happens than meets the eye' (Lindblom, 1979, p. 139). The cumulative effect of such change can be great. To quote Lindblom:

A fast-moving sequence of small changes can more speedily accomplish a drastic alteration of the *status quo* than can an only infrequent major policy change. If the speed of change is the product of size of steps times frequency of step, incremental change patterns are, under ordinary circumstances, the fastest method of change available. One might reply of course that drastic steps in policy need be no more infrequent than incremental steps. We can be reasonably sure, however, that in almost all circumstances that suggestion is false. Incremental steps can be made quickly because they are only incremental. They do not rock the boat, do not stir up the great antagonisms and paralyzing schisms as do proposals for more drastic change. (ibid., p. 131)

Lindblom's advocacy of incrementalism was based upon the view that it was not only an operating procedure in much policy-making but was also a functional necessity. Within policy sectors, and more significantly within policy networks, incrementalism 'reduces the stakes in each political controversy, thus encouraging losers to bear their losses without disrupting the political system. It helps maintain the vague general consensus on basic values' (ibid., p. 131). Thus, as far as interest group politics is concerned:

> what has been agreed in the past – what is the base – is not itself an arbitrary position but represents a negotiated balance. Current negotiations presumably involve similar interests, conflicts over values, preferences and demands, and accordingly it is likely that any current agreement will differ only marginally from the previous position, unless of course the balance of group power has shifted. (Richardson and Jordan, 1979, p. 23)

However, our focus here is on policy succession – not necessarily the same as incrementalism. As Hogwood and Peters highlight, *incrementalists* appear to argue that all change 'short of wars, revolutions and crises are incremental'. However, it is clear that not all change is of a similar size (Hogwood and Peters, 1983, p. 10). Policy succession specifies the direction of change and allows for change to be greater than a minor adjustment. Thus change need not always be minor and/or humdrum, even if it is built upon previous policies. Moreover, as we shall see, the balance of group power does, indeed, shift under certain circumstances.

TECHNOCRATS AND THE POLICY-MAKING PROCESS

No lesson ... seems to be so deeply inculcated by the experience of life as that you never should trust experts. If you believe the doctors, nothing is wholesome; if you believe the theologians, nothing is innocent; if you believe the soldiers, nothing is safe. They all require to have their strong wine diluted by a very large admixture of insipid common sense.

Lord Salisbury, as Secretary of State for India, 1877

> *How rarely have additions to the public sector been initiated by the demands of voters or the advocacy of pressure groups or the platforms of political parties. On the contrary, in the field of health, housing, urban renewal, transportation, welfare, education, poverty, and energy, it has been, in very great measure, people in government service, or closely associated with it, acting on the basis of their specialised and technical knowledge, who first perceived the problem, conceived the program, initially urged it on the president and congress, went on to help lobby it through to enactment, and then saw to its administration.*
>
> Samuel H. Beer, 'Federalism, Nationalism, and Democracy in America', Presidential Address, The American Political Science Association, 1978

For long periods in the water sector this has been the case. Since the Victorian era technocrats, in this case water engineers, have defined the basic problems facing the sector, and have proposed and implemented the(ir) solutions. Their involvement in the sector throughout the twentieth century is easily charted, although their role has not been without controversy. For example, the Advisory Committee on Water, established by the Ministry of Health in 1919, was criticised for being a very sectional body – the majority of its membership being drawn from three professional associations: the Association of Waterworks Engineers (AWE), the British Waterworks Association (BWA) and the Water Companies Association (WCA). Similarly, the Central Advisory Water Committee, established in 1937 to represent a wider range of interests, appeared to come to conclusions which reflected technocratic thinking. As Hassan points out, while, 'it was a very influential source of advice to government between 1937 and 1945 ... [it] recommended nothing that seriously threatened municipal, corporate or professional water-supply interests' (Hassan, 1993, p. 20). A degree of professional 'capture' of these so-called advisory bodies seems to have occurred.

Professionalism, or more accurately technocracy, that is, decision-making power and criteria being based on technical expertise, is not an especially new phenomenon – it dates back to the seventeenth century at least. In classical political terms technocracy relates 'to a system of government in which technically trained experts rule by virtue of their specialist knowledge and position in dominant political and economic institutions' (Fischer, 1990, p. 17). Technocrats are probably among some of the most successful interest groups in both the UK and the US polities. As Rhodes argues, 'Professional influence is exercised in traditional interest group activities (e.g. lobbying); it is institutionalized in policy networks; and it sets the parameters to decision-making through national level ideological structure' (Rhodes, 1988, p. 79). Technical dominance can create a general consensus which can then lead to policy outputs reflecting the perceptions (and solutions) of technical experts and framed in a way which is difficult for others to challenge. These professional groups can exercise influence without necessarily participating *directly* in the policy process 'since some consequential actors can, without any overt action on their part, have their interests taken into account through the reactions of other core members who anticipate their interests in particular policies' (Laumann and Knoke, 1987, p. 11).

Similarly, Beer identifies what he terms a 'professional bureaucratic complex', as follows:

> The main component in any such complex is a core of officials with scientific or professional training. This bureaucratic core also normally works closely with two other components: certain interested legislators, especially the chairmen of the relevant and specialised subcommittees, and the spokesmen for the group that benefits from the program. (Beer, 1978, p. 17)

One of the strengths of the professions is their homogeneity. For example, Dunleavy (1981) sees professions as groups with a relatively high level of 'internal specificity and identity' sharing 'significant common interests, orientations and values' (ibid., p. 8). They exhibit a tendency to interpenetrate both the public and the private spheres, as well as numerous levels of the governmental system. Dunleavy also stresses the importance of the ideology of professionalism which justifies the maintenance of significant levels of work autonomy. The framing of public policy issues in terms of technical solution and problems also supports Schattschneider's view that the privileged few exercise the power over the choice of conflicts and the definition of issues in society (Schattschneider, 1960). There is also a tendency for policy implementation to be achieved in a manner compatible with professional practices and principles, with considerable erosion of the distinction between policy formulation and policy implementation. As Dunleavy argues:

> In some areas the distinction between formulation and implementation may dissolve altogether; implementation may be constitutive of policy, so that policy is just what professionals in the field do, having no really separate existence at any other level of the decision making process. (1981, p. 13)

Thus, technocrats have autonomy in three distinct senses: first, in their capacity as self-regulators and self-governors; secondly, in their role as autonomous sources of influence in the decision-making process, and thirdly, at the implementation stage of the policy process. The professionalisation process leads to increases in autonomy at all three levels and as such, 'is a political process of obtaining and enlarging on the acceptance by others of a profession's claims to exclusive competencies or expertise in certain areas of social concern' (Laffin, 1986, p. 24). Mosher identifies several principal mechanisms and channels where professionals influence governmental activities. These include: through election or appointment of professionals to high political or judicial office; through the bringing of ideas, modes of thought which exert pressure on political executives and legislative bodies; and (particularly apposite for the British water industry) 'via effective control and virtual monopoly' of significant management positions (Mosher, 1978, p. 146). The structure or style of national policy-making systems can also facilitate the exercise of professional power. For example, in Britain professional influence is facilitated and encouraged through the segmentation and sectorisation of policy making. As Mosher points out, professionals usually have:

> at least one agency somewhere in the executive branch to crystallize or to move or to prevent change in policy, and to channel their goals and views to other, higher level decision-makers. In fact, since a large share of new or changed public policy is generated within such agencies, this pathway of professionals to policy is probably the most important of all. (ibid., p. 145)

Sectorisation of policy-making may be desirable in order to reduce conflict and intellectual overload but it may also lead to excessive political inertia if conflict avoidance becomes addictive (Richardson and Jordan, 1979; Jordan and Richardson, 1982). Under this system problems might never become issues and issues may be contracted rather than expanded. Sectorisation and professionalisation of policy-making leads to consideration of a restricted number of options, with perceived radical or competing approaches – which almost inevitably tend to emanate outside the policy community – often discounted as 'unworkable'. As Laffin points out, there is 'little or no competition in the market place of policy definitions' (Laffin, 1986, p. 125).

TECHNOCRATS AND WATER POLICY IN BRITAIN

Saunders identified the pre-privatised water industry as a component part of the 'regional state' within which all the members shared a common bond in that none of the agencies was subject to popular election. The regional state apparatus developed as a result of the decentralisation of central government functions to non-departmental public bodies, and the 'erosion' of the powers and responsibilities of local government (Saunders, 1983). Because the regional state apparatus is outside electoral control and is completely discrete from the 'pluralistic processes of political competition':

> decision-making appears curiously non-contentious and uniquely apolitical precisely because most of us have enjoyed precious little opportunity to make our voices heard ... The Regional State tends to be strongly non-contentious and readily lends itself to technical and apolitical approaches to highly politicised questions. (ibid., pp. 23–4)

Within this regional structure, Rhodes argues that the water sector can be characterised as a professional network, exhibiting the pre-eminence of professionals (Rhodes, 1988). The system of decision making in water was one which 'places a premium on expertise, substitutes professional ethics for other forms of accountability and, therefore, insulates the policy process from party political pressures' (ibid., p. 59). As shall be seen in Chapter 2, at the outset of the 1974 reorganisation process water professionals were the key participants in the decision-making process. Like many other professional groups, water technocrats were particularly successful in gaining recognition for their 'intellectual and organisational claims' during the service expansion period which ended in the mid 1970s. As Parker and Penning-Rowsell point out, the old river boards and river authorities 'were mainly led by engineers and during the 1974 reorganisation the continuation of engineering dominance was ensured by the application of two recruiting principles, 'passing on the torch' and the 'ring fence' (Parker and Penning-Rowsell, 1980, p. 48). The Water Act 1973 was largely shaped by the inputs of these professionals and the Ogden Report (on management), which followed it, reinforced the calls for a technically and managerially efficient industry through its advocation of corporate management. The professional staffs of national advisory bodies were also dominated by engineers and scientists, and the professional associations (Institution of Civil Engineers [ICE], Institution of Water Pollution Control [IWPC], Institute of Water Engineers [IWE], and so on) were key actors in the water policy sector at that time.

The problem is that while engineers may be well placed to provide solutions to a wide range of technical problems, they are rather poorly placed to 'judge the values and costs of the various water services to people affected' (Porter, 1978, p. 4). Parker and Penning-Rowsell also argue that the hegemony of engineering solutions led to a somewhat narrow approach to problem solving. Problem definition reflected the training background of the engineers and so 'the perception and identification of problems, social goals, priorities or needs and the solutions adopted to meet these stages in the planning process reflect these professionals' interpretation' (Parker and Penning Rowsell, 1980, p. 48).

The notion that professionals and technocrats generally exercise considerable influence in developed societies is convincing – as is the specific argument that professional engineers were able to play a central role in policy-making for water in Britain. Yet one of the main lessons of this case-study of the making of water policy in Britain over a fifty-year period is that this power declined and new groups achieved positions of dominance. Thus, one should be cautious in describing the distribution of power at any given point of time and must not assume that this will never change. A key task for this volume is to describe and analyse the process of change over time. It is clear that the water sector in 1994 is very different indeed from the water sector in 1944 – both in terms of policies, organisational structures, personnel, and the number and power of different groups more or less active in the sector. Somehow, the powerful engineers and water professionals no longer occupy the position of dominance they once enjoyed. In the end, a series of events weakened the power of the professional engineers to frame water problems purely in technical and engineering terms. Over time, it proved to be impossible to constrain debate in this way. As Smith argues, 'the real issues facing the water industry are not so much physical and technical as economic and social' (Smith 1979, p. 214), It is to the gradual emergence – and eventual dominance – of the economic and social (and hence *political*) issues that the rest of this book is directed. In analysing the powers by which these changes took place it is also hoped to shed light on both the utility and the significant limitations of the use of analytical models relying on the analysis of policy communities and policy networks in British politics. It will thus be demonstrated that policy change can sometimes be endogenous to policy communities and networks while at other times exogenous forces are at work beyond the control of what were thought to be key members of the core policy community. In essence, the picture is one of a shifting balance of power, of an increase in the range of organisations and interests involved in policy-making and of a complex process of policy and organisational changes.

POLICY NETWORKS AND THE ANALYSIS OF POLICY CHANGE

Much of this study is concerned with the role of different actors in the policy process. Indeed, the distinguishing feature of policy process theory is its concerns over the pattern of actor participation. In recent years several 'policy networks' terms have gained currency in the process of describing and analysing the pattern of such participation. Indeed, Rhodes (1990) claims that the *policy network* term has become *ubiquitous*. The network concept is seen as an important analytical tool because it makes the connection between the micro-level relationships of groups and government in the policy-making process, and the broader macro-level factors such as the distribution of power in society (Rhodes and Marsh, 1992a).

Policy networks range from closed and restricted policy communities to more open and accessible issue networks. Thus, policy communities are said to have several characteristics which distinguish them from other types of policy network. Policy communities are: based on the 'major functional interests in and of government' (Rhodes and Marsh, 1992a, 1992b; Richardson and Jordan, 1979); comprise a restricted membership which is generally stable; mobilise bias to *exclude* certain groups. All community members share a consensual view with respect to the 'ideology values and broad policy preferences' (Rhodes and Marsh, 1992b) and policy communities exist 'where there are effective shared "community" views' on problems (Jordan, 1990).

Another 'network' model which may be of relevance to this case-study is that of *professionalised networks*. These networks share many of the characteristics of policy communities. They are relatively closed and comprise a restricted and generally stable membership which shares a consensual view on values and attitudes. The interaction within professionalised networks is regularised and these networks also operate as vehicles for the exclusion of those who threaten the basic value structure of the network. According to Rhodes and Marsh the main difference is that:

professionalized networks express the interest of a particular profession and

manifest a substantial degree of vertical independence, while insulating themselves from other networks ... (while) policy communities are either dominated by the government or serve the interests of all the members of the
community, given that over time they develop common interests. (Rhodes and
Marsh, 1992a, pp. 13–21)

Finally there are other related ways of characterising policy actors' interactions
which attempt to capture the increased levels of participation in the policy process –
for example, *issue networks*. The issue network concept was introduced by Heclo
(1978) as a means of rejecting the conventional, rather ordered, Iron Triangle view
of politics in the United States. With the increasing proliferation of groups all
claiming a stake in the policy process, policy areas have become severely crowded
and, as a result, the focus of political and administrative leadership has become
diffuse. With such increasing complexity, it had become more difficult to identify
leaders of policy areas. In fact, Heclo argued that in the preceding twenty years it had
become almost impossible to identify the dominant actors:

> Looking for the few who are powerful, we tend to overlook the many whose
> webs of influence provoke and guide the exercise of power. Those webs, or
> what I will call 'issue networks', are particularly relevant to the highly intri-
> cate and confusing welfare policies that have been undertaken in recent years.
> (ibid., p. 102)

While the issue network concept has several deficiencies, it is worth utilising this
concept because, as Jordan (1981, p. 114) points out, it 'fails to provide a simple
image to policy making'. Issue networks can be characterised as having a large
number of participants with no restrictions on entry. They are fragmented rather than
segmented (ibid.), and participants tend constantly to vacillate in and out of the
network. Interaction is based on consultation rather than bargaining and negotiation,
and the participants do not share the same 'ideology, values and broad policy preferences' (Rhodes and Marsh, 1992b).

  While the network concept will be used in this study, it needs to be remembered
that even its most ardent supporters have entered an important caveat. These characterisations of policy communities, professionalised networks and issue networks
refer to *ideal types*. 'Inevitably, no policy area will conform exactly to either list of
characteristics' (Rhodes and Marsh, 1992b, p. 187). The purpose is to analyse policy
change over time – particularly the effects of exogenous focus on policy actors.
Thus, change may be provoked and shaped by many factors which are exogenous to
policy networks, yet has to be mediated and implemented through them.

NOTES

1. 'Residual rainfall is total rainfall less evaporation; that is rainfall effectively available for uses of all
   sorts as well as flow sufficient to mainain the ecological health of the river' (Kinnersley, 1994, p. 38).
2. There were twenty-nine Statutory Water Companies (SWCs) prior to privatisation. As a result of
   mergers the number has fallen to twenty-one. Some of the companies have remains SWCs, while others
   have converted to Plc status. See Appendix 1.1 for a list of SWCs and Plcs as at 1 November 1994.

REFERENCES

Beer, S. H. (1978), 'Federalism, Nationalism, and Democracy in America', *The American Political Science Review*, vol. 72 (1), pp. 9–21.

Bumstead, J. C. (1979), 'The Politics of Regionalization: a public perspective', *Journal of the American Water Works Association*, vol. 71, no. 12, pp. 708–12.

Dunleavy, P. (1981), 'Professions and Policy Change: Notes towards a model of ideological corporatism', *Public Administrative Bulletin*, no. 33, pp. 3–16.

Fischer, F. (1990), *Technocracy and the Politics of Expertise* (California: Sage).

Foreman-Peck, J. and Millward, R. (1994), *Public and Private Ownership of British Ownership 1820–1990* (Oxford: Clarendon Press).

Gray, C. (1982), 'The Regional Water Authorities', in B. W. Hogwood and M. Keating (eds), *Regional Government in England* (Oxford: Clarendon Press), pp. 143–67.

Hassan, John A. (1993), *The Water Industry 1900–51: A Failure of Public Policy?* (Series No: 93–09) (Manchester: Manchester Metropolitan University).

Heclo, Hugh (1978), 'Issue Networks and the Executive Establishment', in A. King (ed.), *The New American Political System* (Washington: AEI), pp. 87–124.

Hogwood, B. W. (1987), *From Crisis to Complacency?* (Oxford: Oxford University Press).

Hogwood, B. W. and Peters, B. G. (1983), *Policy Dynamics* (Sussex: Wheatsheaf).

Jordan, A. G. (1981), 'Iron Triangles, Woolly Corporatism and Elastic Nets: Images of the policy process', *Journal of Public Policy*, vol. 1, pp. 95–124.

Jordan, A. G. (1990), 'Sub-governments, Policy Communities and Networks: Refilling the old bottles?', *Journal of Theoretical Politics*, vol. 2, pp. 319–38.

Jordan, A. G., Richardson, J. J. and Kimber, R. H. (1977), 'The Origins of the Water Act of 1973', *Public Administration*, vol. 55 (Autumn), pp. 317–34.

Jordan, G. and Richardson, J. J. (1982), 'The British Policy Style or the Logic of Negotiation', in J. Richardson (ed.), *Policy Styles in Western Europe* (London: George Allen and Unwin), pp. 80–110.

Kingdon, J. (1984), *Agendas, Alternatives and Public Policy* (Boston: Litttle, Brown and Company).

Kinnersley, D. (1988), *Troubled Water: Rivers, Politics and Pollution* (London: Hilary Shipman).

Kinnersley, D. (1994), *Coming Clean: the Politics of Water and the Environment* (London: Penguin).

Laffin, M. (1986), *Professionalism and Policy: The Role of the Professions in the Central–Local Relationship* (Aldershot: Gower).

Laumann, E. O. and Knoke, D. (1987), *The Organizational State* (Wisconsin: University of Wisconsin Press).

Lindblom, C. E. (1959), 'The Science of "Muddling Through"', *Public Administration Review*, vol. 19 (Spring), pp. 79–88.

Lindblom, C. E. (1979), 'Still Muddling, Not Yet Through', in A. G. McGrew and M. J. Wilson (eds) (1982), *Decision Making: Approaches and Analysis* (Manchester: Manchester University Press), pp. 125–38.

McDonald, A. T. and Kay, D. (1988), *Water Resources: Issues and Strategies* (London: Longman).

Mosher, F. C. (1978), 'Professions in Public Service', *Public Administration Review*, vol. 38, pp. 144–50.

OFWAT (1993), *Annual Report 1992/3*.

OFWAT (1994), *Annual Report 1993/4*.

Parker, D. and Penning-Rowsell, E. (1980), *Water Planning in Britain* (London: George Allen & Unwin).

Porter, E. (1978), *Water Management in England and Wales* (Cambridge: Cambridge University Press).

Richardson, J. J. and Jordan, A. G. (1979), *Governing Under Pressure* (Oxford: Martin Robertson & Company Limited).

Rhodes, R. A. W. (1988), *Beyond Westminster and Whitehall* (London: Unwin Hyman).

Rhodes, R. A. W. (1990), 'Policy Networks: a British Perspective', *Journal of Theoretical Politics*, vol. 2, pp. 293–317.

Rhodes, R. A. W. and Marsh, D. (1992a), 'Policy Networks in British Politics: A critique of existing approaches', in D. Marsh and R. A. W. Rhodes (eds), *Policy Networks in British Government* (Oxford: Clarendon Press), pp. 1–26.

Rhodes, R. A. W. and Marsh, D. (1992b), 'New Directions in the Study of Policy Networks', *European Journal of Political Research*, vol. 21, pp. 181–205.

Saunders, P. (1983), *The 'Regional State': A Review of the Literature and Agenda for Research*, Working Paper 35, Urban and Regional Studies (Sussex: University of Sussex).

Schattschneider, E. E. (1960), *Semi-Sovereign People: A Realist's View of Democracy in America* (New York: Holt, Rinehart, & Winston).

Smith, K. (1979), *Water in Britain*, (2nd edn) (London: Macmillan Press Limited).

Wildavsky, A. (1979), *Speaking Truth To Power: The Art and Craft of Policy Analysis* (Boston: Little, Brown and Company).`

APPENDIX I.I: Water and Sewerage Companies.

Anglian Water Services Ltd
Dwr Cymru Cyfyngedig
Northumbrian Water Ltd
North West Water Ltd
Severn Trent Water Ltd
Southern Water Services Ltd
South West Water Services Ltd
Thames Water Utilities Ltd
Wessex Water Services Ltd
Yorkshire Water Services Ltd

Water Only Companies

Bournemouth and West Hampshire Water Plcs
Bristol Water Plc
Cambridge Water Company
Chester Waterworks Company
Cholderton and District Water Company Ltd
East Surrey Water Plc
Essex and Suffolk Water Plc
Folkestone and Dover Water Services Ltd
Hartlepools Water Company
Mid Kent Water Plc
Mid Southern Water Plc
North East Water Plc
North Surrey Water Ltd
Portsmouth Water Plc
South East Water Ltd
South Staffordshire Water Plc
Sutton District Water Plc
Tendring Hundred Water Services Ltd
Three Valleys Water Plc
Wrexham and East Denbighshire Water Company
York Waterworks Plc

SOURCE: OFWAT, 1994.

PART 2

Turbulence: The Dynamics of Policy Change

A Gradualist Revolution:
Policy Change 1969–1989

*There is in this country ample water for all needs. The problem is not
one of total resources, but of organisation and distribution.*
Ministry of Health, Ministry of Agriculture and Fisheries, Department
of Health for Scotland (1944), *A National Water Policy* Cmnd 6515

The quotation above from the 1944 White Paper, set out the basic water sharing
problem which faced the British water industry in the post-war period – put bluntly,
the water in Britain falls in the wrong places! The White Paper was prompted by two
major droughts in 1933 and 1934 which 'led to increasing debate within the industry
and outside concerning the desirability of a National Water Policy' (Hassan, 1993,
p. 9). It outlined the need for a national water policy and identified the numerous
defects endemic to the existing system. These included ill-defined inter-governmental responsibilities leading to overlapping and duplication of activities, multi-
plicity of supply undertakings and an extremely poor rural service. The White Paper
concluded that 'modern needs' could only be met through the rationalisation of
existing undertakings into larger units. Simple though this solution might sound,
achieving it was not to be an easy task as it would necessitate major policy and
administrative and institutional change. Thus, nearly thirty years later, in 1973, the
ending of the fragmentation of water services was to be one of the key tenets of the
Water Act 1973. The act was then seen by several commentators (see, Jordan et al.,
1977; Gray, 1982, 1984) as representing a highly innovative response to the basic
water sharing problems, particularly facing the industry in England and Wales in the
early 1970s. However, the highly fragmented and unintegrated nature of the system
had been continually criticised for many years previous to that time. The problem
was not defining 'the problem', but of securing a solution which could find favour
with the array of interested parties involved. For example, many of the proposed
solutions of earlier years also had at their core some degree of regionalised control
– the solution finally agreed in the early 1970s. The Central Advisory Water
Committee's (CAWC) *Third Report*, 1942–3, criticised the fragmented and unintegrated nature of river management in England and Wales over thirty years before

regionalisation was actually introduced, and it recommended the creation of river-basin 'river authorities' with responsibility for prevention of pollution, fisheries, navigation, conservation and land drainage. Although not on the scale planned in 1973, regionalisation had in fact been discussed much earlier. In the 1920s the Ministry of Health attempted to encourage reorganisation with the creation of Regional Water Advisory Boards. These boards were to co-ordinate water 'under-takers' in the provision of joint water supply. Indeed, Hassan claims that 'It was evident that the system and the work of the regional committees was at the core of the Government's policy towards the water industry in the inter-war years' (Hassan, 1993, p. 8).

In that sense, it can be argued that the process of creating a regionalised and inte-grated administrative system (institutionalised by the Water Act 1973) began in 1944 with the publication of the White Paper that formed the basis of the Water Act 1945. The act invested the Health Minister and the Secretary of State for Scotland with statutory responsibility for water services 'to promote the conservation and proper use of water resources and the provision of water supplies in England and Wales to secure effective execution by water undertakers, under his [sic] control and direc-tion, of a national policy relating to water'. There was an early recognition therefore, that water policy was, indeeed, a national and not just a local issue in Britain.

From a policy succession perspective (Hogwood and Peters, 1983), three aspects of the Water Act 1945 were particularly significant. First, the powers of compulsory amalgamation given to ministers signalled the beginning of the process of moving to larger organisational units that could take advantage of the economies of scale, which the multitude of small discrete units could not. Ministers were empowered to order the combination of separate water undertakers, or the creation of joint commit-tees for the efficient provision of water in their areas. Ministers could also order the consolidation of separate undertakings into one operating unit, provided the under-takers were not local authorities. Secondly, larger geographic units signalled the beginnings of the essential move away from the tradition of water related services being contained within local government geographic boundaries. Thirdly, it also marked the very early beginning of responsibility being transferred from locally elected bodies towards indirectly elected/partly nominated organisations.

The 1945 act was significant for several other reasons. It formalised central government involvement in the policy sector; marked the inauguration of a national water policy; broadened the basis of the supply functions, as water undertakers were required to supply water for non-domestic purposes; established a central co-ordi-nating authority; initiated the collection of hydrological data; limited effluent discharges to watercourses and it included provisions for the process of regrouping. Its potential for bringing about subsequent policy and administrative change was, therefore, very considerable.

THE ANTECEDENTS OF REGIONALISATION

The existence of the Central Advisory Water Committee – which brought together the key actors in the industry – was at that time an important factor in policy development. Here, the industry had an institutionalised policy community, on the classic model, for the identification of problems and the processing of issues. Indeed it was CAWC's Third Report, published in 1943 (Cmnd 6454), that recommended that river boards be created with comprehensive jurisdictions over river basins or groups of river basins for land drainage, pollution prevention, fisheries and certain navigational duties. These proposals aimed to reduce the number and range of operating units in the water field, to affect the integration of some water services, and to establish a rational basis for the geographic extent of the authorities' jurisdiction (Mitchell, 1970). The CAWC report eventually lead to the River Boards Act 1948 which was particularly significant in the development of water policy in Britain, because it was the first attempt at comprehensive river basin management. Thus, it constitutes the first step towards the eventual creation of multi-purpose agencies for England and Wales on 1 April 1974. The 1948 act created thirty-two river boards in England and Wales with responsibility for pollution control, land drainage and fisheries (these functions had previously been the responsibility of three separate types of body). The changes in water supply and conservation, pollution control, land drainage and fisheries were not mirrored in the sewage disposal sector, which remained a highly diffuse administrative system. Moreover, there were signs that public policy was lagging behind the trajectory of the actual problems that public policy was designed to address. In particular, the demand for clean water began to outstrip the capacity of the system to meet supply in parts of England and Wales.

After the reforms of the 1940s, CAWC had fallen into abeyance, but with demand for water continually spiralling, the Government re-established the committee in 1955. The final report of one of its sub-committees (the so-called Proudham Report), published in 1962, criticised the unintegrated administrative system of water supply and proposed the establishment of river authorities, whose membership should be between ten and fifteen, to manage water resources of the river basin as a whole. It also proposed a central authority to promote an active policy for conservation and the proper use of water resources. CAWC called for a central executive body to be created to promote an active policy for water, to co-ordinate the activities of the river authorities, and to construct works for water conservation.

Other changes at this time were also directed at reducing the number of operating units. Until 1956 the regrouping process operated on a voluntary basis, which, somewhat predictably, resulted in implementation difficulties. A high degree of hostility and resistance characterised this era, as organisations naturally fought for their survival. The Ministry of Housing and Local Government (MHLG) replaced the Ministry of Health as the lead department in the water sector, and the new department issued two circulars, one in 1956 and a second in 1958. The circulars contained guidelines on how regrouping was to be achieved. Furthermore, they warned that if the Secretary of State was not reasonably satisfied with the pace of change then he

TABLE 2.1: Number and type of water undertaker

Local Authorities	1956	1970
County Borough Councils	53	29
Borough Councils	177	17
Urban District Councils	295	9
Rural District Councils	358	9
Sub-total	883	64
Joint Boards	42	101
Statutory Water Companies	90	33
Miscellaneous	15	–
Total	1030	198

SOURCE: CAWC, 1971.

would use his statutory powers under the Water Act 1945 to secure consolidation. Between 1945 and 1956 the number of undertakings fell by a mere 156, from 1186 to 1030 (See Table 2.1). After ministerial interventions, the number of undertakings fell quite dramatically to 260 in 1969 and finally to 187 immediately prior to the 1974 reorganisation. Of the 700 undertakings regrouped between 1956 and 1966 only 35 (5 per cent) were the result of ministerial compulsion (Okun, 1967).

The regrouping of smaller units into larger ones had several advantages. Significant reductions in the capital and operating cost through the accompanying economies of scale; more efficient development of water resources; larger numbers and a higher quality staff; better services for rural and isolated areas; easier assimilation of new larger water-demanding enterprises (for example, industry) (ibid.). The threat of imposition, combined with the actual lack of a restrictive and formal legislative framework for the regrouping, enabled the rationalisation process to be achieved in a flexible and pragmatic way. Okun has emphasised the importance of this gradual process in laying the foundations for the major legislative change of the early 1970s – that is, that *policy succession* was an important feature of the making of water policy – 'this regrouping was to provide the foundation without which reorganisation on the scale proposed in the Water Act 1973 might not have been attempted' (Okun, 1977, p. 19).

Events continued to present challenges to policy, however. For example the 1959 drought demonstrated that the system was vulnerable. As Kinnersley argues, 'organised control of water resource development and abstractions was also seen as necessary in the early 1960s, following the severe drought of 1959, and due to competition between water companies and anyone else (such as farmers and industry) who wanted new major supplies of raw water' (Kinnersley, 1994, p. 44). Thus the 1963 Water Resources Act was largely a response to the severe drought of 1959 and created the twenty-nine river authorities out of the previous thirty-four river boards, twenty-two of which were situated wholly in England, four wholly in Wales and three straddling the Anglo-Welsh border. These authorities were responsible for the management of water resources in their basins or groups of basins. A Water Resources Board (WRB) was also established, both to advise the minister on national water policy and to advise the river authorities in their duties in the water resource area. The river authorities were composed of between twenty-five and forty-one members with the bare majority being county council and borough council nominees, and the remainder appointed by the appropriate minister.

It is worth remembering that the hydrological concept of integrated river basin management (IRBM) was claimed to be the major innovation of the 1974 reorganisation (see p. 33). Yet, the river boards were significant in that they were the first official recognition of river basins as management units. The placing of the entire catchment area under one authority was a *de facto* recognition of the significance of hydrological boundaries as natural administrative units for water, and the reduction in the number of management units enhanced the opportunity for integrated management. The river authorities (operational from 1 April 1965) which replaced the river boards under the Water Resources Act 1963 contained some notable features which are still in operation today, for example a licensing system for abstractions. As Kinnersley notes, the abstraction licensing system:

> was launched without the phasing-in period for existing and new installations that had applied to effluent discharge controls. But existing abstracters were granted licences of right to take volumes of water which later turned out to be more than some smaller rivers could sustain. Thirty years later, the NRA is now struggling to correct those misjudgements, as reducing licensed volumes is beset with the difficulties of finding replacement sources for the licences. (Kinnersley, 1994, p. 44)

The thrust of the 1963 Act was seen as largely progressive and had a significant impact on the development of the industry. It permitted the development of technical and managerial concepts without which the 1973 Act would not have been considered. The river authorities were significant in the process of policy succession because of their multi-functional operating activities. They were relatively successful in spite of their short (six year) life-span, with the main problem they faced being the (still) relatively unintegrated system over which they had oversight. Kinnersley has aptly summarised the institutional changes which occurred between 1945 and 1970 as 'directed to two purposes: to improve the conduct of particular water sharing activities, and to get better co-ordination between several of these activities as they seemed increasingly to affect each other' (Kinnersley, 1988, p. 92).

In total, the process of policy and administrative change during the post-war period up to the start of the 1970s can be characterised as *non-radical policy succession*. Significant changes had taken place over time – new co-ordinating mechanisms, a gradual reduction in the number of undertakers, tighter pollution controls (for example over effluent discharges via individual consent limits and conditions), and better monitoring of river quality had all been instituted. Yet these policy changes were not keeping pace with the development of the water policy problem itself – policy still lagged behind the rate of change in the problem. Thus, the 1970s saw a shift from non-radical policy succession to a more radical approach to policy innovation, though still based upon a system of policy succession rather than introducing a marked *discontinuity* in water policy and management. The shift was from non-radical policy succession to *radical policy succession*.

AGENDA SETTING AND THE PRESSURES FOR RADICAL REFORM

The signs of a more significant disturbance to the existing system – especially to the range of participation in the policy process – came in 1969. It was then that the possible removal of local authority participation emerged onto the political agenda. However, as late as 1966 the Government had expressed its commitment to the benefits of water and sewage services being controlled by local government, because of the necessity of close co-operation between the duties of planning authorities, and the desirability of political accountability which local government control was thought to deliver. Thus, in evidence to the Royal Commission on Local Government in 1966, the ministry (MHLG) stated 'that it would be unfortunate to separate sewerage from responsibility for housing and planning, which would necessarily result from entrusting it to the river authorities'.

The only interest organisation which at that time envisaged a regionalised system of control similar to that eventually proposed in the 1973 Water Bill was one of the professional water associations – the Institute of Water Engineers (IWE). Even it viewed the prospect as a long-term objective. The IWE, in 1969, argued that:

> water undertakings should be autonomous bodies whose boundaries are determined in relation to the needs of the service rather than that they should necessarily follow local government boundaries … the work of water undertakings and sewerage authorities will have to be related more to hydrological boundary considerations than to existing or proposed local government boundaries. (IWE submission to CAWC, 1969)

The increased availability of *information* was a key factor in bringing about change. A series of reports by the Water Resources Board (WRB) drew attention to the likely future trends for water demand, estimating that it could double by the end of the century. With the levels of available water likely to remain constant, these reports concluded that the re-use of existing supplies might have to form a significant part of the solution to potential problems. Hence, there was a strong technical imperative that radical policy change should be placed on the agenda. In response to the problems facing the industry, the MHLG re-established CAWC (again) to examine the prospects for the *The Future of Water Management in England and Wales* (see pp. 30–3 below for a fuller discussion of CAWC's role in the policy making process). [Scotland's needs were, still, less pressing. In contrast to England and Wales, issues of (water) quantity were not as important in Scotland – even though consumption per head in Scotland is greater than that in England and Wales. This is largely because of Scotland's lower population density and ample sources of water (available from unpolluted upland sources) for all requirements for the foreseeable future]. The memorandum issued by the MHLG to organisations and individuals wishing to submit evidence to CAWC, stated that:

> For the purposes of their study the Committee have decided to make the following assumptions about the position between now and the end of the century. The demand for water in England and Wales will roughly double. There will be a comparable increase in the volume of effluents requiring treatment and also some increase in the complexity of effluents. The demand for water will have to be met primarily from inland sources, including possible estuarine barriers. In view of the extent to which the water resources of England and Wales are already developed this will entail a great increase in the re-use of water. (MHLG, 1969, p. 1)

Water supply and sewage disposal would have to be integrated and operate in a co-ordinated manner. The rationale behind this change was that if those who polluted the water were also those responsible for supplying wholesome drinking water, abstracted from the sources that they were polluting, then they would consider more fully the consequences of their polluting activities. This seemingly anodyne technical argument had, however, considerable implications for the structure and administration of the industry. Making the administrative structures more appropriate for the technical problems to be solved had some important consequences for at least one of the (then) key actors – local government, as shall be seen.

Two other factors were influential in the change of direction. The return of Jack Beddoe, Under Secretary to the Water Division of the MHLG in 1968, and the almost simultaneous publication of the report of the Royal Commission on Local Government, both facilitated a major alteration in the departmental view. Until the arrival of Beddoe, the department had been reluctant to act on the numerous recommendations of the WRB, for three main reasons. First, the recommendations were *de facto* only suggestions, as the WRB possessed no executive powers. Secondly, there was an ongoing conflict between the department and the board which led to the department's refusal to implement any of its recommendations. Thirdly, Parliament was reluctant to act on the WRB's proposals because its reports were highly technical with no reference to political realities. Indeed, the most important factor which kept the water question out of the party political arena was the fact that water was generally perceived as an apolitical cross-party issue. It should be borne in mind that it was a Labour administration that reconstituted CAWC and a Conservative one which acted on its recommendations. The cross-party nature of water was highlighted by a Labour backbencher, Nigel Spearing who, during the passage of the subsequent reforms, argued that, 'matters concerning water, while controversial in the best political sense, have not been unduly party political, except for the great issue of ownership of water and the operation of private undertakings' (HC Standing Committee D, Col. 3, Water Bill, Tuesday, 20 February 1973).

As is often the case in the reform process, individuals, as 'change champions' can play a crucial role. In fact Jack Beddoe is widely credited as being the chief architect of the Water Act 1973. One member of CAWC described the parliamentary bill as *Beddoe's Bill*, and at the parliamentary stage of the policy process the Association of Municipal Corporations had a policy of 'continued and unalterable opposition to this civil servant's bill' (*Local Government Chronicle*, 24 November 1972). While the Permanent Secretary in the department at that time was 'keen on the proposals', it was widely accepted that Beddoe had convinced him of the necessity for change. Such a high profile for traditionally anonymous civil servants was unusual at the time and would still be considered so today.[1]

The first public sign that a departmental change was in the offing came in the autumn of 1968 when Beddoe presented a paper to a symposium of water engineers (Institute of Public Health Engineers, Institution of Water Pollution Control and the Institute of Water Engineers), in which he stressed the requirement for a multi-purpose water industry, organised largely outside the local government remit. He maintained that quality and quantity problems would be better solved under such an integrated system. He constructed a strong case for multi-functional authorities based on extensive regional areas within hydrological boundaries (Jordan et al., 1977). The combination of his personal reforming style and the largely apolitical nature of water meant that elected politicians, be they ministers, front bench spokespersons, or backbenchers, did not influence this key decision-point in the policy process – namely, the agenda setting stage. Beddoe had, correctly, perceived that large sections of the industry had come to recognise that a serious problem existed, and he was able to utilise ideas already debated by fellow professionals within the existing policy community to launch the reform process. In addition, he was opportunistic in the sense that one of the likely opponents from within the policy community – the local government interests – were likely to be preoccupied with more major concerns, the reform of local government itself. Beddoe saw that major change was possible and was able to present a 'solution' at the conference to a 'problem' of which everyone had become aware.

It appears that the actual agenda for reform was set and given shape and direction by Beddoe and his departmental colleagues. This is an unusual role for the department to be fulfilling as it normally acts as a buffer/umpire between the various competing client groups. Here we see civil servants playing the part of *policy advocate*, rather than their usual role of *policy broker* (Sabatier, 1988). According to Sabatier the 'dominant concern (of policy brokers) is with keeping the level of political conflict within acceptable limits and with reaching some 'reasonable' solution to the problem' (ibid., p. 141). However, as he concedes, policy brokers may also act as advocates 'if their agency has a clearly defined mission'. Beddoe gave the MHLG (and subsequently the DOE) that clearly defined mission – to bring about a fully integrated and multi-purpose system for England and Wales.

The idea suited the technocrats in the industry well. However, although several professional groups had identified multi-functionalism and regionalism as a possible option prior to the arrival of Beddoe at the department, no 'advocacy coalition' (Sabatier, 1988) had yet emerged. Once the issue was placed onto the agenda by Beddoe, the professional groups, who were powerful actors within the water policy community, became vociferous proponents of a change in that direction. The proposed reform enhanced opportunities to extend their professional autonomy by turning water completely into a technical and professional issue. The pressure for reform was further bolstered by the engineers' symposium discussed above, the Jeger Committee Report (MHLG, 1970) on the future of sewage disposal and the 1971 CAWC report, all of which embraced the technical arguments for change.

The role Beddoe played in both agenda setting and in processing the issue, contained certain novel features. Water had previously been a relatively low priority within government mainly because of its apolitical nature – itself largely a conse-quence of the professionalisation of decision-making (Jordan, et al., 1977). The issue did not proceed onto the *institutional agenda* (Cobb and Elder, 1972) from the rela-tively common rough and tumble of interest group or party politics. It was placed on the agenda through the internalised world of Whitehall and its associated 'profes-sional' constituency. The issue of reorganisation was one to which the department and the minister, Peter Walker, became strongly committed as a result of Beddoe's enthusiasm. Indeed, Beddoe appeared to exhibit two of the distinguishing features which Downs (1967, pp. 109–10) attributed to *bureaucratic zealots*, 'the narrowness of their sacred policies, and the implacable energy they focus solely on promoting those policies'. The eventual commitment of the department and ministers assured the maintenance and development of the issue (Hogwood, 1987, p. 47).

Beddoe's approach to this policy development was not only zealous, but was also very shrewd. He was the type of civil servant who recognised that policy change need not necessarily be feared. He perceived the water shortage problem as a change opportunity and provided a firm lead by filling the policy vacuum. Beddoe was able to guide the issue through the *systemic* to the *institutional* agenda (Cobb and Elder, 1972). In doing so, he illustrated a more general feature of problem identification in the British policy process. Thus, as Richardson and Jordan suggest:

> it is within the ministry – probably about Assistant or Under Secretary level – that defects in existing policy often reveal themselves. It is at this level that proposals for change can often emerge, or at least the need for a major depart-mental policy reappraisal can be established. (1979, p. 94)

Beddoe convinced other relevant actors, in particular technocrats, that change was possible. A general consensus quickly emerged within the professional policy community about the need for change. The case for reform proceeded smoothly through the systemic agenda to institutional agenda, as a result of several factors. First, there was a general dissatisfaction with the operation, as well as with the antic-ipated future operation, of the existing policy. It was perceived as being inadequate to meet future requirements (for example, as demonstrated in numerous WRB reports). Secondly, there was eventually internal pressure within government. Beddoe's

presentation of the likelihood of potential future water shortages and its ramifications, in public health and political terms, ensured that it was an issue which the
ministerial team would take seriously. If water shortages occurred in the future,
water would become a highly salient political problem instead of an administrative
backwater. Thirdly, as suggested above, a unique opportunity for reform arose with
the simultaneous reorganisation of local government. With sewage disposal at that
time being an integral part of local government services, the Government felt that the
reform process in the water sector would be best achieved in parallel with the major
reorganisation of local government. As one key participant put it, 'while local
government was on the operating table, Jack Beddoe removed their kidneys!'
Fourthly, the issue did enjoy an element of fashionability, since it could be presented
by the Government as part of the process of the 'greening' of public policy.

The origins of change in the sector have been concisely summarised by one key insider
at the time as an admixture of 'a view of difficulties ahead; an occasion not likely to
recur; and forceful personalities in relevant positions with clear ideas of what they
wanted to achieve. None of which would have been sufficient on their own' (Kinnersley, 1988, pp. 96–7). There was a *window of opportunity* for change created by
several factors coming on stream at the same point in time (Kingdon, 1984) followed
by the emergence of an advocacy coalition (Sabatier, 1988) in favour of regional
authorities based upon the concept of integrated river basin management (IRBM).

THE CENTRAL ADVISORY WATER COMMITTEE (CAWC) AND THE POLICY MAKING PROCESS

In 1970 when CAWC began its investigations into the future management of the water
industry in England and Wales there were three main types of water body: 198 water
supply organisations providing water to domestic and non-domestic consumers;[2]
1,300 sewerage and sewage disposal authorities which were either local authorities
or joint boards of local authorities; and 29 river authorities responsible for water
conservation, pollution control, land drainage, fisheries and, in some cases, navigation.
CAWC's remit was:

> To consider in the light of the Report of the Royal Commission on Local
> Government in England and Wales and of technical and other developments
> how the functions relating to water conservation, management of water
> resources, water supply, sewerage, sewage disposal and pollution prevention
> now exercised by River Authorities, public water undertakings, and sewerage
> and sewage disposal authorities can be best organised; and to make recom-
> mendations. (CAWC, 1971, p. 1)

The report which CAWC eventually produced identified numerous weaknesses in the
existing institutional structures, including the 'excessive number of River Authorities which lead to inefficient use of staff and resources'. However, the main problem
which CAWC identified related to the division of responsibility between organisations,
essentially river authorities and the water undertakers. This led to conflicts of interest

which created a situation within which, CAWC argued (para. 131), it may not have been 'possible to achieve the best overall solution'. The committee pointed out that while the undertakers were required to supply water when it was demanded, they did not control the sources. If a conflict emerged between the river authorities and the undertakers, then the only recourse the undertakers had was to the Secretary of State. The committee recommended that the structure should be based on the following criteria: 'If a body is under statutory obligation to supply water, then either it must itself have the powers to enable it to meet this obligation, or there must be another body which has a statutory obligation to make water available to it' (CAWC, 1971, para. 139).

CAWC's role in identifying this weakness was crucial for the newly formed Department of the Environment (previously MHLG) since it permitted the department to do a *volte-face* on its evidence to the Reddclife–Maude Commission on Local Government Reform in 1966 as the urgency of the technical imperative outlined by the *politically neutral* CAWC (essentially the policy community gathered within a committee) permitted the department to claim that it had been persuaded of the necessity for change by rational argument.

CAWC proposed that water resources would be best planned over England and Wales as a whole, and that national planning should include issues of quality and quantity (CAWC, 1971, para. 151). The WRB had only previously considered issues of quantity, thus its remit should be expanded to include quality issues and it should become a national water authority. The new authority was envisaged as adopting a holistic approach to water policy. In addition to taking over the WRB's responsibilities, it would formulate a national plan, which would give comprehensive consideration to all issues cognate to water, give technical guidance to the proposed multi-purpose regional authorities – the regional water authorities, RWAS – collate and publish hydrological data, and carry out and supervise research.

The CAWC report had discussed two main alternative management systems: multi-purpose RWAS or single-purpose RWAS, which could be planning and co-ordination bodies, alongside twenty-nine river authorities, fifty water undertakers and fifty sewage disposal authorities. The *multi-purpose RWA* approach met CAWC's concerns over the conflicts of interest between separate bodies. Each multi-purpose RWA would be akin to the other major public utilities and would be required to make economic charges for its services. The committee 'envisaged that the total amount paid in charges by each category of consumer for each of the services provided by the RWA would be nearly as possible equal to the total cost incurred by the RWA in providing that service to that category of consumer' (CAWC, 1971, para. 181). Authorities would be expected to break even or to reach a previously prescribed level of self-financing, and would regulate pollution to improve river quality in accordance with the national plan. The new regional authorities were to be composed of between ten and fifteen members, appointed by the Secretary of State. The potential losers – the local authorities – were, however, recognised and were given a life-raft in this more radical option. Thus, CAWC argued that:

if it was thought desirable, a portion of them [the proposed RWAs] could be appointed by the major local authorities. The Chairman could be appointed by the Ministers on the basis of his proven ability in guiding complex organisations. The day-to-day management would be in the hands of a number of full-time chief officers under a full-time chief executive. (CAWC, 1971, para. 176)

Recognising that its job was to explore options, CAWC also examined several variations on the single-purpose system and did not actually *recommend* the adoption of any one system. It merely presented the options, leaving the decision to be made by others.

The committee's decision not to make any recommendations was widely and severely criticised. Yet, as has been pointed out, CAWC's failure to reach any conclusive decision on the future shape of the industry could easily have been predicted (Jordan and Richardson, 1977). The composition of the committee was so wide and diverse that participants did not share the same values, even though they were clearly part of the relevant policy community. (Thus, what bound them together was their stakeholder status in the policy area, rather than shared values.) In fact, internally, the committee had voted fourteen to thirteen in favour of multi-purpose authorities. The lack of a clear recommendation suited the DOE, however, as it could then decide for itself.

Thus, the committee was not a source of policy because the fundamentals had already been developed within the department. The department viewed the multi-functional approach as the optimal solution. In particular, Beddoe favoured it and a departmental working party report, which had been completed in spring 1969 before CAWC had been reconvened, also advocated its adoption. More significant, however, Peter Walker, Secretary of State for the Environment, managed to secure Cabinet approval for major multi-purpose reform even before the publication of the CAWC report later that year. Thus, it appears that the ministry and the cabinet had decided policy before the committee had reached its conclusions.

Even so, CAWC was still useful to the department if only for purely tactical reasons, as it provided a degree of legitimation and independent external scrutiny. CAWC's deliberations enabled the Government to claim that its proposals for change were largely a response to technical advice. The image which the Government projected of the CAWC process as external to the department was false (ibid.). The autonomy of the committee was not as great as it appeared because many of its ideas actually emanated from within the department, and the department also monitored closely much of its work. The 'big brother' presence left no doubts as to the department's wishes and preferences (ibid.).

Indeed, CAWC's covert *raison d'être* may simply have been for the department to gauge the climate of opinion within the policy community – or network – of actors there represented. It was probably more of a *consultative committee*, than a *committee of inquiry*. Thus:

critics of the bland report sometimes qualified their criticisms to the effect that at least CAWC had investigated and set out the facts – but in reality the factual description was a thinly re-written version of evidence submitted by the Ministry. CAWC did not inform the Ministry of the state of health of the industry – rather it was vice versa. CAWC's own investigations unearthed (or at least demonstrated) more about the attitudes to change than about the necessity or otherwise of change. (ibid. p. 47)

REGIONALISATION: THE GOVERNMENT'S PROPOSALS FOR CHANGE

The Water Bill involves a radical reorganisation of one of our most vital industries. It makes the new all-purpose Regional Water Authorities (RWAS) responsible for the whole of the hydrological cycle. The RWAS will be responsible not only for water supply but for the recycling of dirty water for further use. (p. v, Foreword to the *Management Structure (Ogden) Committee Report*, by Geoffrey Rippon, Secretary of State for the Environment)

The Government informed the House of Commons on 2 December 1971 that it had decided to regionalise the water services in England and Wales, to take effect on the same day as the proposed local government reform, 1 April 1974. The Government believed that strong regional bodies were required because the water sector was not suited to a strict system of centralised control. This was an admission that the national water policy had little or no practical impact in the sector and that many of the problems which it had failed to address would be better solved at the regional level (Kirby, 1979).

The reorganisation of the Scottish water industry was implemented in May 1975 under the Local Government (Scotland) Act 1973. The reform of the Scottish industry, as Waddington and Hammerton pointed out at that time, was:

merely a by-product of the Local Government (Scotland) Act 1973 ... the reform has stemmed directly from the need to reform local government, and not from any specific desire to reform the water industry as a whole. Indeed, putting water supply back into local authority control directly contradicts the recommendations of the Scottish Water Advisory Committee, whose 1966 report led to the establishment of the present water boards. (1974, p. 212)

Thus, given that the Local Government (Scotland) Act 1973 returned responsibility for water to the local authorities, the Scottish reform process in 1975 was to a certain extent the reverse of the changes occurring in England and Wales.

The 1974 reorganisation in England and Wales was to include all water related services except land drainage and fisheries of which the Ministry of Agriculture and Food (MAFF) had successfully managed to retain control. The anomalous separation of land drainage from other water related functions lies in the traditional ties between MAFF and the agricultural drainage field (see Jordan et al., 1977). All attempts, prior to 1989, to transfer the land drainage function from MAFF were successfully combated by the farming lobby, backed by senior civil servants within the ministry, who feared that land drainage would be swallowed up by the more pressing needs of water supply and sewage disposal (Jordan et al., 1977). With the two exceptions of land drainage and fisheries, the Government was convinced of the urgent requirement for all the water related functions to be considered within the hydrological cycle – as opposed to following political boundaries – and that they should be controlled by all-purpose authorities. The DOE summarised the Government's aims as follows:

> the time has come to bring together, under all-purpose management structures, all aspects of the hydrological cycle, literally from source to tap. ... the solution must go beyond a mere reduction in the number of operating units ... The basic principle of the 1963 (Water Resources) Act, that water resources should be managed comprehensively on the basis of river basins, taking full account of all relevant interests, needs to be carried forward. (DOE, 1971, Circular 92/71, para. 8)

The circular concluded that the complete integration of water services was essential and that there was an urgent requirement for authorities with a clear sense of purpose. These organisations should also take a comprehensive long-term view of all cognate aspects of water management, as well as 'taking successful and cost-effective action to safeguard water supplies and protect the environment' (DOE, 1971, Circular 92/71, para. 9).

The question remained, however, of precisely how these principles should be implemented – in particular the question of how many regional authorities there should be had to be resolved. (For example, an earlier CAWC report (in 1969) had outlined the prospective boundaries for between seven and thirteen RWAs). Jack Beddoe hoped for a maximum of six authorities and wanted smaller compact executive boards, placing greater stress on managerialism and efficiency than on democracy or accountability. The bargained outcome was ten, with local authorities gaining a statutory majority representation of RWA membership. David Kinnersley maintains that Jack Beddoe lost out for two main reasons. First, local authorities' assets were transferred to the new regional authorities without any compensation being paid to them beyond the transfer of any relevant debt. Secondly, whilst the efficiency argument was persuasive for the utility functions of water and sewage services, the creation of all-purpose authorities exercising regulatory functions (for example, being self-monitoring and having the power to prosecute those failing to meet statutory requirements) required a degree of political validation (Kinnersley, 1988, p. 98). At that time, the climate of opinion was such that these general questions of accountability still carried some weight.

LOBBYING AND THE WATER ACT 1973

The DOE issued several consultation papers between January and September 1972 (see Table 2.2) and a total of 180 groups responded to these documents. It was in the consultation process that the *technical imperative* behind the reorganisation had to be tempered by the political realities of the interest group structure within the water sector. Having decided upon radical change, a process of bargaining ensued. This left

TABLE 2.2. Consultation papers issued by DOE in 1972.

6 January	'The Place of the Water Companies in the New System'
20 January	'Safeguards for Staff'
20 January	'The Welsh National Development Authority'
7 February	'Practical Arrangements for Implementation'
6 March	'Operational Areas: Fringe Problems'
6 March	'Local Law and Related Matters'
27 March	'Public Health Functions Relating to Local Authoritie'
29 March	'Constitution of Regional Water Authorities'
18 April	'Public Participation in Water Management'
18 April	'Economics and Finance'
June-July	'Pollution Control'
9 August	'The Amenity Use of Water Space and the Reorganisation of the British Waterways Board'
10 August	'The National Water Council'
22 August	'Staff Commission for England and Wales'
18 September	'Future Organisation of Land Drainage'
18 September	'Fisheries'
25 September	'Grant'

SOURCE: Adapted from Okun, 1977, p. 51.

some major issues unresolved and, as events turned out, to be dealt with in the second major reorganisation, in 1989. (See Chapters 3 and 4.) Consistent with the history of the sector up to 1973, the 1973–4 reforms also laid the foundations – albeit without conscious intent – for future policy change, thus ensuring the pattern of policy succession described.

As usual in examples of major policy change, big issues had to be 'unpacked' into smaller and more manageable policy problems. It is these that are examined now.

Integrated River Basin Management and the Statutory Water Companies

Civil servants at the DOE initially proposed that the regional water authorities (RWAS) would take over the statutory water companies' (SWCS) functions and assets, so that the *raison d' être* of the reorganisation – integration based on the hydrological cycle – would not be compromised. The Central Advisory Water Committee (CAWC) had also recommended that the RWAS acquire the thirty-one SWCS.

The Conservative administration, however, had pledged to halt, and indeed reverse, the expansion of the public sector. While the nationalisation of the SWCS would have been intrinsically small, the symbolic significance was regarded as too great. A 1971 DOE Circular rejected the initial civil service proposal and argued that:

> consideration of the desirable forms of organisation within the public sector must be distinguished from proposals for a further increase in the size of the public sector. There must be a strong presumption against any such proposals. The company undertakings are in general viable and efficient and the Government see a continuing role for them as agents of the RWAS. (DOE 92/71, para. 29)

The Conservative administration remained resolute in its conviction and the Water Act 1973 left the SWCs as autonomous entities. Their survival was a result of three main factors. First, the Heath Government was in difficulties with Conservative backbenchers over its application to join the EEC – hence a number of unrelated concessions were made as the price of support for this controversial policy. Secondly, ideology was important – Conservatives did not want to be seen as expanding the public sector. Thirdly, the lack of parliamentary and bargaining time forced the Government to seek quick solutions to a number of specific problems – a pattern which, as will be apparent, was also evident in the privatisation proposals much later.

The retention of the private water companies was an anomaly which undermined the logic of both regionalisation and IRBM. In a letter to *The Times* (20 December 1971) B. J. Nicholls, a member of CAWC, pointed out that the retention of the SWCs was:

> an illogical compromise which no doubt is the result of considerable political pressure which these bodies are able to bring to bear in the corridors of power ... the Government has lacked the political courage to treat all water undertakings in the same way. Presumably to try to avoid the tag of 'nationalization' they are proposing that the 31 SWCs should remain as agents of the RWAs. The excuse for preferential treatment is that the company undertakings are 'in general viable and efficient'. This statement is ludicrous when one considers that out of 31 companies, 18 supply less than 250 000 people each and seven of those supply less than 150,000 people ... These statistics show this proposal for what it is – a political expedient rather than a technical appraisal of the situation.

The local authority interests – represented by the Association of Municipal Corporations, the Rural District Councils' Association and the Urban District Councils' Association, all opposed the retention of SWCs. Indeed, the contradictions inherent in the Government's political concession were highlighted by the British Waterworks Association (BWA) which maintained that if the SWCs were acceptable as agents, then those local authorities which had been supplying water should also be acceptable. The BWA argued that:

> It is clear that the original concept of the RWAs as all purpose management bodies led by a small team of high calibre members and officers is disappearing as the Government's proposals unfold. Instead, the proposals are producing a fragmented and ponderous organization abounding with overlapping responsibilities and the opportunity to streamline and improve on the present structure is being lost in the process. (cited in Jordan et al., 1977, p. 331)

It is interesting to note that while the overwhelming majority of the respondents opposed the Government's intentions, key policy community and professionalised networks 'insiders', such as the Confederation of British Industry (CBI) and the Institute of Public Health Engineers (IPHE), approved of the Government's plans.

Managerialism and the Transformation of Organisational Ethos

As in the case of privatisation, policy change was also intended to bring about organisational change – particularly changes in organisational culture. Moreover, the new organisations would be unable to absorb the large numbers of existing staff, in particular those located in the higher echelons of the old organisations. The Government, therefore, offered early retirement to those who wished to leave the industry prior to reorganisation. In doing so it failed to recognise that there were also risks in encouraging departures. In practice this policy had some unintended consequences as the take-up rate was extremely high. Consequently, the new organisations were deprived of many highly experienced water managers whose participation in the embryonic and formative years of the RWAs would, according to several industry insiders, have been invaluable.

The Government also proposed to appoint some chief executives from outside the existing industry – the 'ring fence' was to be breached. Its determination to press this proposal demonstrated the depth of its commitment to the doctrine of new managerialism. From the Government's perspective, managers from outside the industry were not shackled with the public service attitudes which were felt to inhibit the existing management. New managers were expected to enhance and develop the concept of 'water' as a commodity rather than a public service. This intended shift in organisational ethos – which was indeed implemented – again paved the way for future policy changes, in particular, the Water Act 1983 which finally excluded the local authorities. Ultimately, it also facilitated privatisation.

During the passage of the 1973 Water Bill, the Secretary of State established a Management Structure Committee (MSC) (more commonly know as the Ogden Committee) 'to consider possible forms of management structure with a view to producing guidance on this matter for RWAs' (MSC, 1973, p. 1). The report reflected broader changes in public sector management at that time and it followed closely the recommendations of the Bains Committee Report, which also proposed the adoption of corporate management structures for local government. The recommendations of the Ogden Report were generally accepted and were particularly significant because of their place in the evolving professional and organisational culture in the water industry. The recommendations covered three main areas: the authority, the headquarter's management structure and the divisional structure. The Ogden Committee proposed that, in time, the RWAs should move towards a multi-functional managerialist approach which would foster multi-disciplinary consideration of policy and planning. It urged the new authorities to develop a corporate approach to management and to see the problems of their regions as a whole, avoiding both local constituency or special interest perspectives (ibid.). The committee concluded that, in future, it would not be possible to separate quantity from quality considerations – they would have to be considered and managed together. The RWAs would be required to follow a holistic managerial approach to the water cycle, managing it as a whole within hydrological constraints (ibid.). Though apparently detailed and esoteric, these recommendations possibly reflect a much broader and much more profound change towards a less accountable and more centralised exercise of power in Britain – a trend which has continued to this day (Richardson, 1994).

The National Water Council and the Water and Space Amenity Commission

The Government concurred with the CAWC that a National Water Council (NWC) should be established to act as a central spokesbody for the industry as a whole, and to provide services of general benefit to the industry. The 1973 act established the NWC and the Water and Space Amenity Commission (WSAC).

The NWC's advisory duties fell into two main categories. First, policy issues. These included common financial policy, implementation of current legislation and liaison with other non-departmental public bodies. Secondly, technical issues. Joint NWC/DOE standing technical committees were established to serve the industry in its widest sense, examining a wide and diverse range of technical and scientific issues. The NWC was primarily an advisory body with no planning or executive powers, and was supposed to be the main line of communication between the RWAs and central government departments. The RWAs, however, enjoyed direct access to ministers and were not required by statute to work through the council. However, once set up, the council did perform an important role in consultation processes between RWAs and interest groups – mainly producer groups. For example, it had regular meetings with groups such as the Chemical Industries Association (CIA), the Confederation of British Industry (CBI), the National Farmers Union (NFU) and so on.

The WSAC was financed by the NWC and was composed of the ten RWA chairmen, the NWC chairman and eleven ministerial nominees. Its duties included advising the Secretary of State on the formulation, promotion and execution of recreational and amenity aspects of the national water policy. The WSAC appeared to be of significance in that the Government had responded to the claims made by amenity and recreation interests during the passage of the legislation. The resources allocated to the WSAC, however, did not match the title of the authority. It had five full-time staff and lacked grant aiding powers. As John Dodwell, General Secretary of the Inland Waterways Association pointed out in 1972, while welcoming the establishment of the WSAC 'there appears to be a breakdown in the Government's logic in not giving the new Commission teeth' (*The Daily Telegraph*, 26 September 1972). Indeed, the commission might be described as a *placebo*, as it gave the appearance of tackling the problem, but in reality it did very little (Stringer and Richardson, 1980).

Local Authority Concessions

In terms of getting the radical reforms accepted, a series of concessions had to be made – not least to a (hitherto) key interest such as the local authorities. Thus, the Government had initially proposed that water authority chairmen were to be appointed by the minister for a five-year term, and that the RWA membership should be small, with a significant part of its membership drawn from local authorities. Many members would also be appointed by ministers for their wide and diverse interests, such as fishing, navigation, amenity, agriculture, recreation and industry while the chief executive should be appointed by ministers and members of the water authority. The Government also proposed creating autonomous Regional Consultative Councils (RCCs) to deal directly with consumer problems.

The then Leader of the Greater London Council, Sir Desmond Plummer, accused the Government of transferring the nation's water resources over to 'faceless bodies who will be unaccountable to the public for water and sewage control' (*The Daily Telegraph*, 21 August 1972). Local authority associations called on the Government to ensure that the RWAs were subject to democratic control and public accountability. They wanted two-thirds of the RWA membership to be given to local authority nominees. The local authority associations stated that the RCCs idea should be scrapped. In a joint statement the Association of Municipal Corporations, the County Councils' Association, and the Association of Urban and Rural District Councils said that they were 'deeply disappointed' with the Government's proposals. They argued that important local services such as water supply and sewage disposal services which 'should be the direct responsibility of the future local authorities ... are ... closely linked with other local authority responsibilities such as local amenity, local housing, and industry and planning' (*The Guardian*, 4 December 1971).

This issue became the most significant one for the four local authority associations as they saw the last vestige of their power in the water sector disappearing. The associations sent a deputation to the Secretary of State, Peter Walker, backing their claims with a threat to boycott working parties already set up to plan the changes in the industry. As Sir Frank Marshall, Chairman of the Association of Municipal Corporations, put it, the association has recommended a policy 'not so much of non-cooperation as reluctant hesitation'. He criticised the consultation process because of the 'much less open attitude of the DOE' compared with the Department of Health and Social Security (DHSS)' (*Municipal Review*, No. 513, [September] 1972). The consultation process was defended by Eldon Griffiths, Parliamentary Under Secretary of State. He said that the Government had circulated some 40,000 copies of fourteen consultation papers (issued before September 1972: three others were issued and subsequently received well over 1,000 responses). Griffiths stated that, 'we fully recognise the interests of local authorities and have undertaken to give them a substantial share of the membership. As a result of our continuing consultation discussions, I am confident that we can find a solution' (*Local Government Chronicle*, 6 October 1972, p. 1689).

In a somewhat earlier letter to the local authority associations, the Secretary of State had said that he had given the question of local authority representation 'a good deal of further thought' and that he was impressed by the force of the local authority representations. He had pledged to give local authorities a significant role in the water sector. He argued that on the one hand the RWAs must have a high degree of freedom to manage the day-to-day affairs of their organisations over a wide range of areas such as finance, investment programmes, sewerage and sewage disposal services. On the other hand, the locally elected representative was envisaged as having 'an essential and integral part to play in the operation of these functions' (*Municipal Review*, no. 373, September 1972).

The matter was finally resolved by conceding greater representation to the local authorities, in order to ease the passage of the Water Bill. However, in retrospect, the Water Act 1973 represented an intermediate stage towards the complete exclusion of local authority interests. Local authority associations had hoped that the concession that they gained over the membership of RWAS would deliver local democracy and political accountability to the water industry. However, the concession did so only in a very broad sense, in that it involved, on a formal basis, elected representatives in RWA decision-making processes. Their fears of professional dominance of the policy-making process were largely realised. As Gray points out, decision-making was 'largely concentrated in the hands of Water Authority officers and vested interests with little scope existing for participation from outside' (Gray, 1982, p. 157).

In fact, the final position of the local authorities on the RWAS turned out to be even weaker than expected. Their nominees actually ceased to be seconded local authority members, and became individual nominees on an *ad hoc* body. Thus, Chilver draws a useful distinction between *representatives* and *nominees*. Representatives take a brief from their parent organisation to the secondary body, whereas nominees do not (Chilver, 1974). The actual practice of the RWAS, once set up, was that local authority members did not carry a brief to the RWAS, if anything the reverse was true – *they appeared to carry a brief from the RWAS to their local authorities!* The situation was compounded by the fact that, unlike the nominees proposed by the Secretary of State, local authority nominees generally did not possess any special technical expertise in any water related area. In many cases they lacked even a general interest in water. Consequently they were generally unable to make any meaningful contribution to RWA proceedings. Thus, the shift towards a more managerial, technical and specialised form of policy delivery further weakened local and democratic accountability. In addition, the size of the RWA boards had changed considerably from that originally proposed by CAWC. CAWC proposed that boards would have between ten and fifteen members, not fifty or so.

Local authority participation on the RWA boards was also at odds with the principle of 'managerialism'. The hybrid membership has been criticised for being neither sufficiently representative of the public, nor wholly based upon managerial expertise criteria (Gray, 1982). 'The belief that the Water Authorities require only small managerial boards to secure effective management is balanced by the desire to ensure that an element of political accountability is present in the industry' (ibid., p. 160). Similarly, Cordle and Willetts highlighted the inherent confusion that existed in that there 'still seems to exist a need for a clearer consideration of the role of local authority nominees on RWAS – a purely managerial role, a consumer representative role, a "reporting back" role, or a combination of all three' (1984, p. 44). Keating and Rhodes have also questioned the effectiveness of local authority representatives on RWAS. They argue that if the representatives were not to represent the special concerns of their own local authorities, then professionals should have assumed direct control of the industry (Keating and Rhodes, 1981). The new organisational culture tended to emphasise the apolitical character of water services, notwithstanding the veneer of local authority participation.

Looking back, the local authorities were sold a pup in 1975! Their participation turned out to be a sham and the concessions made to them by the Secretary of State during the passage of the legislation were largely a matter of expediency. Time was running out as water reorganisation was planned to be implemented on the same day as local government reorganisation – April Fools' Day, 1974. The DOE also realised that it would have been needlessly controversial to exclude local representation on RWAS totally when their position could be effectively neutered anyway. Thus, the stemming of the worst of the local authorities' opposition to the radical restructuring of water in England and Wales enabled the Government to proceed quickly to create the regionalised and integrated system of control it favoured. While all this was going on, Scottish local authorities retained their existing role, unchallenged!

POLICY DEVELOPMENT: THE ROAD TO PRIVATISATION 1974–1989

Immediately after the 1974 reorganisation, the water industry faced a harsh financial and economic environment, similar to other parts of the public sector, demonstrating that policy sectors cannot escape broader trends in the economy and society as a whole. The RWAS' establishment, rather unfortunately, coincided with the first oil crisis, the resultant spiralling of inflation and, eventually, IMF pressure on the Government to reduce public expenditure. Several other factors also made the RWAS' financial debut a rather harsh one. First, the general anti-inflationary measures introduced in the economy in the early 1970s eventually led to a moratorium being imposed on water supply charges in 1973. Thus expenditures were 'out of balance with incomes on transfer day' (Jenkins, 1976, p. 245). Secondly, the new authorities inherited a physical asset structure which was at best dilapidated and required extensive capital investment programmes. Thirdly, sewerage and sewage disposal services had already seen a drop in standards as a result of the political pressures on local government to keep rate levels down. Fourthly, exceptionally high interest rates had been introduced by the Government as a tool of economic management. Fifthly, the lack of reserves and working balances presented serious problems. It has been estimated that the industry inherited a massive debt of £2.2 bn. (at 1974 prices) which was a direct effect of financing capital from loans rather than revenue. RWAS were therefore acutely vulnerable to the impact of high interest rates (over 17 per cent in early 1975) on the funding of their capital expenditure. Finally, the introduction of commercial principles was a significant move away from the previous local authority procedures which involved subsidies via the rate support grant (RSG) (ibid.). The profitability principle, aimed at encouraging economic efficiency and the generation of surpluses, allowed the Secretary of State to require the RWAS to achieve a specified minimum rate of return on assets, and to reduce the requirement for borrowing in order to finance capital schemes. The self-financing directive which the Government introduced had an immediate and dramatic effect (Parker and Penning-Rowsell, 1980).

Water charges were raised immediately the RSG subsidies were withdrawn. From their inception, the RWAs found themselves in the rather unenviable situation of having ceilings imposed on capital expenditure, notwithstanding a backlog of much needed investment. Self-governing the sector might be, but events elsewhere in the economy had a major impact on this self-governance.

Charges spiralled immediately after the 1974 reorganisation, with the average household bill rising by 41 per cent in 1974/5. The problems were a direct result of the removal of a significant subsidy for expensive waste water treatment. Ending the subsidy had significant ramifications. When the service was subsidised, all households paid for the service whether they used it or not. The Water Act 1973 stated that consumers were to be charged for the services they actually received. The termination of cross-subsidisation lead to enormous regional disparities and the Government was forced to introduce the Water Charges Equalisation Act. This was the first step towards a return to *de facto* cross-subsidisation.

It was no great surprise, therefore, that the RWAs suffered severe public relations problems when they presented their customers with their first separate bill for water and sewerage services. The response was totally hostile, with the RWAs criticised for being remote and impersonal large-scale bureaucracies. This view was supported by the local authorities, even though local authority nominees comprised the majority of RWA membership!

Local authorities criticised the fact that the RWAs had the power to levy taxes yet were not directly elected bodies. In response, the RWAs maintained that they were democratically accountable because they were responsible to Parliament via the appropriate minister, and because they were open to public scrutiny and pressure from numerous sources. Thus, there were two competing criteria of legitimacy – electoral and technical – with opposing perspectives on definitions of accountability. Local authorities understood accountability to mean political accountability to a constituency. In contrast RWA officers saw accountability in terms of the efficient performance of the industry. The situation was exacerbated by the lack of coincidence between local authority boundaries and the river basins on which the RWAs were based. Thus:

> The absence of elected authorities corresponding to water regions in turn reinforced the case for their being appointed and *ad hoc* rather than elected and multifunctional. Thus, the way was opened for conflicts between water authorities and local government and within the authorities themselves. These have concerned the 'legitimacy' of the RWAs in the eyes of those who have to deal with them and the criteria by which they make decisions. (Keating and Rhodes, 1981, p. 488)

Problems of accountability and influence were compounded by the fact that central professional bodies claimed to possess a high degree of understanding about the commercial and managerial problems confronting the industry. As Rhodes points out, 'When such expertise is allied to professional organisations ... expertise and professional values can rival political values as the basis for decisions; the policy system becomes professionalised and insulated from the political system' (Rhodes, 1988, p. 115).

The 1973–4 reforms, though radical and based upon previous experience, therefore had within them an inbuilt instability. The political compromise over the local authority interest – devised to satisfy one of the (then) key members of the policy community – had produced some kind of 'policy mess'. Eventually, the difficult question of accountability had to be resolved by further policy change. In 1981, therefore, the Government published *The Membership of Regional Water Authorities. A Consultation Paper From the DoE*. The paper was based on a review of the industry, which the Government had instigated. It had done so for two main reasons. First, a Monopolies and Mergers Commission (MMC) Report on Severn Trent RWA and its two associated water companies recommended changes to the membership of RWAS. It recommended a reduction in size and a change in the composition of the membership on the grounds that the exisiting membership had led to a waste of resources, increasing bureaucracy and a slowing down of decision-making. It was further argued that consumers were not well represented under the present arrangements, and that, consequently, the size of the membership should be reduced and that it should not be predominantly based on local authority representation. The MMC estimated that if the Severn Trent membership was reduced to the same size as the boards of nationalised industries (approximately twelve), then an annual saving of £650,000 (at 1981 prices) could be achieved. Secondly, the Department of Trade and Industry (DTI) had published a consultation document in December 1981 which dealt with the general question of consumer representation on non-departmental public bodies. Thus, changes were about to take place elsewhere in the public sector and this cleared the way for RWAS to be brought within the remit of the nationalised industries consumer councils system.

The consultation document reviewed a number of options but favoured the so-called 'small option' of between ten to fifteen members appointed wholly or partly by ministers and major local authorities, with complementary consultative committees being created in each area to deal with consumer complaints. The paper criticised the existing system and argued that it was as questionable whether having a majority of local authority representatives on RWA Boards as a link between RWAS and customers had proved to be effective (DOE, 1981). The Department argued that very few individuals knew that they had a local authority representative on their RWA. Echoing the MMC report, the DOE paper stated that:

> The present system of membership results in RWAs of generally large and unwieldy size much bigger than is needed for management of essentially executive organisations. It tends to lead to the proliferation of committees, bureaucracy, avoidable expense, and slowing down of decision making. (DOE, 1981, p. 7)

Gray (1984) has argued that the influential MMC's criticisms of the RWAS were at best questionable. First, the role of local authority representatives was highly ambiguous.

Many people, including the representatives themselves, were unsure whether they were policy-makers and planners, and/or public relations people. Secondly, the size argument was unsupported by the available evidence because RWAs were required by statute to have at least three committees – the average was five, the smallest three and the largest seven – hardly a proliferation. Finally, he argues, the claims over the 'excessive' costs due to the membership size of RWAs was founded on a rather shaky assumption, since:

> savings anticipated from a reduction in membership size do make sense if, first, the ineffectiveness of members is real, and, secondly, if improvements to effectiveness cannot be made. While the former is possibly true the latter, unstated, assumption is open to debate. (Gray, 1984, p. 15)

As suggested, the real problem was not size. It was the creation of RWAs dichotomised along two competing bases of legitimacy – electoral and technical. Following the consultations based upon the DOE's consultation paper of 1981, the Government decided to push water reform one step further by abolishing the institutionalised link between the RWAs and local authorities. The Water Act 1983 removed the statutory requirement that local authority nominees comprise the majority on RWA boards. Relevant ministers were given powers to appoint all the RWA membership, and the membership size was to be no less than nine and no greater than fifteen. RWAs were permitted to terminate sewerage agency arrangements with district councils if they were not satisfied with the service the councils provided. The NWC and the WSAC were abolished. The RWAs were to make special arrangements for consumer representation, and the authorities were permitted to exclude the media and the general public from meetings of the authority and its committees. In total, this package of policy changes moved the water industry even further from its traditional administrative roots. After 1983, many boards became much more malleable instruments for the chairmen to secure their objectives. As Saunders points out:

> With the removal of local authority members, the Board has been (fully) depoliticised and incorporated, through the chairmen, into the managerial structure and ethos of the authority. (1984, p. 7)

The RWAs developed a direct 'one-to-one' relationship with the DOE, on the conventional nationalised industry model of ministry/industry sponsorship. Effectively, the community of actors involved in water policy was fairly tightly drawn – the DOE and the industry, with policy commonly being determined in meetings between the WSA chairmen, DOE officials, and DOE ministers. However, another policy actor – the Treasury – was also a key (if somewhat shadowy) player. Much of the interaction between the industry and its sponsoring ministry, the DOE, concerned ceilings on borrowing and charge setting. Once agreement was reached over the total financial package, the authorities were free to allocate resources as they wished, on the nationalised industry model. The relationship gave the RWAs a significant degree of autonomy to run the industry as they wished. They had, effectively, been given the 'franchise for public policy' (Jordan and Richardson, 1982). RWAs determined their own objectives within a strict financial framework set by the Government.

This, of course, raises the difficult question of where power lay? Two contrasting images of power in the sector can be constructed – again quite familiar to students of the nationalised industry/government relationship. On the one hand, the Government was clearly in control of some key variables that were central features of the environment in which the industry operated – namely finance and charges. On the other hand, the industry was 'left to get on with it' once these key variables had been determined. In a sense, the water sector was a mixture of state power *and* the franchising of public policy. However, the industry, like others in Britain, was to a degree also being carried along by broader changes in values in society at that time – such as 'managerialism', which acted to its benefit, and what King has termed a 'mood change' (King, 1985) in Britain which emphasised the need to cut public expenditure and taxes. In the end, as shall be apparent in subsequent chapters, this 'mood change' had some specific consequences in terms of tougher financial controls on the industry and provided the 'spark' for a major discontinuity in policy development.

These broad shifts in values and in policy fashion did not, however, completely sweep aside the notion that accountability was important for what was still a publicly owned industry. This value had to be accorded at least lip service in the form of consumer representation. (Again, a familiar piece of symbolic or placebo policy for the nationalised industries as a whole). Consumer Consultative Councils (CCCs) were established in each RWA region, and were comprised of between ten and forty members representing a wide variety of interests, including local authorities, industry, agriculture, voluntary associations and so on. In addition to the CCCs, Regional Recreation Conservation Committees (RRCCs) were created covering the whole region and were composed of numerous recreational and environmental groups. These councils and committees were largely symbolic in nature. Major policy decisions for the sector were made by a process of bargaining between state actors (DOE, Treasury, MAFF for some issues) and representatives of the industry in a straightforward example of policy community politics. The broader issue network was confined to the periphery of the policy process in these new structures. The claim that the structures were largely symbolic is supported by the complete lack of interest shown in these bodies by major producer groups (for example, the CBI, the NFU and so on). The producers continued to lobby through the traditional routes of informal and regular contact directly with the RWAs, which reflected their insider status, or directly with the Government. As the Southern Water Chairman informed Saunders:

> we have regular meetings with groups like the NFU, the CLA and the CBI ... so all that's been going on irrespective of these consultative councils ... I can't speak to every bloody shopkeeper. We have been in constant discussion with the major groups. I think the consultative councils will widen the discussion ... I will continue to talk with these groups so that I shall have two lots to talk to instead of one lot. (Saunders, 1984, p. 8)

This was not new. Long before the 1983 reforms, the Chief Executive of Thames Water Authority had said that, 'we have contacts with the CBI and the NFU and are always willing to meet conservationists or other organised groups by arrangement' (Morrison, 1975, p. 45). As Saunders has commented, while these discussions may involve both types of participant, it seems very unlikely that the outcomes will be the same for both sets of participants (Saunders, 1983). While access to the Government and RWAS may not be restricted solely to such mutually self-interested groups (that is, agricultural, industrial and professional), these groups are traditionally strong and politically astute, and 'make better use of these opportunities and generally present arguments with which the Government (and the RWAS) is likely to agree' (Parker and Penning-Rowsell, 1980, p. 248). Privately, one insider has observed that, although his RWA had to create consumer consultative committees, 'like the theory of public accountability in the 1973/4 reforms, they were also irrelevant' (Private correspondence, October 1990).

Thus, it appears that the Water Act 1983 structured the industry as the framers of the 1973–4 reform had originally envisaged, until the local authority associations managed to secure concessions from Peter Walker during the passage of the 1973 bill. Sir Gordon Jones, Chairman of Yorkshire Water Services, believes that 1983 was a watershed year for the RWAS:

> most, if not all, of the Water Authorities started to think of themselves as businesses, albeit public owned and subject to financial and other constraints … all ten introduced business practices to the maximum extent compatible with that … there is no doubt that the prevailing culture and ethos within the Water Authorities changed markedly after 1983 or so, with more of an emphasis towards the definition of corporate goals and objectives, the introduction of Business Plans, management training and on quite a large scale, and a greater degree (albeit still not very much) of customer orientation. (Private correspondence, 28 May 1991)

CONCLUSIONS: THE WATER ACT 1973, POLICY SUCCESSION AND THE POLICY PROCESS

The Water Act 1973 ended the disintegrated nature of service delivery in the water sector in England and Wales. The Water Resources Act 1963 had paved the way for the 1973 act by advancing the concept and practice of IRBM and this, combined with the regrouping process, had its 'logical' conclusion in the ten multi-purpose RWAS. Consequently, greater hydrological links with the operational units was achieved and, in theory at least, financial resources were increased via economies of scale. Yet the water sector appears to exhibit a long-term 'reform dynamic' familiar in other policy areas. Thus, Elcock argues that:

> reorganising government agencies has been a long-standing preoccupation of British public administrators. Structural change has been undertaken in the hope and belief that it would solve some of the major problems confronting those agencies and improve their performance. (1991, p. 44)

He also warns that there is a danger that reorganisation may be addictive because those who lose out in the previous reorganisation begin almost immediately 'to press for further reorganisation to meet their demands' (ibid. p. 62). There is some evidence of this in the water sector. A decade after the 1973–4 reorganisation, the industry was restructured again under the Water Act 1983. This in turn was succeeded by privatisation in 1989. Currently, the Government is establishing an Environmental Protection Agency which will rationalise some aspects of the regulatory structure of the industry. The Environment Agencies Act will amalgamate the NRA, Her Majesty's Inspectorate of Pollution (HMIP) and local authority waste regulators into one organisation. Thus, reform appears to have become a permanent feature of the system.

Though the role of the state *vis-à-vis* other actors was of considerable importance, this role was confined to the relatively narrow issue of financing – the state's preoccupation at that time. State policy in terms of clear policy guidelines for the sector was absent, however, except in a purely formal sense. For example, one clearly defined goal of the 1973 act was the promotion of a national water policy – a policy goal first espoused in the 1944 White Paper, *A National Water Policy*. However, little was actually achieved in this area beyond the reduction in the number of operating units, and the final amalgamation of the remaining units into the ten RWAs. Yet it might be argued that the 1973 Act created organisations which were rather autonomous from direct central or local government control. They were largely free to provide the service as they wished within the relatively loose policy framework of central supervision or control but within increasingly strict financial controls. This view has been confirmed by Sir Gordon Jones:

> although my experience of the Public Sector is limited to about five or six years in Yorkshire Water, the degree of Government interference in the water industry was quite low, and we were left on a fairly loose rein subject only to severe financial constraints on how much we could borrow. There were, of course, second order targets, such as reductions in operating costs, numbers employed, disposal of assets and the like, but they were fairly minimal: in addition, there were nudges about charges, but no explicit directives. (Private correspondence, 28 May 1991)

Gray argues that the dominance of hydrological factors in shaping the institutional structure of the sector had several consequences. First, all other factors, be they political, social or economic, found themselves secondary to the predominance of the technical imperative. Secondly, the outcome of the dominance of such technical factors was that the operating units were strangely hybrid. The authorities created in 1973–4 were not pure nationalised industries. (Yet they did share some common characteristics with these organisations, such as an organisational structure similar to other non-departmental bodies.) Nor were they any longer part of the local government service. Yet, as we have seen, their membership was based on a majority of members nominated from local government (Gray, 1982, p. 148). As he suggests, however, politics was also important, as the retention of the SWCs had demonstrated so clearly. Other concessions made during the consultation process show that while the main lines of policy may be viewed as largely being a result of a technical imperative, they were also shaped by an admixture of technical, political and economic factors (ibid., p. 148).

Another key aspect of the 1973 act was that it highlighted a significant degree of influence by water technocrats. Their input essentially finalised the removal of the management of water and water related services from any direct electoral control and replaced it with appointed managerial style boards to run each RWA. Managerial efficiency was replaced at the expense of participation by outsiders in the policy-making process. As Saunders has suggested, the reorganisation of the industry had undermined:

> both electoral and participatory democracy within the reorganised industry. The gap that was left was filled by the water professionals themselves who claimed legitimacy for their domination of planning and policy-making by reference to their technical expertise. (1985, p. 34)

The relative dominance of water technocrats was short lived, however. They too were subject to the effects of broader changes. Between 1973 and 1983 economic developments and structural changes in the management of RWAs loosened the technocratic grip on power. The power base of the technocrats was quickly eroded as corporate actors, especially finance directors, became more influential within the organisations as the Government tightened its financial grip. Policy change also began to redistribute power between professions, as well as between different units of government. As Gray points out:

> Between 1968 and 1977 the work of the Water Directorate in the MHLG and, subsequently the Department of the Environment (DOE) has altered from a concern with engineering and capital approvals for individual schemes ... to a more general approach aimed at overall performance and activities. The main centre of work is now concerned with cash-limits and financial performance, including with the implications of these for future WA (Water Authority) plans. (1984, p. 12)

Here, again, is an exercise of state power and, therefore, a qualification to the 'autonomous industry' image. The Government's increasing concern with monetary policy had the effect of changing the organisational agenda in the water authorities – and consequently of elevating the importance of finance directors over engineers. Up to about 1983 the internal politics of the RWAs had been a power struggle within the framework of corporate management – with people like directors of resource planning and directors of scientific services losing out. In the end, by the early to mid 1980s, RWAs tended to be managed by a close working relationship between the director of finance and the chairman.

What of policy change? Wildavsky maintains that:

To understand where future policies are likely to lead us we need to know about past policies. For, as policy becomes its own cause, the future problems in which we are increasingly interested are a response to our past solutions ... policy solutions are the temporary and partial reduction of tension. (1979, pp. 83 and 390)

Characterisations of the 1973–4 reorganisation as a radical policy innovation are, therefore, qualified if one takes account of the historical development of the industry. Viewed from a greater longitudinal perspective, change can be seen as exhibiting numerous elements of policy succession. This view was confirmed by civil servants to Jordan and Richardson in the mid 1970s:

It was possible to argue that the 1973 Act was a mere continuation of a process of reducing the number of operating units and alleviating competition between them. Such an image of felicitous evaluation was presented to us in interviews at the DOE. (Jordan and Richardson, 1977, p. 308)

In practice, policy succession and 'radical' innovation may be quite similar in that they are both purposive attempts at policy change. They differ in that genuine innovation relates to the involvement of government in a *new* area of activity whereas policy succession attempts to replace an existing policy. Thus, policy change paves the way for policy change and, in the case of water, successive policy change paved the way for innovative policy change. The 1944 White Paper and the Water Act 1945 paved the way for the changes introduced in the Water Resources Act 1963, which prepared the way for the Water Act 1973, which in its turn lead to the half-way house to privatisation, the Water Act 1983. The Water Act 1983 essentially removed a hitherto powerful actor (local government), imbued the water authorities with private sector management practices and ultimately led to wholesale privatisation. At the point of privatisation some kind of policy discontinuity can be seen – in the sense that the industry was moved from the public to the private sector and from a system of essentially private regulation to a system of public regulation. While definitely facilitated by the long succession of policy changes described in this chapter – and therefore in one sense some kind of 'logical' end point – there is no particular reason to believe that the problems which the industry faced by 1989 *necessitated* a move to the private sector. That the option of tackling the industry's (by then) considerable problems within the public sector was never really examined was due to the coincidence of a number of factors and events, to which we now turn.

NOTES

1. Beddoe later became Chief Executive of the Severn Trent Regional Water Authority, after the 1974 reorganisation.
2. Within this category there were three main types of 'water undertaker': Statutory Water Companies (swcs), local authorities and joint boards of local authorities.

REFERENCES

Central Advisory Water Committee (CAWC) (1943), *Third Report, 1942–43*, Cmnd 6454 (London: hmso).
Central Advisory Water Committee (CAWC) (1971), *The Future of Water Management in England and Wales* (London: HMSO)
Chilver, R. C. (1974), 'Forms of Organisation', in B. Funnel and R. Hey (eds), *The Management of Water Resources in England and Wales* (Farnborough, Hants: Saxon House).
Cobb, R. W. and Elder, C. D. (1972), *Participation in American Politics: The Dynamics of Agenda Building* (Baltimore: The John Hopkins University Press).
Cordle, P. and Willetts, C. (1984), 'Links between Regional Water Authorities and Local Authorities' (County Treasury: West Midlands County Council).
Department of the Environment (DOE) (1971), *Reorganisation of Water and Sewerage Services: Government Proposals and Arrangements for Consultation*, Circular DOE 92/71.
DOE (1981), *The Membership of Regional Water Authorities. A Consultation Paper from the DOE* (London: DOE).
Downs, A. (1967), *Inside Bureaucracy* (Boston: Little, Brown and Company).
Elcock, H. (1991), *Change and Decay?: Public Administration in the 1990s* (Essex: Longman).
Gray, C. (1982), 'The Regional Water Authorities', in B. W. Hogwood and M. Keating (eds), *Regional Government in England* (Oxford: Clarendon Press) pp. 143–67.
Gray, C. (1984), 'Values and Change in Inter-Governmental Relations', *Public Administration Bulletin*, no. 44 (April), pp. 2–18.
Hassan, John A. (1993), *The Water Industry 1900–51: A Failure of Public Policy?* (Series No: 93–09) (Manchester: Manchester Metropolitan University).
Hogwood, B. W. (1987), *From Crisis to Complacency?* (Oxford: Oxford University Press).
Hogwood, B. W. and Peters, Guy (1983), *Policy Dynamics* (Oxford: Oxford University Press).
Jenkins, R. C. (1976), 'Financing the Water Cycle', *Water Pollution Control*, vol. 75, pp. 244–51.
Jordan, A. G., and Richardson, J. J. (1977), 'Outside Committees and Policy-Making: The Central Water Advisory Committee', *Public Administration Bulletin*, no. 24, pp. 41–58.
Jordan, A. G., Richardson, J. J. and Kimber, R. H. (1977), 'The Origins of the Water Act of 1973', *Public Administration*, vol. 55 (Autumn), pp. 317–34.
Jordan, A. G., Richardson, J. J. and Kimber, R. H. (1978), 'Lobbying, Administrative Reform and Policy Styles. The Case of Land Drainage', *Political Studies*, vol. 26, no. 1, pp. 47–64.
Jordan, A. G. and Richardson, J. J. (1982), 'The British Policy Style or the Logic of Negotiation?', in J. Richardson (ed.), *Policy Styles in Western Europe* (London: George Allen & Unwin), pp. 80–110.
Keating, M. and Rhodes, M. (1981), 'Politics or Technocracy? The Regional Water Authorities', *The Political Quarterly*, vol. 52, pp. 487–90.
King, A. (1985), 'Governmental Responses to Budget Scarcity', *Policy Studies Journal*, 113, vol. 3, pp. 476–93.
Kingdon, J. (1984), *Agendas, Alternatives, and Public Policies* (Boston: Little, Brown and Company).
Kinnersley, D. (1988), *Troubled Water: Rivers, Politics and Pollution* (London: Hilary Shipman).
Kinnersley, D. (1994), *Coming Clean: The Politics of Water and the Enivorment* (London: Penguin).
Kirby, C. (1979), *Water in Great Britain* (Harmondsworth: Penguin Books).
Management Structure Committee (Ogden Committee) (1973), *The New Water Industry: The Management Structure* (London: HMSO).
Ministry of Health, Ministry of Agriculture and Fisheries, Department of Health for Scotland (1944), *A National Water Policy*, Cmnd 6515 (London: HMSO).
Ministry of Housing and Local Government (MHLG) (1969), 'Central Advisory Water Committee Memorandum to Organisations and Individuals Submitting Evidence' (London: MHLG).
Ministry of Housing and Local Government (MHLG) (1970), *Taken for Granted*, Report of the Working Party on Sewage Disposal (London: HMSO).
Mitchell, B. (1970), 'The Institutional Framework for Water Management in England and Wales', *Natural Resources Journal*, vol. 10 (July), pp. 566–89.
Morrison, A. (1975), 'Multifunctional Expertise', *Municipal Journal/Municipal Engineering Supplement*, 4 April 1975, pp. 3–4.
Okun, D. A. (1967), 'Regrouping of Water Supplies in the United Kingdom', *Public Works*, June, pp. 153–54, 206.
Okun, D. A. (1977), *Regionalisation of Water Management* (London: Applied Science Publishers Limited).
Parker, D. and Penning-Rowsell, E. (1980), *Water Planning in Britain* (London: George Allen & Unwin).
Rhodes, R. A. W. (1988), *Beyond Westminster and Whitehall* (London: Unwin Hyman).

Richardson, J. J. (1994), 'Doing Less by Doing More: British Government 1979–93', *West European Politics*, vol. 17, no. 3, pp. 178–97.

Richardson, J. J. and Jordan, A. G. (1979), *Governing Under Pressure: The Policy Process in a Post-Parliamentary Democracy* (Oxford: Martin Robertson).

Sabatier, P. A. (1988), 'An Advocacy Coalition Framework of Policy Change and the Role of Policy-Orientated Learning Therein', *Policy Sciences*, vol. 21, pp. 129–68.

Saunders, P. (1983), *The 'Regional State': A Review of the Literature and Agenda for Research*, Working Paper 35, Urban and Regional Studies (Sussex: University of Sussex).

Saunders, P. (1984), *We Can't Afford Democracy Too Much: Findings from a Study of Regional State Institutions in South-East England*, Working Paper 43 Urban and Regional Studies (Sussex: University of Sussex).

Stringer, J. K. and Richardson, J. J. (1980), 'Managing the Political Agenda: Problem definition and policy making in Britain', *Parliamentary Affairs*, vol. 23, pp. 23–39.

Waddington, J. I. and Hammerton, D. (1974), 'A new look for water management in Scotland', *Effluent and Water Treatment Journal*, April, pp. 211–17.

Wildavsky, A. (1979), *Speaking Truth To Power: The Art and Craft of Policy Analysis* (Boston: Little, Brown and Company).

3

Policy Discontinuity:
Privatisation as a Challenge

INTRODUCTION: IDEOLOGY AND PRAGMATISM

We have absolutely no intention of privatising the water industry. The Government have no plans to urge that upon the water authorities. There has been some press speculation about it in the past, but there is no intention to do so.

> Neil MacFarlane, Parliamentary Under-Secretary of State
> for the Department of the Environment,
> HC Debates, 20 December 1984, col. 457

My right hon. Friends and I will be examining the possibility of a measure of privatisation in the Industry.

> Ian Gow, Junior Environment Minister, HC Debates,
> 7 February 1985, col. 1142

In the last six years we have made the water authorities fit and ready to join the private sector ... Privatisation is the next logical step. It will bring benefits to the customers, to the industry itself and to the nation as a whole.

> Kenneth Baker, Secretary of State for the Environment,
> HC Debates, 5 February 1986, col. 287

The privatisation of the water industry was one of the most controversial, turbulent and complex privatisations of the 1980s. From start to finish the process included four Secretaries of State for the Environment (Jenkins, Baker, Ridley and Chris Patten), eight water ministers (Belstead, Caithness, Gow, MacFarlane, Moynihan, Howard, John Patten, Trippier), and one of the largest restructuring bills ever presented to Parliament, containing some 192 clauses and 27 schedules.

Conventional wisdom perceives privatisation as an example of policy innovation, and one of the cornerstones of Thatcherism. This chapter (together with Chapter 4) illustrates that the process of water privatisation is best characterised as more a case of muddling through, leaving many issues and problems to be resolved at the implementation stage, than a purposive well thought-out steering from the centre. Ideological motivations on the part of the Conservative Government played a role in the agenda setting and formulation stages of the broad privatisation programme. The processes and policy outcomes of privatisation, however, question the notion of an ideologically driven Thatcherite policy innovation. The evidence on water privatisation suggests a rather more complex interpretation. The picture is of an uncertain and stumbling Government, a divided industry, the exercise of personal leadership in the development of policy, fluidity of group influence and the pragmatic necessity for ultimately negotiating with key interests in the policy process.

All policies have a history and this can either constrain or facilitate what might follow in the future. In this case, the history of the policy sector was far from constricting. Indeed, as Chapter 2 suggested, the foundations for the privatisation of the water industry in England and Wales were laid by the 1973–4 reorganisation. Ten regional water authorities (RWAs) were created and were given control over every aspect of water management in their particular region. The 1973–4 reorganisation (itself a radical policy change) had followed the common pattern of water policy-making: most of the established interests were to some extent accommodated in the final policy outcome. Dominated by technocrats, the water policy sector conformed fairly closely to the model of a tight policy network in which technical expertise was the main basis for consensual decision-making – that is, water was a good example of a professionalised policy network (Rhodes, 1988). Only the local authorities really lost out in the change processes and even they did not go away empty handed.

Yet, as has been argued, the policy sector saw further important changes in the post-1973 period as financial aspects increasingly became more important and as organisational cultures began to change within the RWAs. The seeds of more fundamental change were sown in 1973, after which water came to be seen as an economic good, akin to that provided by other public utilities. Since the creation of the RWAs in England and Wales, water has been seen less and less as a service and more and more as a commodity (Saunders, 1985). The moves described in the previous chapter – the further restructuring of the industry through the Water Act 1983, the shift from historic cost accounting (HCA) to current cost accounting (CCA) which overtly pushed the RWAs towards an ethos which stressed commercialism, and the final exclusion of local authority representation on RWAs[1] – all, in some way, facilitated the eventual privatisation, without it actually having been planned.

Thus, the decision to privatise may not be as radical as it initially appears (even though it was a clean break with the past), when one takes account of the history of policy developments. Over time, the industry had become more 'managerialist', and the degree of conventional public accountability had declined. However, it was still a considerable leap from the reformed water industry to a *private* water industry. Indeed, the Government was not planning to privatise the water industry. If further change was to take place, the catalyst had to come from elsewhere.

PRIVATISATION STUMBLES ONTO THE POLITICAL AGENDA

In February 1985 the Treasury Orders on Rate of Return for the water industry provoked and annoyed the management of some of the then RWAs. In January 1985, several of the RWA chairmen reminded their customers that it was the Government that was to blame for increased charges. In particular, the Thames Chairman, the late Roy Watts, stated that his board objected to the repayment to the Government of an extra £40 m. in loans and to the consequent increase in charges of 10 per cent to cover it. Thames had budgeted for a 6 per cent increase and Watts volunteered Thames as the first candidate for privatisation – indeed he had first suggested privatisation in 1984.

Watts maintained that Thames had become essentially a revenue-raiser for the Treasury, similar to the electricity and gas industries. He stated that, 'Repaying loans early to the National Loans Fund (NLF) is just the same as paying taxes to the Treasury .... [the Government is] abusing the monopoly power of the utilities' (*Management Today*, January 1985, p. 110). By his intervention, Watts played a key role in the agenda setting stage of the privatisation process, and heralded the beginning of what David Kinnersley described as 'a long period of confusion and false starts' (Kinnersley, 1988, p. 136). His intervention was not entirely opportunistic, however. It reflected the strong financial position of his own RWA. While his call for independence from the Government was not founded on any detailed organisational blueprint, it represented a logical development in the Watts' approach to the management of Thames. Thus, it was not a purely random event. Since his arrival at Thames he had, according to Jim Boudier, Finance Director at Thames Water, 'generated organisational change within Thames ... imbuing the organisation with a greater business sense' (Interview, October 1990). Watts saw Thames as akin to an American utility company rather than a public service organisation and it is important to note, therefore, that changes in organisational culture may, in the event, be as important as formal legislative and institutional developments in the policy process.

Following Watts' comments, the late Ian Gow, the junior Environment Minister, announced, during the Treasury Orders debate on 7 February 1985 (it is believed without the knowledge of his department), that the Government was at least prepared to consider change. The use of the term 'Government' was, perhaps, an example of poetic licence! For example, as late as 31 January 1985, Prime Minister Thatcher, had been unenthusiastic about the prospects of water privatisation. In December 1984 the Government had issued a categorical denial that it had any intention of privatising the water industry (see the quotation from Neil MacFarlane cited above). In response to a written Parliamentary Question, the Prime Minister had replied that:

> The Government would welcome new ideas on privatisation. However, the Water Authorities are natural monopolies for many of their functions and *we need to be particularly careful when considering replacing a public monopoly by a private one*. Because of the environmental and public health responsibilities, any proposal to privatise them would also raise issues of regulation. (HC Debates, 31 October 1985, col. 292w, emphasis added)

Yet one week later Gow said that:

> Some of my right hon. and hon. Friends have suggested that the Water Author-
> ities might be transferred to the private sector and I understand that that
> prospect would not be unwelcome to the Chairman of Thames ... The transfer
> of Water Authorities, which form a natural monopoly, presents special prob-
> lems, not least because of their regulatory functions. Nevertheless, my right
> hon. Friends and I will be examining the possibility of a measure of privatisa-
> tion in the industry. (HC Debates, 7 February 1985, col. 1142)

The inherent confusion in the conflicting governmental statements was further
compounded by the publication of the Ministry of Agriculture, Fisheries and Food
(MAFF) Green Paper in March 1985: *Financing and Administration of Land
Drainage, Flood Prevention and Coast Protection in England and Wales* (Cmnd.
9449). This paper discussed the alternative methods of financing the RWAs' land
drainage, flood prevention and coast protection activities. Nowhere was privatisation
mentioned. Indeed, when the House of Lords debated the Department of the Environment (DOE) Discussion Paper on water privatisation (issued one month after the
MAFF document, on 1 April 1985), Baroness Nicol drew attention to the fact that:

> It [the MAFF Green Paper] set out to examine all the possible financial alterna-
> tives which are open for these operations. Nowhere that I can find is privatisa-
> tion mentioned as an alternative ... We have to ask: does the MAFF know what
> the DOE is doing, does the DOE know what action the MAFF is taking, or do they
> just fall out with each other and not discuss these matters at all? (HL Debates,
> 22 April 1985, cols 992–3)

Privatisation of the water industry therefore appeared to arrive on the political
agenda rather suddenly and without any formal policy co-ordination within the
machinery of government, although Ian Gow had discussed the possibility of privatisation with Nigel Lawson (Chancellor of the Exchequer), and with several Conservative backbenchers prior to the announcement. In his memoirs, Nigel Lawson
stated that he had 'encouraged him [Gow] to drop the ... hint about the prospects for
privatisation' (Lawson, 1992, p. 230). A threatened Conservative backbench revolt
over the Rate of Return Order (which saw nineteen Conservative MPs vote against
the Government and twenty-eight abstain), was also particularly influential in
catalysing the Government's interest in privatisation – an interesting example of the
role of backbenchers in encouraging policy change (Judge, 1993). Roy Watts had been
keeping the 140 or so MPs in the Thames region well briefed on this issue and had,
therefore, developed something of a potential parliamentary lobby in favour of *at
least examining the possibility of privatisation*. In a sense, this was the start of the
emergence of an 'advocacy coalition' in favour of major policy change (Sabatier,
1988). It appears that there had been no departmental consideration of possible models
for a privatised water industry. Moreover, water privatisation was at or near the
bottom of a rather long (official) Treasury list of possible candidates for privatisation.

Thus, there appeared to be no need for the department to give it active consideration. The Whitehall machine was, uncharacteristically, slow to spot that a mood change was taking place, right in its own backyard! A Water Authorities Association (WAA) working group set up when privatisation appeared on the systemic agenda (Cob and Elder, 1972) stated that, 'informal soundings at official level confirmed that the Government started from the basis of no firm plan or even outline framework' (Internal WAA Memo, April 1985).

PRESSURES BEHIND PRIVATISATION: AN ADVOCACY COALITION EMERGES

A strong driving force behind privatisation was the water authority management, in particular, Thames. They had developed a strong motivation for change, in part because the Government's financial policies had forced them to seek alternatives to the existing system of political and financial control. Whether by design or not, the Conservative Government had been 'encouraging' the support for privatisation from the management of all of its public corporations, through a process which, Steel and Heald have pointed out, made 'life unnecessarily unpleasant for the nationalised industries [and] thus became a convenient spur to a change in management attitudes towards denationalisation' (Steel and Heald, 1984, p. 17). The financial pressures on the Government itself were the prime motivation for the succession of changes in the relationship between it and public corporations, combined with a feeling on the part of the Conservatives that managerial performance in the corporations could be improved. Again, these moves facilitated privatisation rather than being part of some general design for shifting the public sector into the market-place.

Whatever the Government's precise motivation, water managers came to the conclusion that privatisation, with its apparent freedom from governmental interference, was the most feasible option. The RWAs viewed the present (pre-privatised) financial framework as unsatisfactory, as it involved:

1. Control by the Government of RWA borrowing levels.
2. Restriction of access to sources of borrowing.
3. Financial targets set by the Government with the intention and effect of reducing borrowing and increasing charges.
4. Levels of operating costs determined by the Government.
5. Control by the Government of the form of accounts involving the publication of accounts based on the historic cost convention whilst charges were based on the current cost convention (leading to unnecessary complexity and lack of clarity).
6. No *overt* control on the level of prices charged but a high degree of covert control often not perceived by the customer.

These factors, according to Michael Carney, then Secretary of the Water Authorities Association, essentially meant that:

nationalised industries ... [had] to operate with one hand firmly and permanently tied behind their backs by Treasury constraints and the arcane requirements of public finance ... the other arm of nationalised industries ... was occasionally tied behind their backs by the capricious operation of the political process. This has resulted in erratic control of pricing, stop-go programmes of capital expenditure, significant changes in priorities for capital investment, acceleration of particular schemes to placate particular political interests and equivocation and fudging about standards ... our exit from the public sector will not only free our operational arms ... but should overcome the million and one hidden requirements which are inherent in political and public life. (1989, pp. 9-11)

The pre-privatised financial framework left the regional water authorities trapped in the short-termist philosophy of the governmental system. Roy Watts claimed that:

Short-termism meant volatility, uncertainty, changing political priorities. Negotiations with government meant second-guessing and duplication, with government independently going over similar ground. What you didn't spend by 31 March you lost, because the government machine is short-term and cash-based. (Watts, 1990, p. 8.1)

Thus, the Government's central concern with public borrowing meant downward pressure on public investment – including water industry investment, and price increases which were designed to creat negative EFLs (external financing limits) in order to reduce public expenditure and the total PSBR (public sector borrowing requirement). Once privatisation as a concept had been established, 'problems with EFLs began to be recognised by Treasury ministers as a powerful weapon for persuading the top management of public enterprises that denationalisation would liberate them from irrational *public sector constraints*' (Heald, 1988, p. 35). Bill Harper, subsequently Deputy Chairman of Thames Water Utilities, has argued that it was the combination of new 'managerial attitudes and the financial situation of the industry which gave rise to a call both from the industry itself and from the Government to examine the prospects of privatisation' (1988, p. 218). Thus, strategic management changes, financial restructuring and, most importantly, the imbuing of the then public sector management with new attitudes led management to become one of the most vociferous proponents of privatisation and for them to mobilise support for this change. By then, privatisation of British Telecom, and other parts of the public sector, had been shown to be technically possible and not to present major political risks.

There were, however, more tangible benefits for the industry's managers. If the industry moved into the private sector they would be faced with the same opportunities and risks existing in that sector. Based on the experience of earlier privatisations, more flexible remuneration packages might emerge. In the event, Roy Watts received £160,000 (including a £27,300 performance bonus) in the year to 31 March 1991. This represented a 119 per cent salary increase. The Welsh Chairman, John Elfed Jones, received £143,000 (including a performance bonus of £35,000); the Anglian Chairman, Bernard Henderson, received £91,000 (eventually moved to a part-time basis and receiving £71,000) and the North West Chairman, Dennis Grove, received £144,000. These rises constitute 74 per cent, 49 per cent and 48.4 per cent salary increases respectively (*The Daily Telegraph*, 4 July 1991). Another incentive was, of course, share options. For example, following privatisation the chairmen of Severn Trent Water, Thames Water and Welsh Water could have sold their shares on the 17 June 1991 and realised £69,000, £71,000 and £78,300 respectively (HC Debates, 18 June 1991, col. 154). The new Chief Executive of Thames, Michael Hoffman, could have made £420,000 if he took up his share option in July 1993, in addition to his 17.9 per cent pay rise of 1 July 1993, which gave him an annual salary of £250,000 (*Daily Telegraph*, 26 July 1993).

From the Government's perspective, privatisation of water had at least two attractions – like other privatisations, it could deliver revenue to the Exchequer in the short term. In the longer term, however, it transferred commercial decision-making to the management, making the Government no longer responsible or accountable for all the industry's ills. Thus, after privatisation, David Gadbury, Director of Planning Southern Water Plc, when commenting on the introduction of a new charging system, said that 'before privatisation we might have been able to get away with imposing a new charging system by blaming government or Brussels, or anyone' (Gadbury, 1990, p. 13.2).

There was one other major incentive which encouraged the Government to join the growing advocacy coalition in favour of privatisation – the prospective investment programmes required because of Britain's membership of the European Community. Indeed, this was probably the most important factor in the Government's decision to privatise water. By 1989 the industry was facing a ten-year investment programme needed to meet a backlog of neglect – estimated by Sir Terrence Heiser, Permanent Secretary at the DOE, at £24.6 bn. By 1992 the estimated cost of this programme had increased to some £26.6 bn as a result of the decision to end sewage sludge dumping at sea by 1998 and because of the acceleration of the programme to achieve compliance with the EC Bathing Waters Directive (HC, Committee of Public Accounts, 1992, qu. 26).

Thus, although water privatisation had arrived on the Government's agenda almost by accident, the idea turned out to have very considerable advantages for the Government. As suggested above, other privatisations had demonstrated that privatising utilities was perfectly practicable, and that it might even have political as well as financial benefits. Even though Roy Watts' initiative took the Government by surprise, the Government both found it difficult to say 'no' and discovered that saying 'yes' had lots of advantages! Thus, Ian Gow's (almost) 'off the cuff' remark started a complex policy process, costing millions of pounds, and which saw the doubters in the industry gradually warm to the idea launched by Watts.

The agenda setting process did not, therefore, conform to any model of a British policy style (Jordan and Richardson, 1982) or to any model of policy-making based upon policy communities or policy networks as key determinants of policy change (Richardson and Jordan, 1979; Marsh and Rhodes, 1992). The hitherto well-ordered policy community in water (Jordan et al., 1977) had not really taken the issue on board, the Government had not really considered it, and even the main proponents appeared to have no clear ideas of how it might be achieved, or of what political obstacles might be encountered with rival interests, or indeed, of the possible legal implications because of Britain's membership of the European Community (EC). Moreover, parts of the industry itself were, at best, sceptical of the whole idea.

In the event, the small advocacy coalition that eventually led to the Government's 1986 water privatisation proposals was the catalyst for the political mobilisation of several hundred interest groups, all claiming an interest in the water policy sector. The lobbying activities of this loose and extended issue 'network' (if indeed, 'network' can be used in this context) continued until late 1989 when the industry was finally privatised and a completely new, and extremely complex, regulatory regime was established (see below, Chapter 5).

INAPPROPRIATE CONSULTATION STYLES AND THE 1985 WATER PRIVATISATION DISCUSSION PAPER

Once the Government had declared its willingness to examine the prospects for water privatisation, it set in motion a consultation process which, in contrast to the agenda setting process generally conformed to the 'standard operating procedures' contained within the British 'policy style' (Richardson and Jordan, 1979; Jordan and Richardson, 1982). The DOE's privatisation discussion paper was circulated to water authority chairmen and other governmentally defined interested parties. This was partly an attempt to buy time in view of the lack of preparatory policy work within the Government, and partly to gauge more accurately the industry's opinion before consulting more widely on privatisation. Reflecting the Government's own uncertainty, Ian Gow's covering letter (1 April 1985) which accompanied the discussion paper said that, 'I enclose the promised paper on water authority privatisation. Our thinking is still at an early stage. I would like to have your views on these issues before I consult more widely'.

At the outset, the department had some notion of a relevant core of insider groups – essentially those interests and individuals who had been members of the rather stable water policy community in the past. This restricted perception of an initial policy community relating to privatisation had significant ramifications for policy developments. Indeed, it was the cause of the first controversy, as the Government was criticised for the limited scope of the consultation exercise. Baroness Nicol condemned the department for:

> this very limited consultation. Even in flying a kite, you need to fly it over a wide area. The views which should have been sought should have included those of the local authorities, the Ministry of Agriculture, Fisheries and Food, conservation bodies and consumer organisations. Without their views any decision or further action on the lines of this document would be made on insufficient evidence and most of us here would find it completely unconvincing and scarcely worthy of consideration. (HL Debates, 22 April 1985, col. 992)

Replying on behalf of the Government, Lord Skelmersdale, while acknowledging that the discussion paper had been sent to water authority chairmen and to the chairman of the Statutory Water Companies' Association, pointed out that it was not a formal consultation document – neither was it confidential, as a copy had been placed in the Library of the House and was freely available on request to the Department (HL Debates, 22 April 1985, col. 996). His reply suggests that, at that stage in the process, the department had a rather partial conception of who really counted, and this produced a narrowly defined policy community for what was a new policy issue. As the minister himself described it, the Government believed that, 'the views of those most directly involved – the water authorities and the statutory water companies – will be particularly useful at this early stage' (HL Debates, 22 April 1985, col. 996). This illustrated the power of government to decide *initially*, who get access to and who is excluded from policy communities and networks. But, as we shall see, the Government could not control the *consequences* of an exclusive approach. Thus, deciding 'who matters' can be done only in the context of the dynamics of a policy issue. As the issue developed, then so the definition of 'who mattered' had to be widened.

The DOE (1985) paper outlined the Government's privatisation policy aims as follows:

Privatisation was seen as a way of:

1. Freeing enterprises from state control so that decisions could be taken for sound business reasons.
2. Increasing efficiency, enterprise and competition.
3. Involving employees in the ownership and success of the companies in which they work.
4. Reducing the size of the public sector.
5. Spreading ownership more widely.

The paper stated that operational activities like water supply and treatment, and disposal of liquid waste, were capable of privatisation, and asked for views on 'whether it would be practicable to separate the operational and regulatory functions, and to transfer the latter to a public sector body set up outside government' (DOE, 1985). The paper also sought opinion on whether:

> pollution control and river management in general, together with nature conservation, recreation and land drainage, are best kept in the public sector, or whether it would be possible to impose them as obligations on the private sector operational bodies, with the setting and policing of these obligations to be carried out externally. (DOE, 1985)

During the initial discussion period on privatisation there were, however, intra-departmental tensions. The Water Directorate within the DOE, after a restricted consultation process which essentially involved the RWAs alone, decided that the environmental protection functions could be privatised with the authorities and that only economic regulation would be needed. This went against the recommendations of the DOE's newly established think-tank, the Central Policy Planning Unit (CPPU), which reviewed environmental protection policy as part of the new environmentally friendly image of the Government prior to the 1987 election. The Planning Unit's report had been drafted after a wide consultation exercise with industry, environmental groups and within governmental departments. It stated that water pollution was likely to become a much more politically significant environmental problem in the near future. It criticised the reductions in the RWAs' monitoring of river quality and the infrequent use of the prosecution weapon against offenders. The CCPU (like the Royal Commission on Environmental Pollution) called for the establishment of an integrated pollution inspectorate, irrespective of privatisation. It was reported that the CCPU report had stated explicitly that 'the water authorities' pollution control functions should not be privatised' but should be transferred to the proposed environmental inspectorate. The report apparently echoed the concerns that civil servants at the DOE's environmental protection divisions had over environmental safeguards (ENDS Report 132 January 1986, p. 3).

The water industry itself – represented by the Water Authorities Association (WAA – subsequently to become the Water Services Association, WSA, after privatisation) – was aware of intra-departmental tensions. Privately, the association recognised that the Government would be unlikely to agree to privatisation of their existing regulatory and service functions *in toto*. Nevertheless, in spite of this recognition in private, the authorities proceeded to press the Government in public for privatisation *in toto*, possibly hoping to exploit the divisions within the DOE (see below).

THE INITIAL RESPONSE TO PRIVATISATION

The Water Minister, John Patten, revealed that the Government had received a total of forty-three responses to the Department's Discussion Paper of which 'seven supported the principle of privatisation and eleven opposed it. The remaining 25 commented on practical issues, without expressing a view on the merits of privatisation itself' (HC Debates, 16 January 1986, col. 680w).

The main professional body, the Institution of Water Engineers and Scientists (IWES) responded by arguing that the principle and practice of IRBM (central to the 1973 reforms) must be preserved, and that it was essential to retain within a single structure the environmental management of each area, including the regulatory functions of resource management and pollution control. The privatised water authorities should be subject to licences with some form of national audit to ensure that licence conditions were adhered to.

Leaders of the water industry, represented by the WAA, were divided but not sufficiently so for the privatisation movement to be stalled. Initially, several water authority chairmen maintained that they could see no materially significant short or medium term improvement resulting from privatisation. Thames was the most enthusiastic authority, whereas Welsh and North West opposed the proposals outright, and Anglian and South West questioned the likely benefits of privatisation.

It is worth noting that if the industry as a whole had come out against privatisation, it would have been considerably more difficult for the Government to continue with the proposal – especially in view of the likely adverse reaction by investors. Within the industry, despite the managerial enthusiasm for greater freedom, there was an initial reluctance to enter into controversial political territory. Michael Carney, Secretary of the WSA outlined the industry's stance. 'The political decision on privatisation of water was a matter for Government, not for the water authorities' (Interview, April 1991).

The official WAA stance, was in fact, quite misleading – both at the time and with hindsight. It is probable that privatisation would not have reached the political agenda had it not been for the Watts' initiative. He was largely responsible for exercising that supreme instrument of political power – agenda setting. Hence, the 'politics isn't our business' formula was a little disingenuous. The WAA stance was also misleading because (as the process unfolded) the industry became very enthusiastic for privatisation and led the advocacy coalition in favour of it, playing a central role in ensuring that the policy would be a 'success'.

In so far as the WAA had an official or public view in 1986, it believed that the authorities should be privatised as they stood, with their environmental, service and regulatory obligations embodied in the general terms of the licences issued to each authority. Probably five of the RWAs wanted to oppose privatisation if it meant losing the system of IRBM. The industry had to balance the advantages of greater financial autonomy against the disadvantages of weakening IRBM. The WAA's response to the Government's discussion paper therefore advocated the retention of the concept of IRBM. The assocation saw no clear distinction between the operational activities of RWAs and environmental regulation functions. It argued that 'It would be quite wrong to envisage a structure which separates water resources from water supply, or pollution control from water resources'. It also publicly rejected a suggestion that private authorities could not be expected to exercise regulatory functions, arguing that the private authorities could operate under a licence system similar to that operated by the Office of Telecommunications (OFTEL) which would guarantee the public interest.

Internally, however, the WAA Working Group on Privatisation (established once the industry learned that the Government was serious about some measure of privatisation) recognised that privatising the water authorities as they stood could lead to difficult internal conflicts between commercial and important regulatory objectives. It was believed that these conflicts were easier to resolve in a public sector organisation whose prime duties were not profit orientated. Consequently, the working group concluded that:

> a privatised authority would presumably not be allowed to continue all its present regulatory functions, attractive though that would be from the authority's own point of view, and we have accordingly envisaged a new regulatory body, responsible to, but at 'arm's length' from, the Department of the Environment. This would undertake quality control functions for clean and for

dirty water purposes, as well as assuming the direct regulatory functions at present carried out by the Water Authorities themselves. (internal WAA memo)

This formula kept WAA members on board and the more active support from leading figures such as Watts enabled the issue to move forward. In the event, the Government adopted the official WAA line, and in February 1986 it issued a White Paper, *Privatisation of the Water Authorities in England and Wales* (Cmnd. 9734). The RWAS were to be privatised *in toto*:

> The principle of integrated river-basin management ... has worked well since it was introduced by the Water Act 1973 and will be retained. The water authorities will be privatised on the basis of their existing boundaries. The Government intends that the water authorities should continue to carry out their responsibilities for the management of rivers, control of pollution, fisheries, environmental conservation, recreation and navigation. (DOE, 1986, pp. 2–3)

The key question which arises here is why the department did not recognise that the transfer of the regulatory functions to the private sector would prove unworkable? This is especially important, bearing in mind that the industry itself had (covertly) identified it as a serious problem. Several factors explain why the department produced a White Paper which did not anticipate the regulatory problem and the political row it stimulated. First, the department had received no prior warning about the prospect of privatisation from its ministers. Secondly, the industry was still part of the public sector, and enjoyed a high degree of *trust* to conduct its affairs in the public interest. In particular, it was assumed that existing laws and obligations were being fully implemented. Thirdly, the department had developed a genuine arms-length relationship with the RWAS on the nationalised industry model. The authorities themselves were subject to financial constraints on their borrowing and were also subject to second-order targets such as reductions in operating costs. But they were, as Sir Gordon Jones, Chairman of Yorkshire Water Plc has described it, 'left on a fairly loose rein' (Private Correspondence, 28 May 1991). Fourthly, the department had reduced its commitment to detailed monitoring of the authorities and had reduced the number of its monitoring staff. Fifthly, the decision to retain regulatory functions within Water Service Public Limited Companies (WSPLCs) was explained by reference to the benefits of IRBM. There is now some discussion within the industry that the technical concept of IRBM was never quite as important in practice as was universally claimed. But there is no doubt that the department, along with most water professionals, genuinely believed IRBM to be of central importance at the time. It was a 'policy theory' to which most of the key policy actors subscribed. A sixth factor was that the department was also very concerned to address questions other than the regulatory regime for water quality. It had a central concern to resolve other regulatory issues, such as financial regulation, and general questions of control of private monopolies, as these problems were especially acute given water's monopoly status. Finally, a more cynical view was that:

in reality it was dictated by the need to ensure that the Water Authorities would not themselves swell the ranks of those opposed to privatisation and by the Treasury's edict that the process must not result in an increase in public sector service manpower. (Ends Report 133, February 1986, p. 10)

From the department's viewpoint, once privatisation was on the agenda and the Government was committed to it, it was necessary to try to maintain the advocacy coalition which had formed around it.

PRIVATISATION IN TURMOIL

It was predictable that the White Paper would be criticised by those groups not part of the main policy community (as defined by the DOE) – both for its content and for the dearth of prior consultation. In a sense, a competing advocacy coalition had developed and was operating in a rather different – and more public – decision-making arena. The response of these outsider groups was a clear sign that this particular issue would be difficult to process via policy community politics and that a wider issue network of groups would mobilise in the policy process. According to the Royal Society for the Protection of Birds (RSPB), the Government's White and Green Papers illustrated a 'lack of prior consultation [which] has resulted in government not identifying significant areas of environmental concern'. This, in fact, proved to be absolutely correct. As we shall see, the regulatory issue was a major policy problem – in both technical and political terms. The limited circle from which the privatisation initiative emerged failed to address this as a major problem to be solved and appeared to take no account of the broader political environment in which they were operating.

In the event, the DOE faced a deluge of opposition, both inside and outside the Government, to its proposals for regulating the industry. The opposition comprised bodies of varying degrees of influence, including the Council for the Protection of Rural England (CPRE), the Institute for European Environmental Policy (IEEP), the Country Landowners Association (CLA), the Institution of Water and Environmental Management (IWEM), the Confederation of British Industry (CBI), the Chemical Industries Association (CIA), and the trade unions. Even MAFF was unhappy about certain aspects of the proposed legislation, as its policy space was again being threatened. One potential interest, virtually absent from the process, was the local authorities. In contrast to their involvement in the 1973–4 reforms, local authorities appeared to be of much less relevance. They had gradually been excluded from the sector and failed to seize this opportunity to re-enter the policy area, in part because of other more important concerns. In practice, the pro-privatisation coalition was not a winnable coalition in the absence of a solution to the environmental regulation issue. It was not surprising, therefore, that the water privatisation process was derailed.

There were three decisive factors which forced the Government to shelve its 1986 proposals. First, widespread opposition, in particular from the CBI and from the environmentalists. The CBI's opposition was expressed both in its formal response to privatisation plans and in private meetings with ministers. While the CBI informed the WAA that there was a widely held view within its membership that the RWAS were not the most natural candidates for privatisation, it nevertheless welcomed privatisation, but rejected the model proposed. The confederation stated that it had 'substantial reservations concerning the privatisation of the water authorities' control functions, especially those relating to environmental control. It would be inappropriate to transfer these functions to the private sector'. Its position, prior to and after the publication of the 1986 White Paper, was very similar to that of the environmentalists and the CLA, i.e. it was 'wrong in principle that one privatised company should exercise statutory control over the affairs of another private company'. It argued that:

> Where a breach of a discharge consent is involved, or a pollution incident created, the WSPLC as a private sector company would have powers to prosecute another company or individual for a criminal offence. Not only do we know of no parallel to such a situation, we consider it would be wrong.

The CBI's view was that an easy solution was available. The WSPLCs' regulatory functions could be transferred to a separate regulatory agency based on areas of WSPLCs. Alternatively, these functions could be removed from the WSPLCs and made the responsibility of the proposed Director General of Water Services (DGWS).

The second significant factor was the arrival of Nicholas Ridley as Secretary of State at the DOE in May 1986. As we shall see in Chapter 4, he was a particular type of minister, he came to the problem with a coherent intellectual framework, and he proved to be a major influence on the final shape and direction of the privatisation of water. The third, and possibly most decisive factor, was the influence of the EC, which demonstrated that it had become a significant actor in the making of national water policy.

THE EC AND PRIVATISATION: THE EROSION OF NATIONAL SOVEREIGNTY

The EC influenced the privatisation process, indirectly and directly, at several points, significantly altering the shape and direction of policy. The EC's first *sortie* on water privatisation occurred in December 1986. The Government had temporarily managed to postpone an appearance before the European Court of Justice by issuing orders to RWAs to comply with EC bathing water quality standards (approximately half of the 350 beaches were below standard[2] – see Chapter 7). However, the Commission informed the Government during the summer of 1986 that it wanted more expedite action. Though not directly concerned with privatisation, this intervention by the EC had the potential to wreck the privatisation process. This was recognised by the DOE which wrote to North West Water Authority regarding the problems at Blackpool, stating that it was concerned about 'possible action against the UK in the European Court during the passage of a water privatisation bill through Parliament or when the authorities are being sold to the private sector' (See ENDS Report 137, June, 1986, pp. 22–3).

The Government was also forced, by the possible threat of legal action over alleged non-compliance with the 1980 EC directive on drinking water quality, to adopt the EC's interpretation of Maximum Admissible Concentration (MAC). The British Government reluctantly made the necessary concessions to avert any possible threat to water privatisation. In spite of the fact that the DOE viewed the EC's interpretation of MACs as scientifically indefensible (ENDS Reports 154, November, 1987, pp. 9–10; and 155, December, 1987, pp. 19–20), and that Nicholas Ridley told the House of Commons on 2 December 1987 that following legal advice 'the term "maximum admissible concentration" in the EC drinking water Directive should relate to individual samples and not to averages over a period. This is a technical point. It concerns the appearance of water supplied and does not have health implications' (HC Debates, 2 December 1987).

However, the most significant and potentially fatal threat which the EC presented to water privatisation was the legal controversy raised by the CPRE and the IEEP over the question of whether WSPLCs would constitute *competent authorities* under EC law. Nigel Haigh, Director of the IEEP wrote to *The Times* on 13 May 1986, questioning whether the privatised water companies would constitute such competent authorities. He pointed out that:

> water pollution is governed by European Community law and a particular Directive requires all discharges into water containing certain dangerous substances to be authorised by a 'competent authority'. I know of no case in any member state where a 'competent authority' for the purposes of an EC water Directive is a private body ... Will the Commission be able to satisfy itself that a private body answerable to shareholders albeit one on to which certain duties have been placed and subject to some government supervision, constitutes a 'competent authority'? The Commission has to satisfy itself on the point since it has a duty to ensure that Directives are properly applied. If this matter is not resolved before the water authorities are sold to private hands the Commission may at any time challenge the British Government before the European Court. (*The Times*, 13 May 1986)

Ministers publicly claimed that there would be no doubt that the WSPLCs would be acceptable to the European Commission as competent authorities, charged under numerous directives with authorising effluent discharges. This view was challenged by a leading European lawyer, Professor Francis Jacobs, who had been consulted by the CPRE. He said that none of the relevant directives clearly defines competent authority. He argued that:

> while there is no obvious objection arising out of the terms of the Directives themselves to the WSPLCs performing the role of 'competent authorities' ... there can be no doubt, we think, that when the phrase 'competent authority' is used by the drafters of EEC legislation, they assume that the bodies designated as such will be public bodies, arms of government or state ... in cases where

EEC legislation has specified a 'competent authority' it has invariably been a 'public' or 'governmental' body. (Jacobs and Shanks, 1986, pp. 13–14)

Professor Jacobs concluded that:

the European Court, if the question were raised before it, might well decide that, at least in relation to some of the functions assigned to the 'competent authorities' by the EEC directives in the field of water pollution, the UK Government could not properly assign them to the WSPLCs. (ibid., p. 18)

As Nigel Haigh highlighted, the crucial point which the Jacobs opinion made was that:

if the Government presented a Bill to Parliament giving powers to the WSPLCs to act as 'competent authorities' for implementing EC Directives, then it would be open to a public interest body (such as the CPRE) to raise the matter in a national court who would then refer the matter to the European Court under Article 177. The CPRE made it clear that they would do this. The Government therefore knew that they could not avoid protracted proceedings before the European Court which at least would cast a pall of uncertainty over any attempts to float the WSPLCs on the stock exchange. It was this point that shook them. (Private Correspondence, 28 May 1991)

This was confirmed by Robin Grove-White, the then Director of the CPRE, who was informally sounded out by civil servants at the DOE about the likelihood of such a case being brought to court (Private Correspondence, 7 June 1991). The Royal Commission on Environmental Pollution (RCEP) also argued that it might 'be prudent for the Government to satisfy itself more thoroughly on this point'. Water industry trade unions questioned whether WSPLCs would be accepted as competent authorities, and the WAA sought private legal advice, in anticipation of problems ahead.

The European Commission, through Commissioner Stanley Clinton Davies, issued a veiled warning that the proposed transfer of pollution control functions to the private sector might be inconsistent with EC legislative requirements. Replying to a parliamentary question tabled by the British MEP, Ken Collins, Clinton Davies stated that:

The Commission does not know of any private body operating in a Member State as a competent authority under Council Directive 76/464 EEC (which deals with discharges of dangerous substances) ... the Commission takes the view that the 'competent authority' in the sense of the said Directive can only be an authority, empowered by each Member State, which acts, in performing its functions, in the general interest. (OJ No. L 129, 18 May 1986, p. 23)

It appeared that the competent authority had to be completely separate and independent from the recipient of its authorisations. Clinton Davis noted, however, that the final interpretation of EC legal provisions is the responsibility of the Court of Justice.

This answer appeared to contradict a Parliamentary reply given on 17 June 1986 by the Water Minister, John Patten. He said that 'My Department has discussed our proposals for privatising the water industry with the Commission. We have no grounds for believing that the water services plcs would not be accepted as competent authorities for the relevant purposes' (HC Debates, 17 June 1986, col. 502w).

The WAA were well aware of this problem and were monitoring the situation very closely. An internal report, circulated within the WAA in February 1987, stated that one solution to this problem was for the Government to create a separate body as a competent authority. The report warned the Association that it should develop a fall-back position 'if the department (DOE) fails to maintain in Brussels that the WSPLCs could be competent authorities' (Internal WAA Report, February 1987). The recognition of potential problems and the development of a fall-back position within the WAA remained a completely internal matter. Publicly the association continued to lobby the department for acceptance of WSPLCs as competent authorities.

This 'competent authority' issue illustrates the *ad hoc* nature of the development of the Government's privatisation plans. The proposals were drafted without reference to this issue, and effective dialogue with the Commission, both before and during the drafting of proposals, was obviously not occurring. The WAA eventually pressed the Government to settle the EC issue, arguing that the DOE should either clarify this situation with the EC, or indemnify the authorities against a possible charge in the courts. In late May 1987, the DOE finally conceded that the water authorities were unlikely to qualify as competent authorities and also that the game-keeper/poacher role could not continue after privatisation. The WAA believed that the gamekeeper/poacher difficulty could have been successfully combatted, but that the EC issue could not be won if the 'DOE is no longer prepared to fight' (Internal WAA memo). The WAA recognised the Government's need to accommodate certain influential groups in the rival advocacy coalition, in particular the CBI and the CPRE, and began looking for satisfactory solutions with such groups. Thus, although the WAA was clearly a core insider group, it recognised that the issue might be processed with the involvement of a much wider interests who, though disparate, were of a common position on this one issue. It therefore began to search for a consensus within this wider network of policy actors.

As a result of the strong opposition to the detailed contents of the proposals and the difficulties presented by the competent authority issue, the privatisation of the water authorities was postponed – a major setback for the Government. On the 3 July 1986 Nicholas Ridley, announced in the House of Commons that:

> ... the Department's consultations with the water authorities have shown that, while preparations for privatisation are well under way, more time is needed to prepare the necessary legislation. I have therefore concluded that we are unlikely to be able to introduce the Bill in the next Session ... (However,) I reaffirm the Government's intention to proceed with water privatisation as soon as practicable. (HC Debates, 3 July 1986, col. 1256)

The failure of the original proposal for the privatisation of water reflected an inappropriate choice of consultation processes by the Government. The issue had been raised by the water industry, and it had been resolved by the Government in close, almost exclusive, co-operation with the water industry. As revealed by later events, the perception that this major policy could be processed under such *monopolistic* standard operating procedures was clearly wrong. Other important policy actors, including extra-territorial areas such as the EC, could not be that easily discounted. If water privatisation was to be placed back on the rails by Ridley, policy solutions which satisfied a much wider range of interests had to formulated. It is to these attempts that we now turn, in Chapter 4.

NOTES

1. The move from HCA to CCA was particularly significant because it is claimed that current cost accounting overstates asset values and understates profitability. For example, in 1988–9 the RWAs accounts estimated 'the net book value of assets at £8.7bn. in historic cost terms and £34.5bn. in current cost terms' (NAO, 1992, p. 25).
2. Initially under the quality directive Britain designated a mere two water, land-locked Luxembourg designated some forty.

REFERENCES

Carney, M. (1989), 'Water Industry Directions', paper presented to *IBM International Utilities Conference*, London, 13–15 June 1989.

Cobb, R. W. and Elder, C. D. (1972), *Participation in American Politics: The Dynamics of Agenda Building* (Baltimore: The John Hopkins University Press).

DOE (1985), *Water Authority Privatisation: A Discussion Paper* (London: DOE).

DOE (1986), *Privatisation of the Water Authorities in England and Wales*, Cmnd. 9734 (London: HMSO).

Gadbury, D. (1990), 'Future Pricing Methods', *Financial Times European Water Industry Conference*, London, 26 and 27 March (London: *The Financial Times*), pp. 13.1–13.3.

Harper, W. R. (1988), 'Privatisation in the Water Sector', in V. V. Ramanadham (ed.), *Privatisation in the UK* (London: Routledge), pp. 215–25.

Heald, D. (1988), 'The United Kingdom: Privatisation and its Political Context', *West European Politics*, vol. 11, pp. 31–48.

House of Commons (HC), Committee of Public Accounts (1992), *Seventh Report, Sale of the Water Authorities in England and Wales* (London: HMSO).

Jacobs, F. and Shanks, M. (1986), 'Joint Advice. Re: Water Authority Privatisation' (Unpublished report commissioned by the CPRE).

Jordan, A. G., and Richardson, J. J. (1977), 'Outside Committees and Policy-Making: The Central Water Advisory Committee', *Public Administration Bulletin*, no. 24, pp. 41–58.

Jordan, A. G., Richardson, J. J. and Kimber, R. H. (1977), 'The Origins of the Water Act of 1973', *Public Administration* vol. 55 (Autumn), pp. 317–34.

Jordan, A. G. and Richardson, J. J. (1982), 'The British Policy Style or the Logic of Negotiation?', in J. Richardson (ed.), *Policy Styles in Western Europe* (London: George Allen & Unwin), pp. 80–110.

Judge, D. (1993), *The Parliamentary State* (London: Sage).

Kinnersley, D. (1988), *Troubled Water: Rivers, Politics and Pollution* (London: Hilary Shipman).

Lawson, N. (1992), *The View from No. 11* (London: Bantam Press).

Marsh, D. and Rhodes R. A. W. (1992) (eds), *Policy Networks in British Government* (Oxford: Clarendon Press).

Rhodes, R. A. W. (1988), *Beyond Westminster and Whitehall* (London: Unwin Hyman).

Richardson, J. J. and Jordan, A. G. (1979), *Governing Under Pressure: The Policy Process in a Post-Parliamentary Democracy* (Oxford: Martin Robertson).

Sabatier, P. A. (1988), 'An Advocacy Coalition Framework of Policy Change and the Role of Policy-Orientated Learning Therein', *Policy Sciences*, vol. 21, pp. 129–68.

Saunders, P. (1985), 'The Forgotten Dimension of Central–Local Relations: Theorising the "regional state"', *Environment and Planning C: Government and Policy*, vol. 3, pp. 149–62.

Steel, D. and Heald, D. (1984), 'The New Agenda', in D. Steel and D. Heald (eds), *Privatising Public Enterprises* (London: RIPA), pp. 13–19.

Watts, R. (1990), 'The UK Water Industry after Privatisation – Opportunity and Challenge', *Financial Times European Water Industry Conference*, London, 26 and 27 March (London: *The Financial Times*), pp. 8.1–8.4.

4

Mobilising Consensus:
Selling Privatisation

INTRODUCTION: THE EMERGENCE OF THE NATIONAL RIVERS AUTHORITY

*I came to the conclusion early in 1987 that environmental regulation
was needed as well as price regulation in respect of the water industry
... I couldn't see how the necessary improvements in water quality could
be secured without it, or how disputes between water companies and
polluters could be resolved, if both were private companies ... I had to
overcome strong resistance to my plan to set up a National Rivers
Authority (NRA), both from some of my officials and later from the water
company chairmen. But I insisted, Cabinet agreed unanimously, and I
announced the establishment of the NRA as the 1987 election broke. This
decision delayed privatization by nearly two years, but I am convinced
it was an essential feature of running the water industry ... it was
another of the benefits of privatization. It could never have been done if
water had remained publicly owned. The Government can't regulate
itself.*

Nicholas Ridley, 1991, pp. 63–4

The quotation above, from the late Nicholas Ridley, the former Secretary of State for
the Environment, illustrates perfectly the policy problem which the Government
faced – and the enormity of the decision, taken by Ridley, to halt the privatisation
process in mid stream. Water privatisation had proved to be a good (or bad) example
of issue expansion in the sense that what had been seen by the Government and the
industry as a relatively technical issue capable of being processed in the usual way
had been transformed into a much broader issue involving important questions of
general principle. To Ridley's considerable credit, he both recognised the principle
and saw that the only viable solution – if the EC and the range of British interest that had
mobilised around that broader issue were to be satisfied – was to create a new and independent regulatory body to oversee the environmental aspects of the water sector.

Once this key decision had been taken and after the renewed success in the 1987
general election the Conservative administration was able to pursue its manifesto

objective of privatising the water industry. The Government decided to create the National Rivers Authority (NRA) to act as an environmental quality regulator. The regulatory responsibilities eventually transferred via the Act to the new body (essentially created out of the regulatory functions of the existing RWAs and involving a transfer of the associated staff) were as follows:

1. River quality and the quality of inland and coastal waters.
2. Land drainage and flood control.
3. Management of water resources.
4. Fisheries.
5. Recreation and conservation.
6. Navigation.
7. Licensing and abstraction of water.
8. Independently monitoring river quality and discharges from sewage treatment plants.
9. The enforcement of water quality objectives.

The creation of the NRA removed many of the objections which had bedevilled the earlier proposals and effectively weakened the rival advocacy coalition which had objected strongly to the original proposals. More importantly, however, it created a public body which qualified as a competent authority under EC law and, therefore, removed the main threat of a legal challenge which could have wrecked the whole privatisation process.

While the proposal to create the NRA solved the most pressing problem, the road ahead was not without its difficulties. The Government still had to convince the key non-governmental actor – the industry driven pro-privatisation coalition – that privatisation would remain viable and advantageous, even with the separation of the environmental regulatory functions.

Even at this stage in the processing of the privatisation issue, the Government did not have a fully worked-out series of clear objectives for water privatisation. These were to emerge much later and were essentially the result of the details of policy thrashed out between Government and industry. Only after the final details had been agreed did the Government state its main objectives. In the event, these were:

1. To improve the efficiency of the industry through its transfer to the private sector.
2. To promote wider share ownership and to encourage customers and employees to become shareholders.
3. Consistent with achieving the objectives, to maximise sale proceeds and ensure a healthy aftermarket in the shares of each company.
4. To maintain the momentum of the privatisation programme as a whole.
5. To transfer the water authorities to private sector ownership and control within the lifetime of the present Parliament.
6. To privatise all ten water authorities together (HC, Committee of Public Accounts, 1992, para. 6).

WATER INDUSTRY HOSTILITY TO CHANGE

Ridley's bold decision was not without risk – in particular it ran the risk of alienating the key interest backing privatisation – the industry itself. As suggested in Chapter 3, the industry had, privately, feared that the DOE would not maintain the 'privatisation *in toto*' line. The WAA's worst fears were, in fact, realised in the text of a letter handed to Sir Gordon Jones (Chairman of the WAA) and other key industry negotiators (William Courtney, Roy Watts and Michael Carney) by Nicholas Ridley. The letter outlined the proposals for the creation of the NRA, although the public announcement of the creation of the NRA was made by Nicholas Ridley in an election speech to his constituents at Chedworth on the evening of 18 May. The letter stated that:

> The White Paper proposals that regulatory and river management functions should be transferred to private companies has met with steadfast opposition, even from groups who have otherwise been very sympathetic to the privatisation of the utility functions of water supply, sewerage and sewage treatment. We have proposed a substantial framework of governmental controls over WSPLCs' exercise of their regulatory functions, but this has not moved the opponents of this aspect of our policy from their view that so important a power of decision over the activities of others should not be placed in private hands. *It is a view which I do not think can or should be resisted ...* We intend therefore to introduce the necessary legislation in a new Parliament to ensure that the National Rivers Authority is established and the water PLCs placed in private ownership as quickly as practicable. (Emphasis added)

The meeting with Ridley (who was accompanied by John Patten and a senior DOE civil servant) had been requested by the WAA to discuss the current situation and to establish the Government's intentions. Effectively they were *told* of the decision that only water supply, sewerage and sewage disposal would be privatised, and that the NRA would be established. This key decision was certainly not a 'bargained outcome' resulting from consultations with the key groups. It was the result of a process of 'internalised decision-making' (Jordan and Richardson, 1982) which effectively ignored the main interest – the industry itself – and did not directly involve the other sets of actors either. The latter did not 'participate' in the conventional sense, though it is clear that they occupied what Dudley has termed an 'empty seat' (Dudley, 1994, pp. 229–30) in the internalised discussions. Had they not been accommodated, it would have been impossible to contract, rather than expand, the water privatisation issue. The meeting between Ridley and the WAA set out the parameters for the rest of the consultation process and the following day the Conservative Party Manifesto (1987, p. 36) stated that the RWAs would be privatised:

> leaving certain functions to a new National Rivers Authority ... to take over responsibilities for ensuring strict safeguards against the pollution of rivers and water courses and to pursue sound conservation policies. The water supply and sewage functions of the Water Authorities will be transferred to the private sector.

Possibly overtaken by events, the WAA initially opposed the creation of the NRA. This was not surprising as civil servants had been reassuring WAA officials as late as 19 November 1986 'that there had been no change of plan and that the White Paper package was being pursued' (Internal WAA memo, 20 November 1986).

After the Queen's Speech in July 1987, the water authority chairmen issued a 'strongly worded statement' which called on the Government to abandon its plans to create the NRA because it 'would not be in the best interest of customers, employees, shareholders or government' (Pearce, 1987, p. 25). On this critical issue the WAA appeared (in its public stance) to move from the inner to the outer circle of the policy process. Internally, the water authorities themselves were, however, divided over the issue, with the South West Chairman, Len Hill, the only chairman to speak publicly against privatisation itself, claiming that the NRA plans were an 'act of political expediency', which would 'destroy the economic, engineering and environmental benefits that have been achieved' (ibid., p. 25). In contrast John Bellak, the Severn Trent Chairman, gave his unqualified support for the Government's plans, whilst Roy Watts, who up until then had been the most fervent supporter of the Government's privatisation plans now found himself opposed to certain fundamental elements of the revised proposals. Thus, the privatisation coalition was, at least potentially, unstable.

Watts described the Green Paper as 'short on costs, short on vision and short on consultation'. Once again we see the lack of consultation as an issue in its own right – again raising doubts about the universality of policy-making models which emphasise the centrality of consultation and negotiation and/or the centrality of policy networks. Watts claimed that IRBM must be retained and that a costly quango such as the NRA merely added another layer of regulation to an already *byzantine regulatory system* (*The Financial Times*, 17 July 1987, emphasis added). His main concern was that the splitting-up of Thames would mean that it would lose a great deal of its expertise which it needed to win overseas river management contracts. Thames had already started to diversify prior to privatisation (see Chapter 6). Deprived of this specialised expertise, Thames stood to lose 10 to 20 per cent of its expected profits, which in turn might reduce Thames' flotation price by £100m. Watts also wanted Thames to be floated first and not held back by some of the less attractive water authorities. However, having played a key role in setting the agenda, he found himself dislodged from the centre of the policy process as a more crowded policy environment emerged.

MINISTERIAL INTERVENTION: THE ROLE OF A 'POLICY INITIATOR'

The image of the policy process that emerges from these events is of a system of decision-making which was somewhat episodic. Thus, while the initial policy-making process was limited to core insider groups, the succeeding policy phase witnessed a more open involvement of participants from outside this restricted core. In Sabatier's terms, two rival advocacy coalitions emerged. The abandonment of the original proposals following this wider involvement was, as suggested above, succeeded by a period when policy-making became 'internalised' (Jordan and

Richardson, 1982), that is the Government virtually ceased consultations with the affected interests, even with core insider groups at the heart of the pro-privatisation coalition. Thus, for a time, a third, and quite different, model of policy-making appears the most applicable. The change in policy style towards an internalisation of policy-making after a period of consultation has a rationale: government makes up its mind after hearing all points of view.

Interest groups need not be, however, entirely passive in the face of a period of non-consultation. To be successful they need to judge when to advance, when to retreat, and how best to secure the best deal if the climate of opinion shifts against them. The WAA was fully aware of these lobbying rules. Although it was not privy to the department's thinking at this stage, it was preparing itself for the creation of some sort of environmental regulatory organisation. In April 1987 an internal memo (with a restricted circulation), indicated that discussions at a 'high level' within the Government suggested that the DOE may be about to make an 'announcement concerning the creation of a National Regulatory Authority – NRA'. Formally DOE officials denied the rumours, but personnel changes within the department suggested to industry sources that work on water privatisation was either to be 'slowed down or at least given lower priority' (Internal WAA memo, April 1987). Their advance intelligence was excellent, the decision to establish the NRA (the memo even got the acronym correct) was in fact taken in February of that year (Interview with civil servant, April 1991).

It would be a mistake to see these policy shifts as always related to 'pressure'. There was, as outlined, considerable pressure on the Government, but the NRA decision also reflected much more closely the new minister's own personal views. Ridley was never particularly keen on the original proposals which he inherited from his predecessor, Kenneth Baker. Ridley had the foresight to recognise the inherent problems of overlapping and conflicting functions between the public and private sectors. He was convinced that the proposal that one private company could prosecute another for a criminal offence was impracticable and unworkable. Thus as Margaret Thatcher confirmed in her memoirs, the decision to slow down the policy process and to establish the NRA was his *alone*.

> It was Nick Ridley … who, when he became Environment Secretary, grasped that what was wrong was that the Water Authorities combined both regulatory and supply functions. It made no sense that those who were responsible for the treatment and disposal of sewage, for example, should be responsible for regulating pollution. (Thatcher, 1993, p. 682)

The lack of consensus following the original proposals created a policy vacuum for ministerial initiative. The emergence of two rival advocacy coalitions had, far from producing deadlock, created an opportunity for radical policy change. Ridley was the type of minister capable of seizing such an opportunity. He was assisted by the fact that a Paving Bill was needed in order to give the RWAs powers to prepare for privatisation, in advance of the actual legislation. The need to prepare and introduce a Paving Bill gave the department a useful breathing space.

In terms of Headey's typologies of ministers, Ridley's role in the policy-making process clearly illustrates the scope for ministerial leadership in policy development. Ridley saw his ministerial role as deciding 'policy objectives', firmly believing that 'Government should govern' (Interview, June 1991). In Headey's terms Ridley was a classic 'policy initiator'. Such ministers, instead of accepting the existing objectives and priorities of their departments, succeeded in exacting policy programmes based on objectives defined by themselves (Headey, 1974, p. 191). This is exactly what Ridley did.

It could be argued that he belonged to a special breed of policy initiator because while achieving a high degree of success in imposing his policy objectives on his department, he was also largely successful in that his policy achieved its intended aim. Unlike his predecessors, he recognised the 'intellectual first principle' that the environmental regulatory functions would have to remain under public control. He devised an intellectual framework within which this policy problem could be solved, and had few inhibitions about imposing it, even against the industry's wishes. This was not Nicholas Ridley's first experience of going 'against the grain' (Dudley, 1989). He had played a key role in imposing a more competitive structure against the wishes of the National Bus Company (NBC) management during its privatisation. Dudley concluded that in the case of the NBC privatisation Ridley 'had won his case against both the Treasury and NBC management' (ibid., p. 29).

Ridley, with the aid of his water minister, Michael Howard, was successful within the DOE for two main reasons. First, they did what all successful policy initiators must do. They focused a great deal of their ministerial attention and time on a policy which they themselves defined as important. Secondly, they temporarily shifted the main focus of the DOE from local government matters to water matters. Also, a senior civil servant (Patrick Brown, who had previously overseen the bus privatisation programme with Ridley) was transferred from the Department of Transport to the DOE to oversee water privatisation. With ministerial and departmental concentration firmly on water, Ridley and Howard had successfully pursued an impositional policy style as they had imposed the NRA on the industry. The existence of a countervailing (to the industry) advocacy coalition in favour of an independent regulatory agency for environmental matters undoubtedly assisted them in this task. Moreover, as shall be seen, ministers were soon able to demonstrate a willingness to consult on the detailed implementation of their key policy decision with legislative action. Having – almost brutally – slammed the door on the industry's face – they were about to reopen it, once the 'big decision' had been reached.

The decision to create the NRA failed to conform to either policy community or issue network models of decision-making. There had been no consultation, although it has to be conceded that the views of all interested parties were fairly well known through their responses to the 1986 White Paper. The decision was taken by a conviction politician, concerned with making what he perceived to be the *right* decision, irrespective of what others believed, and notwithstanding the political consequences. As suggested above, the main potential risk was losing the industry's support for privatisation. However, the likelihood of the risk being materialised was probably low. In addition to the offer of the resumption of consultation, Ridley knew that the internal dynamics of the WAA had been working in his favour during the period of internalised policy-making. Thus, Ridley recognised that the RWA chairmen had reached a consensus over the desirability of privatisation, and that they were keen to reach a workable solution. There had been a gradual shift of opinion within the WAA, with early doubters and opponents becoming enthusiasts. To come out now in strong opposition to privatisation would have been risky. After all, Thames set the privatisation band-wagon rolling, eventually taking most other authorities along with it. Arguably, the water industry had more to lose than the Government. The RWAs had gone too far down the privatisation track to turn back. To oppose the scheme on this issue was, to say the least, politically inappropriate. Moreover, the *incentives* discussed earlier were still on the table – and senior figures and managers in the industry could see the positive benefits which their colleagues in other privatised utilities had gained since privatisation. All in all, a very good deal was still guaranteed!

THE RETURN TO POLICY COMMUNITIES POLITICS

Not surprisingly, the WAA decided to accept the imposition of the NRA, and to play a full role in negotiations. To have acted otherwise would have been irrational as, by November 1987, the Government had received 349 responses to its NRA proposals. Of that total, 179 supported the creation of the NRA, only 39 opposed it, and 131 expressed no view, but offered comments on aspects of its operation (DOE, 1987). Having faced a policy disaster, the Government had devised a solution which met with very broadly based support. Moreover, the water authorities soon realised that a unified voice on major policy issues was vital in order to present an effective front to the DOE as well as to the Treasury. Like all effective core insider groups (Maloney, et al., 1994), the WAA accepted the prevailing climate of opinion and worked for practical concessions in a 'realistic' approach (see Holbeche, 1983). Even so, in public, the chairmen of the water authorities continued to oppose the department's plans to create the NRA, until a few weeks prior to the publication of the actual Green Paper that outlined the nature of the proposed NRA.

'Business as usual' soon replaced internalised policy-making. For example, responding to a Parliamentary question, Nicholas Ridley revealed that he had met water authority chairmen as early as 25 June 1987 and that their meeting had been 'friendly and useful'. He further claimed that his plans had the backing of the overwhelming majority of chairmen:

> We have now entered into discussions to get the detail right. I believe that all the interests that are concerned with water will welcome the setting up of the NRA. If one chairman [Mr Watts] is out-voted by the other nine, I think that we have endorsement from the water industry that we are on the right lines and that we are finding the right solution. (HC Debates, 15 July 1987, col. 1130)

At the June meeting Nicholas Ridley informed the chairmen that he regretted not having been able to discuss the NRA proposals with them at an earlier date. This was unavoidable, he claimed, because he required the consent of his ministerial colleagues before proceeding with consultations. He claimed that 'although the change in policy had been considered within Government in the early months of the year, the final decision to endorse this change had been taken only after the Prime Minister had decided to call the Election' (Internal WAA memo, 1 July 1987). He also told the chairmen that the NRA consultation paper's prime audience was the 'outside world, rather than the industry itself and that the Government wanted to conduct *deep and detailed consultation* with the water authorities alongside carrying the consultation paper forward' (Internal WAA memo, 1 July 1987, emphasis added). Thus, it appeared that two kinds of consultation were being carried out, with the industry being offered the *grande lux* model!

The WAA accepted Ridley's position and indicated to him that while they also regretted the lack of consultation to date, they wanted to 'move forward in coopera-tion with Government, towards a quick and successful privatisation' (Internal WAA memo, 1 July 1987). Sir Gordon Jones told the governmental team that the WAA would be holding a press conference on 26 June 1987, and 'that they would stress that the industry intended to work with the Government to find mutually acceptable solutions to the problems posed by privatisation. The Secretary of State said that it was desirable to avoid any impression of a split between Government and industry' (Internal memo, 1 July 1987). The pro-privatisation coalition had been put back together again, despite its tumble.

As with other privatisations, management support was crucial to a successful outcome. While the WAA was left in no doubt that a NRA would be established and that its basic functions were non-negotiable, it was assured that the way in which the NRA would exercise such functions remained open to discussion. The Government told the WAA that as far as the NRA proposals were concerned 'the precise boundaries are subject to negotiation ... [however], the decision to set up some sort of NRA is irrevocable' (WAA memo, 27 June 1987). The new unanimity was some kind of rewritten history. As we suggest, water authority chairmen had been deeply divided over this issue and had even hinted at one stage that they might be forced to oppose privatisation altogether. In a letter (20 March 1987) to all RWA chairmen, the WAA Chairman, Sir Gordon Jones, had said that:

> we are not concerned with the merits or demerits of privatisation as such, but rather with how it is to be achieved; we support an approach that will work in the best interests of our consumers, our employees, and our shareholders, *but not 'privatisation at any price', particularly if the price is so high that it prevents effective management and control.* (Emphasis added.)

Indeed, the WAA had produced an internal paper entitled 'Strategy for Non-privatisa-tion'. This internal memo considered the prospects that privatisation was to be substantially or indefinitely delayed. It stated that the 'Authorities should have a clear view about the strategy required to operate successfully within the public sector'. The paper stated that:

> It should be possible to achieve these 'freedoms' (i.e. 'more freedom to arrange our financial affairs, more freedom to provide commercial services, more freedom to manage the business without Government interference') for Water Authorities operating within the public sector ... This paper starts with the presumption that our strategy should be to seek to achieve greater financial freedom, commercial freedom and management freedom and goes on to iden-tify some of the major questions which then need to be addressed.

In a sense, the WAA was privately conceding that there was an alternative policy to privatisation which could achieve many of the claimed benefits of privatisation. Indeed, this paper is the only example we could find of anything approaching an 'options search' by any of the key actors involved. In the end, the WAA drew back from such radical rhetoric and accepted that privatisation *if it was to happen meant privatisation plus the NRA*. The chairmen had to accept that other influential actors – not usually active in the policy sector (such as the CBI, the EC and almost all of the environmental groups) all opposed the WSPLCs retaining the environmental regula-tory functions. Between July 1987 and July 1988 the Government and the WAA settled their differences and reappeared from their internal negotiations as a united team in preparation for privatisation. From this point on the WAA became the key non-governmental actor in the run-up to privatisation. Consultation was not only back – it was very *intensive* and very *exclusive*.

The WAA was reassured by its contacts with other privatised utilities. For example, two previously privatised industries (British Telecom and British Gas) informed WAA officials that '*everything is negotiable even up to the eleventh hour, and that funda-mental changes of principle can be made at every stage of the privatisation process*' (Internal WAA memo, 27 June 1987). These contacts further claimed that 'their best bargaining time had been when their Bills had been on the Parliamentary timetable' (Internal WAA memo, 27 June 1987).

After adopting an impositional policy style, the Government had shifted back towards a more consensual and negotiative policy style. It successfully re-created the old policy community. This was crucial to the Government, because of the pivotal position of the water authorities *vis-à-vis* their role in both the flotation, and subse-quently in implementing privatisation. The Government also needed to maintain the industry's political and public support for the privatisation – still a politically contro-versial issue.

With the management back on-side the Government (and industry) set about the task of breaking down privatisation policy into a series of more manageable, bargainable sub-issues. Thus, it can be seen that once the *big* privatisation issues were settled at the meso-level, the achievement of practical/workable policies were devolved to a series of micro-level policy networks. This had a number of advan-tages for both the Government and industry. Detailed issues could be processed through the standard operating procedures, largely in secret. The proposals could also be de-politicised and transformed into a series of *technical* problems to be resolved by fellow professionals. Finally, it meant that if any serious further conflict arose, it could be prevented from 'contaminating' the processing of other important issues within the privatisation remit.

The return to a negotiative policy style was reflected in the WAA's own handling of privatisation. It 'unpacked' privatisation into a series of manageable sub-issues through the establishment of an intra-associational privatisation policy structure (see Figure 4.1 for the WAA's organisational response to privatisation after 1987). A WAA Study Group established to 'consider critically the options for privatisation', concluded that 'an approach in parallel with the work being done in DOE is essential if Water Authorities are not to be disadvantaged when serious detailed discussions with Government are held' (Internal WAA memo).

This structure enabled the necessary expertise to be located at the appropriate times and towards the appropriate issues. The DOE for its part established three Privatisation Divisions as well as a fourth Water Division for the processing of routine business in the Water Directorate.

Two key fora kept privatisation policy on course: first, the Ministerial/ Chairmen's Group which decided policy. For example, on two occasions Michael Howard drew up a shortlist of outstanding issues 'due for resolution'. At one meeting a list containing twenty-eight outstanding issues were discussed or at least bargained. As one member of the WAA negotiation team – David Baldcock – stated that, 'He won some and we won some. After all Mr Howard had to concede something to us' (Interview, April 1991). Secondly, the full-time staff at the WAA headquarters, who handled the day-to-day issues as they arose, scrutinised legislation after policy had been settled, 'to ensure that the actual words reflected the policy'. This group also carried out legislative work in Parliament which entailed attending debates and committee meetings, briefing MPs and reporting back to the Steering Group. Contact between WAA and DOE officials was on a daily basis, and weekly progress meetings were held between WAA and DOE co-ordinators. The WAA had moved from being frozen out of the governmental process to a position of symbiosis.

Differences occurred at certain times and over certain issues during the negotiation process, and both the WAA and the DOE teams felt they were making little headway. During this intensive negotiation process tensions sometimes arose between both sets of officials. Indeed, relations had become so strained at one point that the WAA sought a stronger *political* direction in the process. For example, a WAA memo maintained that WAA options were receiving:

> very negative responses (from civil servants) which were modified only slightly after pressure, and the general inflexibility of civil servants in discussions as they press for 'their model' rather than jointly agreed models, contrasts with the more flexible statements made by Messers. Ridley, Belstead and Moynihan in public statements and during informal discussions with chairmen. Clarification by, and stronger direction from, Ministers is essential. (Internal Memo, 13 November 1987)

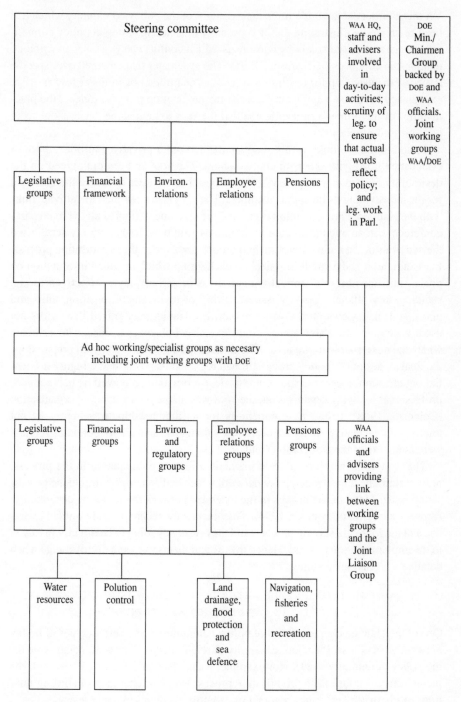

FIGURE 4.1: The WAAS organisational response to privatisation after 1987.

Yet this conflict did not undermine the existence of the policy community which had been re-created – illustrating that it is possibly misleading to depict policy communities as characterised solely by consensus. Much conflict can exist, yet a symbiotic relationship continues (Richardson, 1995). The stalemates that emerged over specific issues were pushed up for resolution at the WAA chairmen/DOE minister forum. Also, expediency became a significant factor in the negotiation process. Indeed, the practicalities of the printer's timetable enabled the WAA to gain some concessions from hard-pressed officials!

In addition to its links with governmental and other privatised utilities, the WAA established links with other influential actors. The WAA and the CBI agreed on the desirability of a common approach, where possible, in order to secure the best deal for the industry and its business customers. The WAA also attempted to cultivate links with the National Farmers Union (NFU) and the CLA, and it lobbied all the main party conferences in an attempt to gain parliamentary support. It also closely scrutinised the activities of the main environmental groups involved in the privatisation process. For example, it had a small 'dossier' on each group which included information on goals, staff, membership, annual budget, areas of activity, style, effectiveness and standing, key officials, priority issues, history of involvement, position, aims and plans, and their views on the water authorities. Having recognised that actors not usually involved in water policy could exercise influence, it needed to estimate where the next trouble might arise. The association was, therefore, well prepared for the final stages of the policy process. It had regained its position as a highly influential organisation, located at the centre of decision-making. As well as being a very professional lobbying organisation, the WAA was also a *policy capable* organisation (Coleman, 1988). It had no competitors for its membership, was highly (if not totally) representative of its membership's domains, and all its potential recruits were members of the association (ibid., p. 57).

The WAA was, therefore, able to maintain effective participation in the process, notwithstanding the extended issue network which had developed around the privatisation issue. Many of the groups in the extended network could not be described as *resource rich* (Maloney et al., 1994). They lacked the technical and political expertise and the lobbying staying power – and they were not going to be directly involved in the implementation process. Hence they found themselves at a disadvantage when detailed negotiations resumed.

A NEGOTIATIVE STYLE RETURNS: THE SHOW IS NOT OVER UNTIL THE FAT CHEQUES ARE SIGNED

One of the claimed characteristics of policy communities and certain types of policy network is, of course, the relative stability of relationships. This is especially true for the policy community model (for example, Richardson and Jordan, 1979). Yet, the picture drawn so far of the privatisation process is one of changing or shifting relationships between key policy actors. For example, elements in the industry had been enormously powerful in placing the privatisation issue on the political agenda; the industry as a whole then played a crucial role in determining the shape of the original privatisation proposals. Up to this point one of the key actors in the existing policy community had managed to exercise the supreme instrument of political power – the power to decide what politics is about (Schattschneider, 1960). They had also played a crucial part in defining policy options. Yet, the policy process had finally stalled while the Government began to sort out its ideas once it had realised that the regulatory issue, raised by the extended issue network, was a significant political and legal obstacle to privatisation. At this point the industry became powerless and excluded. Similarly, the WAA was faced with little room for manoeuvre once the NRA idea was made public. It had no option but to negotiate over details.

In July 1988, after a lull in activity, the Permanent Secretary at the DOE, Patrick Brown, sent a letter to the RWA chairmen asking that they speak with one voice. At a meeting with RWA chairmen in September 1989, the Government was 'prepared to abort the November flotation of the industry if they fail to back the privatisation fully and as one' (Internal WAA memo). The July 1988 letter called on the WAA to establish a compact team consisting of a 'small number of people to negotiate with the Government'. The significance of the word *negotiate* was not lost on the WAA and it accordingly created a new small negotiating team which had daily meetings with DOE officials and weekly meetings with the chairmen. The WAA privatisation structure outlined in Figure 4.1 was therefore further supplemented in response to DOE pressure.

On 20 July 1988 the Government announced that the ten water authorities would be privatised in one single flotation. It was reported that 'Mr Ridley, (was) flanked by the 10 authority chairmen in an unprecedented display of unity aimed at underlining close cooperation in the run-up to privatisation' (*The Financial Times*, 21 July 1988). The decision to float all ten companies simultaneously was later reported as being taken 'at the behest of the chairmen after an agreement not to promote one water company over another'. (*The Financial Times*, 7 September 1989)

With the main lines of policy decided and the dust having settled, the RWAs found themselves in a very strong bargaining position. They had every incentive to bargain for decisions which secured the financial position of the privatised companies. The Government wrote off the industry's £5,028.4 m. debt,[1] including £4,526,069,946 (NLF), and £447,258,437 (Public Work Loans Board) (Hansard, 29 January 1992).

The DOE maintained that the NLF debts 'had to be written off because such loans cannot be made to private sector companies' (HC, Committee of Public Accounts, 1992, para. 20). The industry was given a further £1.6 bn *green dowry* cash injection; cost-pass-through concessions relating to new legal requirements including EC directives and the possible costs of installing domestic water meters (estimated at somewhere between £150 to £200 per household) were granted (see Table 4.1). Beneficial corporation tax treatment was granted which meant that the water companies would not pay mainstream corporation tax, on average, for seven years because of the £7.7 bn of unused capital allowances available to be offset against pre-tax profits. All of

TABLE 4.1: Cost of sale to HM Government.

Water service companies	Debt written off (£m)	Debentures issued to HMG (£m)	Additional shares
Anglian	813.4	61.0	–
Northumbrian	447.5	–	122.6
North West	1,041.6	–	329.7
Severn Trent	831.4	–	360.0
Southern	264.8	–	46.3
South West	129.4	–	265.9
Thames	100.0	11.9	–
Welsh	432.8	–	276.0
Wessex	311.2	–	81.3
Yorkshire	558.7	–	89.0
TOTALS	4,930.8[1]	72.9	1,571.8

Net cost to HM Government	£m
Proceeds of issue	5,238.9
Debt written off	(4,930.8)
Debentures issued	72.9
Cash injection	(1,571.8)
Net cost to HMG	(1,190.8)

NOTE 1. Debt written off excludes an amount of £97.6m relating to the activities of the predecessor Water Authority not vested in the Water Service companies.
SOURCE: Price Waterhouse (1990).

these concessions suggest that the WAA's return to insider lobbying had been extremely effective. The NRA issue was a major defeat, but the rest of the package represented a quite excellent deal for the industry. A subsequent report from the City investment analyst, Credit Lyonnais Laing stated that, 'With the benefit of hindsight the financial framework set up at the time of privatisation was rather generous' (cited in HC Debates, 18 June 1991, col. 164).

This is not to suggest that the RWAs had a completely clear field on which to play. Their strength varied according to the nature of the issue under discussion. They made financial gains aplenty. Yet on other matters, other interests prevailed. For example, the WAA maintained that the proposed separation of regulatory responsibilities for environmental and economic regulation could lead to problems. The association argued for the merger of the two proposed regulators, the NRA and OFWAT, into one organisation. In a letter to Nicholas Ridley, the Chairman of the WAA, Sir Gordon Jones, expressed his anxiety about adding to the number of regulators in the water sector:

> The special features of the water industry, namely its monopolistic character and its environmental and public health impact, should be regulated by preferably

one body to deal with charges, performance standards and environmental standards. This one body would handle any inspection functions thought to be necessary, including HMIP and EC competent authority functions. The regulatory body should not engage in operational activities directly. Ideally, this single body should be an independent statutory body reporting to Parliament through one Department of State. The regulatory body would be required, in setting the financial regime for the PLCs, to take into account their cost consequences for standards set by Government. (Letter from WAA Chairman to the Secretary of State for the Environment, 24 June 1987)

The DOE stated that it saw 'no case for combining the DG and the NRA', and had two main reasons for rejecting the WAA's proposals. First, the department believed that the separation of the two bodies was essential because the two bodies needed to be accountable for 'two quite distinct tasks'. The NRA would sets standards, and OFWAT would consider whether new obligations required changes in the economic formula (Internal WAA memo, 3 November 1987). Secondly, the department stated that the NRA would be:

under a considerable amount of Ministerial control … It will be a quango, in the traditional mode, which allows considerable Ministerial interference. It is essential that the DG should not be susceptible to Ministerial influence. OFWAT will be a non-ministerial government department, with its own voted expenditure, quite separate from the DOE. Its independence of ministers, as with OFTEL (Office of Telecom Communications) and OFGAS (Office of Gas Services), is ensured through legislation. (Internal WAA memo, 3 November 1987)

Even on this issue, however, the WAA did not come away empty handed. At a critical meeting during the privatisation process, on 25 June 1987, the Secretary of State indicated that:

the Government fully recognised that, *if a tightening of environmental regulation imposed additional costs on the industry, these would have to be taken into account by the regime of economic regulation.* (WAA memo, 27 June 1987, emphasis added)

It is particularly significant that the Secretary of State gave a hint that any additional costs, which the development of an environmental regulatory agency might impose on the industry, might be eligible to qualify for the cost-pass-through provisions of the economic regulation system. Such hints were not lost on the industry's negotiators. They accepted that the separation of the regulators was inevitable and began working for the best deal under that regulatory model so that the privatised water companies would operate under favourable implementation rules. Thus, the industry knew that the distinction between policy and implementation was perhaps rather academic. What really mattered, after privatisation, was that the new companies would be able to generate profits, notwithstanding regulation. This objective was, of course, shared fully by one key interest which played only in the shadows of the water privatisation process but which was, nevertheless, important – namely City investors.

Consultations were taking place one-on-one with the department and *individual* RWAs. The setting of the initial K factors witnessed a period of intensive and relatively quick negotiations. As the subsequent National Audit Office (NAO) report on the privatisation of the RWAs highlighted:

> In order to keep the timetable for floatation (an essential requirement in view of the Government's subsequent privatisation programme) Ministers needed to agree K profiles by 31 July 1989 ... Meetings between the Minister and Chairmen failed to produce agreement and the last week of July became a period of intensive review. (NAO, 1992, pp. 2–3)

Determining the initial K level for each company was a very complicated bargaining process but, despite its enormous importance, was of low political salience. It became part of the private management of public business (Richardson and Jordan, 1979). To assess the level of the initial K, each authority developed asset management and investment plans which were submitted to the department. These outlined the RWAs' estimates for operational expenditure over the succeeding twenty years. The department's advisers then assessed the plans for consistency and 'reasonableness'. The plans were generally accepted by the assessors, with slight modifications, and in total amounted to an investment expenditure for the first ten years after privatisation of £24.6 bn (at 1989–90 prices) (NAO, 1992, p. 43).

Detailed negotiations with water authority chairmen over the initial level of K took place between May and August 1989. The water authorities also had some long and arduous negotiations with the Inland Revenue over the capital allowances and future taxation, which lasted from January to November 1988. Again this was an issue of considerable public *importance* but of low public *concern*. Thus, K levels were arrived at through a bargaining process within which the two key participants, and their raft of consultants, had a mutual interest in guaranteeing the success of the flotation. These participants were not highly motivated to ensure that a strict regulatory regime was established. Indeed, quite the reverse, the stricter the regulatory regime the less attractive the WSPLCs would have been to potential investors and thus the greater the risk to the success of the flotation. The industry's management also believed that a strong regulatory regime would reduce the managerial manoeuvrability which had been one of the key motivating factors which led them to pursue the privatisation in the first place. As Kay (1993a) highlighted, the water industry was given protection against two main kinds of risk. First, the K setting methodology 'was based, to a greater extent that in other utilities, on detailed plans submitted by individual companies ... Second, the K regime provided for a variety of automatic adjustments to prices to reflect cost changes, and also for further pass through in a range of relevant changes in circumstances' (ibid., p. 5). *The Financial Times* leader on the day the Water Act 1989 received the Royal Assent stated that:

> each water board is scrambling to negotiate the endowment of a nice fat K which will cushion it from too much regulatory pain in future. It is very hard

to be confident that in the very limited time available, civil servants can get the balance right, especially when confronted with the political imperative of making all 10 water boards attractive to the City. Indeed most of the difficulties with privatisation arise from the government's arbitrary timetable. (*The Financial Times*, 6 July 1989)

As Downs points out there is an 'inverse relationship' between the range of the search for alternative solutions and the pressure of time. Where there are strict time constraints, he argues that a 'minimal number of alternatives will be considered'; that decision-makers will attempt 'to restrict the number of participants' and that *secrecy* will be used to prevent knowledge spilling out to those who might wish to become embroiled in the process. Secrecy, he maintains, also facilitates the achievement of a consensus on complex issues, 'If a great many people must be consulted in making a decision, it becomes difficult to communicate to each person the issues involved, the possible alternatives, and the responses and views of other consultants' (Downs, 1967, p. 183).

Thus, it appears that K factors were set according to investor requirements rather than regulatory judgements. Expediency became a significant factor in the negotiation process. The NAO later claimed that the Government's 'headlong rush' to sell-off the ten RWAS 'reduced the proceeds from the privatisation ... by £2.1 billion during one week of frantic bargaining with water authorities' (reported in *The Sunday Times*, 16 February 1992). Initially the Government had expected to raise some £5.7 bn. However, following the condensed negotiations the actual sale proceeds equalled £3.6 bn. The Government, while accepting that the concessions extracted by the chairmen 'would reduce the proceeds to the taxpayer ... bowed to the chairmen's pressure because it was determined to make the sell-off a success' (*The Sunday Times*, 16 February 1992).

The Seventh Report of the House of Commons' Committee of Public Accounts concluded that:

> the Department found themselves running out of time to conclude the negotiation for sale on satisfactory terms. By the time their final week was reached they had still not settled terms with the chairmen and the 10 new companies, *who knew the deadline to which the Department were working*. In this final week, the cash injection rose to £1.1 billion and the illustrative net proceeds fell from £5.7 billion to £4.4. billion. (HC, Committee of Public Accounts, Seventh Report, para. 27[a], emphasis added)

The RWAS and investors achieved what can only be described as a very good deal. As Kay has argued:

> the water industry, of all the privatised utilities, was the one to obtain by far the most extensive protection against risks at the time of the flotation. This was partly as a result of the favourable bargaining position the Authorities found themselves in, and partly because of the Government's requirement for a

successful flotation. The terms and conditions of the sale required the City's approval, if it was to have any chance of success. (1993a, p. 5)

'OUTSIDER' GROUPS AND THE DETAILS OF POLICY NEGOTIATIONS

To the end, the privatisation of water proved to be an unpredictable process. Certain issues – such as the K factor negotiations – could be processed in private between an exclusive group of actors. Yet, other issues continued to provide participation and opportunities for interests not usually involved in water policy. For example, the controversy over the transfer of land owned by the RWAs to the proposed privatised companies provided an illustration of industry/government bargaining 'up to the eleventh hour', and of the threat that excluded groups from the wider issue network can pose to decisions made in closed policy-making arenas.

Environmental organisations, such as the CPRE, the RSPB, the National Trust and the Countryside Commission, argued that the main attraction to investors was the land assets which the proposed WSPLCs would own after privatisation. They opposed the rights of the WSPLCs to dispose of such land at a speculative value beyond the reach of organisations like the National Trust. During the parliamentary stages of the Water Bill these organisations jointly sponsored several amendments designed to limit the ability of WSPLCs to sell off land of high amenity value. Initially, they achieved some success in persuading the Government of their case. Yet, later on in the legislative process, these outsider groups claimed that (during the Third Reading in the House of Lords) the Government had reneged on its previous commitments to protect the land assets that the new companies would own. Amendments which had been introduced at the Report Stage by the Government, at the behest of these organisations, were reversed as the Government had second thoughts. Prior to the Government's change of mind at the Third Reading, the Secretary of State was given power to designate areas of land as though they were national parks. This general power was removed in an amendment which added Sites of Special Scientific Interest (SSSI) alongside National Parks and Areas of Outstanding Natural Beauty (AONB) to areas covered by the Bill. While the Government argued that an additional 100,000 acres of SSSI would be brought under the protection of this clause, the CPRE maintained that the effect of removing the *discretionary* power was to 'totally prevent the future designation of any other areas of water company land in the wider countryside – it thereby excluded a number of exceptional landscape areas from possible protection'.

The Government's decision was subsequently defended by Chris Patten, the then Secretary of State for the Environment. He stated that land in AONB, National Parks, the Broads and SSSIs:

> can only be sold with the consent of the Secretary of State. I can require that management agreements or covenants are entered into to ensure its future protection and, for example, that it be offered first for sale to a conservation body. As the Water Act (1989) allows, I have delegated much decision-making to the Countryside Commission, who are well qualified to judge what protection

is needed. This is no 'assets strippers' charter' but a workable framework of protection. (Patten, 1990, p. 2.4)

However, the Water Act, 1989 merely requires that a company '*consult* with the Countryside Commission and, in the case of sites of special scientific interest, with the Nature Conservancy Council' (The Water Act, 1989, p. 158, emphasis added).

Essentially, the land issue had also been resolved by the 'flotation test'. The Report Stage concession to the environmentalists had left too much uncertainty for potential investors. It reduced the WSPLCs' attractiveness to prospective investors. This point was put forcefully by the RWAs' negotiating team and the host of City advisers. The Government removed the offending amendment and proceeded towards the imminent flotation date. The approach of the reorganisation date was like an on-coming train which could not be stopped, and as such, it considerably increased the pressure on the Government to settle all outstanding issues.

The late reversal of an initial victory by the environmentalists was insignificant when compared with the defeat of another 'outsider' group – the trade unions. They were clearly stakeholders in the sector yet had little or no influence. They were not inactive, however. For example, a National Joint Trade Union Water Anti-Privatisation Campaign Committee was formed by all the trade unions involved in the water industry. Trade union activities were co-ordinated through this committee within which the National and Local Government Officers Association (NALGO), as the largest water industry union with some 25,000 water industry members, took a lead role. In fact, trade union involvement marked a change from previous practice in other privatisation campaigns, as the unions became more involved in coalition building. They mobilised with other, mainly environmental, groups, to oppose privatisation – forming a coalition of the weaker outsider groups. As Riddell points out, the problem for these outsider groups is that the 'interests of the Treasury in securing early flotations have been foremost – along with the aims of existing managers' (Riddell, 1991, p. 111).

CONCLUSION: PRIVATISATION AS EPISTEMIC POLICY-MAKING

The sale of the WSPLCs went ahead in November 1989 and represented a success in terms of the Government's objective of promoting wider share ownership, raising revenue for the Exchequer and shifting the industry into the private sector (see Tables 4.2 and 4.3). More significantly, however, it allowed the Government to relinquish responsibility for funding future investment programmes.

Contrasting images of the policy process appear when the process by which water was privatised is reviewed. The characteristics of the relationship between the Government and groups changed over time, from episode to episode. The policy style was not consistent. Thus, we see policy decisions being reached in a variety of ways: some were within the internalised world of government departments; some were entirely the result of government/WAA negotiations and some were the result of the activities and presence of an extended issue network consisting of rival advocacy coalitions. At times the process appeared quite chaotic and outside the control of any

TABLE 4.2: Sale of regional water holding companies.

Water service companies	No. of shares offered (m.)	Gross proceeds from sale (£m)
Anglian	294.7	707.3
Northumbrian	65.5	157.2
North West	355.8	853.9
Severn Trent	353.6	848.6
Southern	163.7	392.9
South West	122.2	293.3
Thames	384.2	922.1
Welsh	144.1	345.8
Wessex	102.6	246.2
Yorkshire	196.5	471.6
TOTALS	2,182.9	5,238.9

SOURCE: Price Waterhouse (1990).

TABLE 4.3: Share allocation by main investor group

GROUP	Before clawback (%)	Clawback (%)	After clawback (%)
Small investors	26.55	+20.325	46.875
UK institutions	54.95	−15.700	39.250
Foreign investors	18.50	−4.625	13.875
TOTAL	100.00	0.000	100.000

This table shows how initial share allocations changed when clawback was triggered.
SOURCE: Hansard, 19.12.89

one group of actors.

Taken at face value, the transfer of the industry from the public to the private sector can be seen as a major discontinuity in the development of water policy. Yet, in a different sense this major policy change may be characterised as part of a longer process of policy succession. As was argued in Chapter 3, preceding policies facilitated the major change that privatisation represented. Looking back, the industry appears to have been on an (unintended) *privatisation trajectory*. The final achievement of privatisation was not, however, the *end* of the policy process. Indeed, as shall be apparent in succeeding chapters, it merely opened up a whole range of policy and political issues and ushered in a more complex and transparent institutional framework for the resolution of problems and conflicts.

A POSTSCRIPT: COMMERCIALISING SCOTTISH WATER

Introduction: Policy Change or a Gift from God?

As indicated, Scotland generally escaped the long series of policy changes seen in England and Wales. Yet, eventually the policy change issue arrived on the Scottish political agenda. Thus, on 21 March 1991, the Secretary of State for Scotland, Ian Lang, announced a review of the structure of local government in Scotland. He stated that the Government believed that Scotland would be better served by a single-tier local government structure. The Secretary of State did not, however, mention water and sewerage services at this point, but merely that the consultation paper would be 'seeking views on possible functional changes and on options for improving the management and efficiency of local government in Scotland' (HC Debate, 21 March 1991, col. 463). It was the consultation paper published in June 1991 – *The Structure of Local Government in Scotland: the case for change* (Dep 7165) – which suggested that, 'the provision of water and sewerage services might best be handled by organisations separate from the new unitary authorities' (para. 23). (Currently, 1994, the water industry in Scotland is the responsibility of the nine Regional and three Island Councils.) Thus, with one small sentence water was pushed to the top of the Scottish political agenda. The opposition parties immediately presented the proposed changes as the Government's pretext for full-scale privatisation of water and sewerage services similar to the situation in England and Wales.

Scottish Water – A Gift from God

In a somewhat cautious move towards policy change the Scottish Office published a consultation paper, in November 1992, on the future of water and sewerage services – *Water and Sewerage Services in Scotland: investing for our future* – which outlined eight possible options for the future structure of the water industry in Scotland. The eight options initially laid out by the Scottish Office were as follows:

1. Placing services within a new unitary authority.
2. Creating joint boards of the new unitary authorities.
3. A lead authority structure.
4. Creating new water authorities.
5. A single national water authority.
6. Joint local authority/private sector schemes.
7. (Full-scale) privatisation through a public flotation.
8. Privatisation through franchising.

The response to this consultation document was phenomenal, to say the least. The Government received 4,834 responses to its consultation paper, including 4,069 submissions from individuals (The Scottish Office, 1993b) (Appendix 4.1 lists the types of respondent to the consultation document). This exceeded the 3,317 responses received by the Scottish Office to its local government reorganisation consultation paper – *Shaping the New Councils* – and indeed, that for the process of privatisation in England and Wales. As was seen earlier, in 1986 the Department of the Environment received a total of forty-three responses to its first discussion paper on water privatisation in England and Wales (HC Debates, 16 January 1986, col. 680w), and by November 1987, when water privatisation in England and Wales had become a 'big' political issue, the Government received a mere 349 responses to its proposals to establish the National Rivers Authority.

Over 92 per cent of respondents to the *Investing for Our Future* paper 'did not specify a preference for any particular option laid out in the consultation paper', while 94 per cent supported public control, and a 'one percent were in favour of privatisation' (The Scottish Office, 1993b, p. 3).[2] In addition to formal consultation responses, the Scottish Office 'received petitions with over 90,000 signatures and over 60,000 pre-printed postcards' all opposing the privatisation option (The Scottish Office, 1993b, p. 7). Indeed, the *Glasgow Evening Times* readership survey found some 27,646 respondents against privatisation with only 353 in favour, and a MORI poll in *The Sunday Times* in September 1992 found 89 per cent of respondents opposed water privatisation while only 67 per cent opposed coal and 49 per cent opposed the privatisation of rail services (Scottish and Westminster Communications, 1993, paras. 4.2 and 4.3). The high level of opposition to the prospect of change led Tom Clarke, the former Shadow Secretary of State for Scotland, to comment that, 'Most people in Scotland – indeed, 98 per cent – believe that water is a gift from God' (HC Debate, 14 July 1993, col. 991). When asked whether privatisation had emerged as the least popular option, Ian Lang replied, somewhat ironically, that 'I don't think that is an understatement' (*The Independent*, 27 April 1993).

The possibility of privatising the industry, as had happened in England and Wales, produced a remarkable consensus over a very wide range of interests in a diverse issue network. Thus, the following interests opposed privatisation: the nine Regional and three Island Councils; forty-six of the fifty-three District Councils, the Institution of Civil Engineers (ICE), the National Farmers Union (NFU) (see Scottish and Westminster Communications, 1993, paras. 6.2, 6.4 and 10.2), the Scottish Landowners' Federation (SLF), the Federation of Small Businesses (FSB), the environmental lobby, all of the main opposition parties and the Trade Unions (National Association of Local Government Officers [NALGO], the Transport and General Workers Union [TGWU] and NUPE). The trade unions feared privatisation on the grounds that it was likely to lead to union derecognition and job cuts. The Confederation of British Industry (CBI) favoured the creation of new authorities and the Scottish Chambers of Commerce (SCC) called on the Government to attract private investment into the sector, additional to government funding. Somewhat unsurprisingly, the water and sewerage companies in England and Wales favoured privatisation. For example, North West Water offered the Scottish Office its services:

> our unique experience ... combined with our international experience would enable us to make a significant contribution as part of any restructuring of the Scottish water and wastewater industry. (Cited in Scottish and Westminster Communications, 1993, para. 13.2).

Most surprising for the Government, however, was the lack of enthusiasm shown by its own party associations and affiliated organisations. Of the nineteen submissions made by Conservative associations and groups only the Economic Affairs Committee of the Scottish Conservative and Unionist Association favoured immediate outright privatisation. John Young, a Conservative district councillor and Vice-Chairperson of the Scottish Tory Reform Group said that 'the Tory rank and file are strongly opposed to the idea (that is, privatisation) ... If the best option is a joint public–private water authority, fine, but I want the public sector to have the controlling interest' (*The Sunday Times*, 30 August 1992). Opponents of the reorganisation of water and sewerage services in Scotland have presented the changes as an attack on local democracy (with the removal from local authority control) and as 'halfway house' to full-scale privatisation. However, Ian Lang described it as the 'best of both worlds' (*Scotland on Sunday*, 11 July 1994). With such a breadth of opposition to the removal of water services from local authority control it appears that the Conservatives managed to propose a policy change which is possibly *even more* unpopular in Scotland than the Poll Tax/Community Charge had been. In the event, the Government attempted a face-saving compromise proposing the formation of new boards, exhibiting a somewhat hybrid (public/private) structure.

The Shape of the New Boards

In July 1993 Ian Lang informed the House of Commons that the Government intended to create three public water authorities 'broadly in line with Option (D) in the consultation paper *Investing For our Future*'. The Secretary of State had, however, decided to extend the consultation period before publishing more detailed legislative proposals. The White Paper, *Shaping the Future – The New Councils*, spelt out more clearly what 'broadly in line with Option (d)' actually meant. The Government envisaged public ownership, but 'with a major role for the private sector in providing and financing much of the essential and large capital investment programme needed over the next decade' (The Scottish Office, 1993a, para. 3.22). The new authorities will assume ownership of the existing assets and will become responsible for their day-to-day operation. They will also finance their services and investment through charging the 'full costs of water and sewerage services' (The Scottish Office, 1993a, para. 3.23).

The three new water and sewerage authorities will be known as the East of Scotland Water Authority, the West of Scotland Water Authority and the North of Scotland Water Authority. The membership of the authority will be between seven and eleven (plus the chief executive of the authority), appointed by the Secretary of State 'from persons who appear to him to have knowledge or experience relevant to the discharge of the functions of the authority' (Local Government etc. [Scotland] Bill, Schedule 7, para. 3). The three chief executive posts were advertised in November 1994. They were to be appointed, according to a Scottish Office spokesperson, on the basis of 'people with the appropriate managerial skills, be they learned in the public or private sector, or indeed both' (*Scotland on Sunday*, 30 October 1994).

The boards' remits includes attracting high levels of private sector investment for improvement programmes – which the Treasury is no longer prepared to fund. Thus, as was the case in England and Wales, it appears that the changes in Scotland are also considerably influenced by factors exogenous to the water sector, with the Treasury exercising considerable influence. Indeed, the irony of the situation is that not only have the changes to the British water industry been influenced by the Treasury, but they have been partially caused by the Treasury through the continued underfunding of the sector – a problem caused by the Treasury and passed on by the Treasury. As Ian Lang argued, the reorganisation of water and sewerage services is required 'because we need about £5 billion of investment in the industry during the next 10 to 15 years ... In the 20 years between 1969 and 1989 – when expenditure was entirely in the public sector – investment throughout the United Kingdom was under £6 billion. Between 1989 and 1999, investment is likely to be closer to £30 billion' (HC Debate, 17 November 1994, cols. 154–5). The Europeanisation of water policy has also had a major impact in Scotland. For example, Sir Hector Monro, replying to a Parliamentary question on the costs of meeting EC standards, pointed out that:

> The European Community directives with most significant financial implica-
> tions for capital expenditure are the drinking water directive and the urban
> waste water directive which are estimated at £1.2 billion and £1.3 billion
> respectively over the next 15 years. (HC Debate, 23 June 1993, col. 209w)

In a sense, what has happened in Scotland in 1994 is a re-run of the England and Welsh experience, except that the political salience of privatisation has been even greater in Scotland and has acted as a more effective constraint on radical policy change.

The new water and sewerage authorities will have to draft codes of practice relating to:

(a) their standards of performance in providing services to their customers;
(b) for procedures for dealing with complaints by their customers or their potential or former customers;
(c) the circumstances in which they will pay compensation if or in so far as those standards are not attained; and
(d) such matters as are incidental to the provisions made under paragraphs (a) and (c) above (Clause 65, Local Government etc. (Scotland) Bill [as amended in the first Scottish Standing Committee and on Consideration]).

The Scottish Water and Sewerage Customers' Council will be created 'for the purpose of representing the interests of customers and potential customers of the new water and sewerage authorities. It will be funded by the Treasury and "contributions" from the new authorities. The Council will have between 8 and 12 members appointed by the Secretary of State' from persons who appear to him to have knowledge or experience relevant to the discharge of the functions of the authority (Local Government etc. [Scotland] Bill, Schedule 9, para. 3). The Council will have three committees, one for each of the water and sewerage areas, comprising between seven and eleven members. It will investigate customer complaints and will advise the

Secretary of State on both the standards of service provided by the new authorities and the authorities' handling of customer relations. Charging schemes have to be approved by the Customers' Council and the new authorities. If agreement cannot be reached the Secretary of State's approval is required. 'The Secretary of State may from time to time by order fix maximum charges' (ibid., Clause 74).

The reorganisation of the Scottish water sector into three new public authorities is analogous in several ways to the process of organisational change in England and Wales during the 1970s and 1980s. First, it will create a regionalised system, which the Water Act 1973 did in England and Wales. Secondly, the 1973 reorganisation of the English and Welsh industries transferred the water and sewerage assets of the local authorities (which have formerly supplied water and sewerage services) to the new regional water authorities. (The transfer date is to be 1 April 1996.) Thirdly, the new Scottish boards are organised along similar lines to the RWA boards reformed under the Water Act 1983, being small and having appointees made by the Secretary of State. Similarly, the status of customers is to be enhanced. Indeed, the direct role of customers may be greater in Scotland because of the role of the customers' council in the setting of charges.

Implementing Without Consensus?

The perception has continued, much to the Conservative Government's frustration, that privatisation is the hidden agenda. Ian Lang stated that Scotland's water and sewerage services are not being privatised 'whether by the back door, the front door, or by any other route. Privatisation is simply not on the government's agenda. The services are remaining in public ownership' (*The Sunday Times* [Scottish Supplement], 27 March 1994). The Government's continued reassurances that full-scale privatisation was no longer on the political agenda fell on deaf ears as the main opposition parties enjoyed the opportunity to exploit further the Government's considerable unpopularity in Scotland. For example, Strathclyde Regional Council organised a referendum which kept the issue alive and demonstrated the continuing high degree of opposition to the Government's plans to remove the industry from local authority control. Approximately 1.2 million people (97 per cent of those who took part in the referendum) voted against the Government's proposals to remove water and sewerage services form local authority control. Only 2.8 per cent (34,000) supported the Government's plans. Some 71 per cent of voters returned their ballot papers (*The Herald*, 23 March 1994).

At the time of writing (early November 1994) the Convention on Scottish Local Government, the Labour, Liberal and Scottish Nationalist Parties and the Scottish TUC have all decided to boycott the new water boards. The Labour Party has stated that the boycott will continue until the Secretary of State guarantees that the Boards will be entirely made up of local authority representatives. The only organisations originally asked to submit names and now remaining on the Scottish Office's list are the CBI, the Scottish Landowners' Federation, the NFU and the Scottish Consumer Council (*Scotland on Sunday*, 30 October 1994). It appears that the Government will leave three or four places vacant on the water boards which could be offered to the elected councillors on the shadow unitary authorities that will be established in April 1995.

NOTES

1. All the authorities except Anglian were sold debt free.
2. It is believed that Ian Lang's favoured option was franchising.

REFERENCES

Coleman, W. D. (1988), *Business and Politics: A Study of Collective Action* (Kingston and Montreal: McGill-Queen's University Press).
Depatment of the Environment (DOE) (1987), *The National Rivers Authority: The Government's Policy for a Public Regulatory Body in a Privatised Water Industry* (London: HMSO).
Downs, A. (1967), *Inside Bureaucracy* (Boston: Little, Brown and Company).
Dudley, G. F. (1994), 'The Next Steps Agencies, Political Salience and the Arm's-Length Principle: Barbara Castle at the Ministry of Transport 1965–68', *Public Administration*, vol. 72, no. 2, pp. 219–40.
Dudley, G. (1989), 'Privatisation "With The Grain": Distinguishing features of the sale of the National Bus Company', *Strathclyde Papers on Government and Politics*, no. 59 (Glasgow: Department of Politics, University of Strathclyde).
Headey, B. (1974), *British Cabinet Ministers* (London: Allen & Unwin).
Holbeche, B. (1983), 'Policy and Influence: MAFF and the National Farmers' Union', *Public Policy and Administration*, vol. 1, no. 3, pp. 40–7.
House of Commons (HC), Committee of Public Accounts (1992), *Seventh Report, Sale of the Water Authorities in England and Wales* (London: HMSO).
Jordan, A. G. and Richardson, J. J. (1982), 'The British Policy Style or the Logic of Negotiation?', in J. Richardson (ed.), *Policy Styles in Western Europe* (London: George Allen & Unwin), pp. 80–110.
Kay, J. (1993a), 'The Economic and Financial Background', paper presented to the Institution of Water and Environmental Management Annual Conference, 'Water Industry Regulation Three Years On', Harrogate, 2 and 3 March 1993.
Kay, J. (1993b), 'Utility Regulation and the Monopolies and Mergers Commission: Retrospect and prospect', in M. E. Beesley (ed.), *Major Issues in Regulation* (London: Institute of Economic Affairs), pp. 58–61.
Local Government etc. (Scotland) Bill [as amended in the first Scottish Standing Committee and on Consideration] (London: HMSO), May 1994.
Maloney, W. M., A, Jordan, G. and McLaughlin, A. M. (1994) 'Interest Groups and Public Policy: the insider/outsider model revisited', *Journal of Public Policy*, vol. 14, pp. 17–38.
National Audit Office (NAO) (1992), *Department of the Environment: Sale of the Water Authorities in England and Wales* (London: HMSO).
Patten, C. (1990), Opening address to the *Financial Times European Water Industry Conference*, London, 26 and 27 March (London: *The Financial Times*), pp. 2.1–2.4.
Pearce, F. (1987), 'Ministers battle for water scientists', *New Scientist*, 2 July, p. 25.
Price Waterhouse (1990), *Privatisation: The Facts* (London: Price Waterhouse).
Richardson, J. J. (1995), 'Actor Based Models of National and EU Policy-Making: Policy networks, epistemic communities and advocacy coalitions', in A. Menon and H. Kassim (eds), *The EU and National Industrial Policy* (London: Routledge).
Riddell, P. (1991), *The Thatcher Era and its Legacy* (Oxford: Blackwell).
Ridley, N. (1991), *My Style of Government: The Thatcher Years* (London: Hutchinson).
Schattschneider, E. E. (1960), *Semi-Sovereign People: A Realist's View of Democracy in America* (New York: Holt, Rinehart & Winston).
Scottish and Westminster Communications (1993), *The Future of Water and Sewerage Services in Scotland: An Overview of Responses to the Scottish Office* (Edinburgh: Scottish and Westminster Communications).
The Scottish Office (1993a), *Shaping the New Councils: Summary of Responses* (Edinburgh: Scottish Office).
The Scottish Office (1993b), *Summary of Responses to the Consultation Paper 'Investing for our Future'* (Edinburgh: Scottish Office).
The Scottish Office (1993c), *Shaping the Future – The New Councils*, Cmnd 2267 (Edinburgh: HMSO).
Thatcher, M. (1993), *The Downing Street Years* (London: Harper Collins Publishers).

APPENDIX 4.1: 'Investing for our Future': types of respondent.

	No. of responses	*Percentage of overall response*
Individuals	4,069	84.2
Regional councils	9	0.2
Water and sewerage depts	1	–
Other organisations	5	0.1
Island councils	3	0.1
Other organisations	1	–
District councils	47	1.0
Community councils	278	5.8
Political representatives/ organisations	123	2.5
Public Bodies	44	0.9
Voluntary/welfare organisations	45	0.9
Medical organisations	15	0.3
Chambers of Commerce	3	0.1
Business associations	4	0.1
Trade associations	5	0.1
Universities	4	0.1
Professional associations	8	0.2
Religious associations	12	0.2
Recreational/sporting groups	67	1.4
Trades unions	21	0.4
Other associations	9	0.2
Water companies	5	0.1
Engineering companies	10	0.2
Financial institutions/banks	12	0.2
Legal companies	4	0.1
Other companies	30	0.6
TOTAL	4834	100.00

SOURCE: The Scottish Office (1993b), Summary of Responses to the Consultation Paper 'Investing for our Future' (Edinburgh: The Scottish Office), p. 9.

PART 3

Calming Troubled Waters?

5

Regulation in the Post-privatised Water Industry: Complexity, Conflict and Consensus

Understanding economic regulation ... means understanding a process of intermediation and bargaining between large and powerful organizations spanning what are conventionally termed the public and private domains of decision-making ... Economic regulation under advanced capitalism – its formation and implementation – invariably involves interdependence and bargaining between powerful and sophisticated actors against a background of extensive state involvement.

L. Hancher and M. Moran, 1989

INTRODUCTION: CONFLICT AND CONSENSUS

So far this book has focused on the process of policy formulation, rather than policy implementation – even though the close interrelationship between the two has been stressed. However, it now addresses the policy process after privatisation. In one sense privatisation can be said to represent the end point of a long process. Yet in another sense it marks the beginning of a new era, as the whole water policy process has been opened up to wider participation and has become more transparent. This has created a very fluid policy environment, characterised by unstable and often conflictual relationships between actors, and hence a high degree of uncertainty. Rather than seeing privatisation as a stable end point, it may be more useful to examine it as a destabilising event and as a discontinuity with past experience.

Thus, if the water industry thought that privatisation would simplify life, it was badly mistaken. Privatisation brought with it a new and extremely complex regulatory regime. A large number of regulators is involved, for example, the Office of Water Services (OFWAT), the National Rivers Authority (NRA),[1] the Drinking Water Inspectorate (DWI), the Office of Fair Trading (OFT), the Monopolies and Mergers Commission (MMC), Her Majesty's Inspectorate of Pollution (HMIP) and the Ministry of Agriculture, Fisheries and Food (MAFF) – as well as the EU, of course (see Figure 5.1). Further changes are planned with the creation of the new Environmental Agency (for England and Wales) bringing together the NRA, HMIP and the waste regulation functions of local authorities. A separate environmental protection agency has been proposed for Scotland.

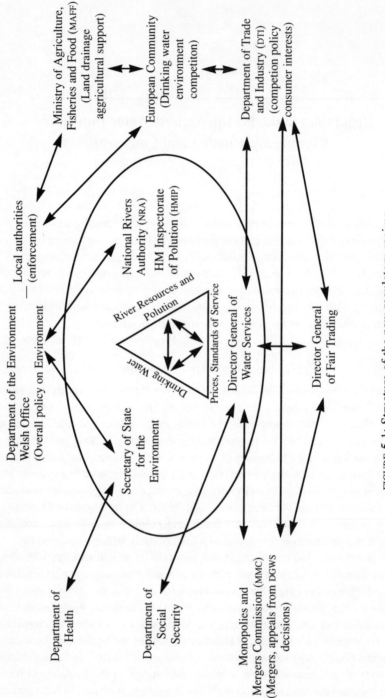

FIGURE 5.1: Structure of the new regulatory regime.

SOURCE: OFWAT, 1993b.

The current regime for the privatised industry is in sharp contrast to the regulatory regime under public ownership. In so far as the industry was subject to regulation prior to privatisation it was largely self-regulation, albeit with increasingly tight financial regulation from the Department of the Environment (DOE).

Moreover, in the post-privatised world the political salience of the sector has increased rather than declined. Consequently, water policy-making has been exposed to the glare of publicity, has provoked public debate and has seen public conflict between some of the key actors. This has not simply manifested itself as a struggle between the new regulatory authorities and the water companies as they naturally search for a consensual *modus operandi*. There have been bitter 'turf fights' between the regulators themselves. Yet, it would be misleading to suggest that the system is besieged by total conflict. In practice, there are many instances of the British tradition of 'bargained regulation'. Some key issues divide the main actors, but there has been a clear recognition that, as mutual 'stakeholders' in the policy area, compromises have to be reached if service delivery is to continue efficiently and effectively. Thus, on the one hand, the regulatory process can be characterised by bargaining and negotiation, operating along the lines of the preferred British policy style while, on the other hand, there is conflict, with in some instances the threat, (and use) of legal sanction to ensure compliance with relevant legislation. The political process has now shifted from the politics of privatisation to the (public) politics of regulation.

Prior to privatisation, the regulatory regime was strongly characterised by consensual and private decision-making in the British regulatory tradition. It is also fair to say that the regulatory system under public ownership was much less rigorous and certainly less complex than under current arrangements. As we have argued, the industry was involved in a mainly arm's length relationship with government, predicated on what one civil servant described to us as a basis of trust in the industry to do a good (and legal!) job. In that sense, water was no different from the rest of British public administration where a strongly held public service ethic was thought to be a more efficient 'regulatory tool' than any set of formal institutional rules or laws. Behavioural norms and values could be relied upon, it was thought, to produce optimum results in terms of service efficiency. The pre-privatisation regulator/regulatee relationship, while being inherently contradictory, survived because of this ethic. As the National Consumers' Council pointed out at the time, 'the regulator (the "sponsoring government department") was also a wholly-owned subsidiary of the only shareholder (the government)' (NCC, 1989, p. 16).

In so far as there was serious conflict it was within government, particularly between the industry's lead department – the DOE – and its financier, the Treasury. On occasions, they appeared to have divergent interests. The DOE generally pressed for more resources to enable the industry to meet its environmental obligations (in particular EU Directives). In contrast the Treasury framed its policy on investment levels and charging policy on the basis of macro-economic concerns – in particular reflecting the growing concerns with the public sector borrowing requirement (PSBR).

Even before privatisation, however, the regulatory structures were not entirely simple. There were several other agencies, besides the DOE and the RWAS, involved in the regulatory process. Britain's membership of the European Community (EC) had introduced a major new regulatory player in the early 1970s (see Chapter 6). Her Majesty's Inspectorate of Pollution had responsibilities and duties which included: advising the RWAS on water pollution concerns, verifying sampling and monitoring procedures, monitoring the implementation of EC water pollution directives and enforcing water quality standards. Local authorities were also charged (under Section 11 of the Water Act 1973) with certain regulatory functions. Even though the regulatory system was already complex, however, it was clearly less burdensome to the industry. The regulatory shoe did not pinch very hard. This was because the central core of the old regulatory system was *self-regulation* .

REGULATION IN A PRIVATISED WATER INDUSTRY

The Economic Regulatory System

Water privatisation differed fundamentally from those it succeeded. Water is first and foremost a 'natural monopoly *par excellence*' (Littlechild, 1988). Consequently, with the sunk costs involved in the established local network of pipes and sewers, 'it is not economic for potential competitors to install rival networks' (ibid., p. 44). Although some forms of competition might emerge, it is difficult to see genuine and extensive competition developing in the industry unless there is a common carriage facility to which everyone has access, as in telecommunication. As a result of this monopoly situation, economic regulation is likely to be permanent, rather than a case of 'holding the fort' until meaningful competition arrives (ibid., p. 45). Successive Conservative administrations have seen monopoly as an anathema and have espoused the benefits of competition and its corollary of choice and consumer sovereignty. Where a monopoly exists, however, Conservative Governments have come to regard regulated private monopoly as preferable to publicly owned monopoly (Vickers and Yarrow, 1990). Yet the Conservatives have also been concerned to avoid 'excessive' regulation. (Indeed, a major deregulation bill is currently, 1994, passing through Parliament). Thus, they see regulation as a 'restriction of freedom' (DOE, 1993, para. 1.2). In an attempt to square these conflicting ideologies, the search has been for as 'light' a regulatory regime as is politically possible. In practice, all the privatised utilities, including water, have experienced 'regulatory creep' as the (rather independent) regulators have responded to public and parliamentary criticisms of their role. In a sense, the 'regulatory bargain' has been rewritten by the regulators, prompting charges that the regulators themselves need to be subject to more effective control.

The water sector is especially challenging in terms of designing an effective regulatory regime. It exhibits several kinds of market failure, and consequently several types of regulatory behaviour: first, regulation to control monopoly behaviour; secondly, regulation to promote competition where possible; thirdly, regulation to control and compensate for *externalities* – for example, pollution control regulations, which are designed to alleviate the problems caused by such externalities;

fourthly, regulation may be used in times of *scarcity*; fifthly, regulation as a mechanism for correcting for inadequate information (see Breyer, 1979, pp. 235–6).

Within England and Wales, there are three core regulators. The Secretary of State for the Environment has responsibility for drinking water quality, the NRA has responsibility for environmental regulation and OFWAT for economic regulation. The British privatisation programme was, undoubtedly, a learning experience for the Government. Early 'models' of regulation tended to be copied. Thus, the economic regulatory system established for British Telecom was the basic datum for succeeding utility privatisations. In the now privatised water sector there are essentially two economic regulators – the MMC and the OFWAT (headed by the Director General of Water Services (DGWS) (sometimes referred to as the DG). The legislative framework for the main economic regulatory mechanisms are set out in the Water Acts 1989, 1990, 1991 and the Competition and Service (Utilities) Act 1992; the instruments of appointment – which is the licence under which the companies are permitted to operate and a basic pricing formula for their products and services – the so-called RPI+K factor. The core of the system of economic regulation is the control which the Director General can exercise over the prices which companies can charge to their customers. The annual increase in prices is restricted to the retail price index plus an addition K which is allocated to each individual company, initially for each of the ten years 1990 to 2000. The K factor is to offset the major investment programmes which are necessary to clear the backlog of investment and to meet rising standards – particularly as set by the EU. Essentially, the K factor is a cost-pass-through mechanism. In the event, the K factors were reviewed in 1994 – in the so-called 'periodic review' discussed below. The level of K is intended to 'ensure that the benefits of increased efficiency will be systematically passed on to consumers in the form of lower prices (lower K values), or alternatively higher standards' (MMC, 1990b, para. 2.16). In setting the K factor, the DG has a statutory duty to ensure that the companies can finance their main functions, that is, the K must be sufficient for the companies to remain in business and to perform their central functions – the supply of clean water and the disposal of waste water and so on.

The privatised water companies were also protected by a golden share, for five years in the first instance (HC Debates, 11 January 1989, col. 842).[2] As Graham and Prosser (1991, p. 141) explain, 'The basis, in general, for a golden share scheme in Britain is that the share capital of the company will contain one special-rights redeemable preference share of £1 held by the Government or its nominee'. The articles of association of the ten privatised companies stipulate that directors must prohibit any one actor or actors in collusion from acquiring a shareholding of more than 15 per cent in the company. The articles can only be altered with the permission of the golden shareholder, the Government. The golden share is likely to be invoked where the Government believes 'there is a clear need to protect a business from unwelcome take-over, for example, on national security grounds, or, as a temporary measure, to provide an opportunity for management to adjust to the private sector' (The Treasury, 1990). According to the former Chancellor of the Exchequer, Nigel

Lawson, the golden share was devised to enable the Government, 'to prevent control of the companies from falling into unsuitable hands. (The term "unsuitable" had to be used, rather than "foreign", to avoid falling foul of [European] Community Law; but everyone knew what it was likely to mean)' (Lawson, 1992, p. 219).

The Role of the Monopolies and Mergers Commission

The MMC now has an important role in the water sector, particularly in relation to licensing conditions, and mergers and take-overs. The MMC can act as a 'court of appeal' for both the DGWS and for the individual companies – for example, the companies can appeal to the MMC against the DGWS's decision on the K factor in the periodic review. Indirectly, via the Director General of Fair Trading (DGFT) and the Secretary of State for Trade and Industry, the DGWS can refer proposed mergers and take-overs to the MMC for adjudication.

Under the Water Act 1991 the 'Secretary of State [for Trade and Industry] must refer to the MMC certain mergers or proposed mergers involving two or more "water enterprises" when the value of assets taken over exceeds £30 million' (MMC, 1992, p. 25). The MMC must decide if the potential mergers are against the public interest. Under the act (as amended by the Competition and Service [Utilities] Act 1992) it must also consider if a proposed merger, reducing the number of water companies, reduces the DGWS' (that is OFWAT's) ability to make meaningful comparisons with regard to comparative competition.

These legislative requirements provoked the MMC's early involvement in the sector. Since privatisation, the MMC has published three reports, one in April 1990 and two in July 1990 (MMC, 1990a, 1990b, 1990c). The first report (MMC, 1990a) examined the proposed merger of three Home Counties water companies – Colne Valley, Lee Valley, and Rickmansworth – because it would have given Compagnie Générale des Eaux (CGE) a controlling stake in the proposed merged company – Three Valleys Water Services. The MMC viewed the Three Valleys merger as against the public interest because of its 'detrimental impact' on the ability of the DGWS to make comparisons between water companies (MMC, 1990a).

The Secretary of State, Nicholas Ridley, while doubtful about the proposed merger referred the matter to the DGWS for further consideration, asking him 'to explore the matter with the companies on his behalf, and report to him within three months' (*Water Bulletin*, 4 May 1990, no. 407). The Minister was particularly keen on the prospects of costs saving for customers as a result of the merger. In January 1991 the three companies were allowed to merge and became collectively known as the Three Valleys Water Services Plc.[3] Through a series of discussion with the DGWS the companies convinced him that a merger would be beneficial to customers. The DG, Byatt commented:

> I have argued strongly against any reduction in the number of companies if it affects my ability to make comparisons of their efficiency. However, I recognise that some mergers will lead to direct gains for customers which can outweigh the benefits accruing from comparative competition. In this particular case

there will be considerable efficiencies to be gained and the benefits from these can be passed on to customers keeping their bills lower than they would otherwise have been (*Water Bulletin*, 10 August 1990, no. 421).

The third MMC report investigated CGE's 29.9 per cent holding in Mid Kent Holdings. The Commission 'recommended General Utilities give undertakings limiting its influence on Mid Kent, but Mr Ridley was "not persuaded" this would ensure public interests were protected' (*Water Bulletin*, 13 July 1990, no. 417). Ridley, called on the DGWS to instruct CGE to reduce its holding to 19.5 per cent.

Thus the MMC has proved to be an important actor in the post-privatised water sector, and is likely to remain so, especially given South West Water's recent appeal to the Commission about its K factor determined by the DGWS's periodic review (see below) in July 1994.[4] The Commission is the regulatory backstop and the ultimate court of appeal. Its recommendations may prove to have a major impact on the future structure of the industry, that is, the number of competitors, and their ownership.[5] However, the Secretary of State for Trade and Industry has also proved to be an important actor, overruling and referring MMC's recommendations whenever it was believed to be necessary.

The Office of Water Services

OFWAT is a non-ministerial government department headed by the DGWS, Ian Byatt,[6] who is appointed by the Secretary of State for the Environment. The primary duty of the DGWS is to ensure that the water and sewage companies (WASCs) and the former statutory water companies, now water only companies (WOCs), carry out their functions in accordance with the terms of their instruments of appointment, and that they are able to finance their activities and secure a reasonable return on capital. Through the licensing system, the DGWS regulates levels of charging, relationships with customers, levels of service and service targets, conditions on maintenance of assets and disposal of protected land. He has a duty to protect the interests of the customers through the facilitation of effective competition between operators, and the promotion of efficiency within the industry. Like all regulators, therefore, he is set the task of securing efficiency gains via the regulatory process – not an easy task. The DGWS is also responsible for appointing the chairpersons and members of the ten OFWAT Consumer Service Committees (CSCs). The DGWS also carries out mandatory periodic reviews, normally at least every ten years. Byatt announced on 31 July 1992 that he intended to carry out a 'periodic review' of the companies' price caps in 1994 (OFWAT, 1992a). This has now been done (see below).

In his first Annual Report, Byatt outlined OFWAT's general regulatory style as setting a framework which safeguards the public interest and which provides incentives to efficient management. In particular, he indicated that he would regulate by reference to outputs – 'what the customer receives and what he or she pays for – rather than by inputs, because the industry should be allowed to allocate its resources in the most efficient way' (OFWAT, 1990, p. 10). The style of regulation was promised to be an open one: 'I shall aim to stimulate debate and explain the reasons lying behind my decisions' (OFWAT 1991, p. 10). An important part of this policy of open-ness is the publication of the so-called 'Dear MD Letters'. These are the DGWS's formal method of communication with the companies. Some thirty of these were published in OFWAT's first year. By May 1992 the figure had risen to seventy-eight, with fifty-four 'Dear Finance Directors Letters' having been sent. Some four years later, in 1994, no one could accuse Byatt of failing to achieve at least his objective of open debate, as we shall see below. The traditional, more private British consul-tative style was also present however. Thus, although the new system promised to be a break with the regulatory past ('In contrast to the past, the water industry will be regulated from outside and not by its own procedures'), there was also a clear promise of a close consultative relationship with the industry ('I shall work with the industry in developing regulatory information'). The DGWS also gave early warning of his concern to develop a public debate about charges. ('I proposed to stimulate a public debate on methods of charging for water and on the structure of water tariffs. I see a major role for the CSCs in this debate') (OFWAT 1990).

OFWAT's determination to develop a technically robust system for monitoring levels of charges was also a clear signal that 'regulatory capture' was rather unlikely, at least in the early years. The initial (rather generous) K factors had been set by the Government for the then privatised companies and for the twenty-nine private water only companies in August 1989 and February/March 1990 respectively. Thereafter the task of overseeing the level and system of charging fell to OFWAT's Charges Control Division. The primary objective of the Division is to 'limit charges to those which would be charged by companies competing directly with each other' – a tough regulatory task in a monopoly supplier situation. In practice, the K factor applies to a basket of tariffs which covers all standard charges to domestic and non-domestic customers, giving companies some individual discretion about how individual tariffs are charged.

The Environmental Regulatory Structure

The National Rivers Authority

As already mentioned, an independent environmental regulator (the NRA), was imposed on the industry for three main reasons: the EC's insistence on a public body being the *competent authority*; the deluge of opposition to the Government's initial (1986) proposal to privatise the RWAs with their regulatory functions intact; and Nicholas Ridley's belief that the gamekeeper/poacher role could not continue after privatisation.

The NRA took over the regulatory and other specific functions which the RWAs had previously held. Its main duties and responsibilities include:

1. River quality and the quality of inland coastal waters.
2. Land drainage and flood control.
3. Management of water resources.
4. Fisheries.

5. Recreation and conservation.
6. Navigation.
7. Licensing and abstraction of water.
8. Independently monitoring river quality and discharges from sewage treatment plants.
9. The enforcement of water quality objectives to be determined by the Secretary of State (*Water Facts*, 1993).

As Kinnersley has argued, there is a crucial difference between OFWAT and the NRA as regulators. Thus, 'the whole point of OFWAT's existence will be to regulate water plcs according to their license obligations. The NRA, by contrast, will be administering river basins including deciding and enforcing constraints on all sorts of companies taking water from rivers and putting effluents into them' (1988, p. 139). This has proved to be prophetic. As the chairman of the NRA pointed out in 1993, one constant theme in the water debate 'is the argument about the right balance between the need for environmental improvement and the cost' (Crickhowell, 1993a, p. 2.1).

The NRA is the so-called 'competent authority' for England and Wales for the implementation of the various EC directives concerning water quality. Central to the NRA's powers is its function in issuing discharge-consents to polluters and the associated conditions to ensure that the discharge will not have a significantly detrimental effect on the receiving waters. The NRA also plays an important advisory role to the Government. For example, in December 1991 the NRA issued a consultation document detailing its proposals for a new classificatory scheme for introducing water quality objectives (WQOs). The Government drew upon the NRA's recommendations in formulating its own WQO recommendations. The NRA is also responsible for licensing abstractions of water and has executive, as well as regulatory, functions in flood defence, conservation and navigation. The agency's general approach to discharge consents has been to set discharge limits which are individually based on local circumstances – as opposed to setting uniform emission standards applicable to all discharges of a particular size or type (NRA, 1994, pp. 8–9).

The Department of the Environment (DOE) and Secretary of State for Wales

The Secretaries of State for the Environment and Wales have important functions regarding the setting up of water quality objectives and, of course, in representing the UK in EC negotiations concerning existing and proposed directives. Their functions are summarised below.

1. Appointing companies to act as water and sewerage undertakers, the Director General of Water Services and individuals to serve on the National Rivers Authority.
2. Elaborating and supplementing the regulatory framework by means of subordinate legislation, for example, to establish standards of performance in relation to the supply of water and sewerage services, to determine standards of wholesomeness of water, to set out criteria for the classification of

river quality and to impose requirements to take precautions against pollution.

3. Approving various codes of practice including conservation and recreational duties, and the exercise of pipe-laying powers.

4. Enforcing certain statutory obligations imposed on water and sewerage undertakers, for example, by making enforcement orders and initiating the prosecution of any water undertaker which supplies water unfit for human consumption. In respect of the National Rivers Authority, the Secretary of State's main functions are:

   a) Paying a grant-in-aid, setting financial duties and controlling overall staff numbers and conditions of service.
   b) Designating water protection zones and making drought orders.
   c) Approving charges schemes for water abstraction and discharge consents.
   d) Appointing technical assessors of water quality.
   e) Applying, in exceptional circumstances, for a special administration order.

The Secretaries of State receive the reports of the Chief Inspector of the Drinking Water Inspectorate, Director General of Water Services and the National Rivers Authority and, in certain circumstances, can give directions to them and receive information from them related to their functions.

The Drinking Water Inspectorate (DWI)

The DWI was formed in January 1990 and was given the task of checking on behalf of the Secretaries of State that water companies are complying with their statutory duties. It does this via a 'technical audit' of each company, consisting of three elements as follows: (see Appendix 5.1 for details)

1. An annual assessment based on information provided by companies of the quality of water in each supply zone, compliance with sampling and other requirements, and the progress made on improvement programmes.

2. Inspections of individual companies, covering not only a general check at the time of the inspection on the matters covered above but also an assessment of the quality of the information collected by the company.

3. Interim checks made on aspects of compliance based on information provided periodically by companies. (Healey, 1993)

One of the main achievements of the DWI has been to produce a massive database regarding water quality, water pollution and degrees of compliance, considerably superior to the levels and reliability of information in most member states of the EC. For example, the Inspectors' Report in 1991 ran to 272 pages, mostly of detailed data drawn from the 3.75 million tests in the previous year. In many respects, it is the DWI's efforts that help maintain the political salience of water, as the data are available for critics to use (and misuse!)

Her Majesty's Inspectorate of Pollution (HMIP), Local Authorities, MAFF and the EU also has some responsibility regarding the control of water pollution. Under the Water Act 1989 (amended by the Water Industry Act 1991), before a discharge of trade effluent containing certain dangerous substances can be consented by the sewage undertakers, the application has to be referred to the Secretary of State for his or her consideration (the substances are identified by legislation). This function is delegated to HMIP. In fact there are overlapping functions between the NRA and HMIP concerning the discharge of industrial waste. As John Bowman, the former Chief Executive of the NRA has pointed out

> in the case of discharges to water HMIP are required to consult the NRA and may not set a lesser standard on the discharge than that required by the NRA ... The situation created by legislation is so complicated that after long discussions HMIP and the NRA have agreed a *Memorandum of Understanding* as to how they will operate the legislation between them without causing unnecessary duplication of effort to themselves or causing unnecessary work by discharges. *There is little doubt that the legislation could have been far more effectively drafted and that the problems created by the legislation were drawn to the attention of the Government at the time.* (Bowman, 1992, p. 572, emphasis added)

This is probably another example of the Government hurrying to privatise without any full 'options appraisal' of the water-policy change – and of its belief that it was not only privatising the industry but was privatising its problems too.

Local authorities have a continuing duty to keep themselves informed about the *wholesomeness*[7] and sufficiency of water supplies in their areas. If they are not satisfied with the quality of water supplied they are required to inform the water companies. If the companies' response to the problem is seen as 'unsatisfactory', local authorities then have a duty to 'notify the Secretary of State, who will consider whether enforcement action is necessary' (Drinking Water Inspectorate, 1991b, para. 2.4).

MAFF also has responsibility for some aspects of water regulation, relating to the environmental impacts of farming and regulating the marine environment. For example, the ministry currently licences dumping of sewage sludge at sea.

Finally, and (probably) most importantly, the EU has responsibility for setting a broad range of Europe-wide regulatory standards which are currently the source of much tension in the sector. The industry feels that it is being squeezed between the conflicting objectives of the European Commission and OFWAT. As Kon and Gibson-Bolton (1994) point out:

> The director general's priority is to restrict price increases for water and sewerage services despite the heavy costs of compliance with EU directives. The European Commission, on the other hand, emphasises the broader economic and public welfare benefits of compliance with EU directives – such as increased tourism and reduced water-related health problems. (*Water Bulletin*, 5 August 1994, no. 617)

REGULATORY CONFLICT: THE NRA VERSUS OFWAT

Following privatisation, regulation of some kind was inevitable, because of the monopoly position of the industry itself, the high political salience of privatisation, and the requirements of EU law. However, the new regulatory structure has not returned the sector to the private management of public business. If the industry had the public policy franchise before privatisation it has not completely regained it after privatisation. Thus, in policy areas where values are contested (for example, the water sector) the area becomes more open to both public scrutiny and more fluid patterns of participation. These contested values – essentially between environmental and economic values – have manifested themselves most clearly in the cleavage between the two main regulators – the NRA and OFWAT – over the costs and pace of environmental improvements. The public dispute between the two regulators would have been unthinkable in, say, the 1950s, 1960s and 1970s. Thus, regulatory conflict, rather than regulatory capture, appears to be a major aspect of the early years of the new regulatory regime.

The NRA and OFWAT illustrate the old adage, where you stand depends on where you sit. Each agency has begun to act autonomously from the Government and has emerged as a key actor in its own right – so much so that a considerable degree of initiative has slipped away from the lead department, the DOE, despite its important functions in such matters as setting statutory water quality objectives and in representing Britain within the EU. Regulatory conflict has led many water companies to appeal to the Government to take action to simplify the system of control and has become part of a wider debate in Britain concerning regulatory structures and regulatory policies after privatisation. For example, on the appointment of Michael Heseltine as Secretary of State for the Environment, North West Water called on him to 'narrow the gap between the objectives of the privatised industry's principal regulators'. Similarly, Northumbrian Water 'claimed it was a "pig in the middle", caught between the National Rivers Authority's calls for rapid anti-pollution improvements, and the Office of Water Services' strict economic regulation' (*The Financial Times*, 29 November 1990). This is not surprising as, broadly, different regulatory styles appear to be in place. Thus, the former Secretary of the WSA, Michael Carney, has argued that there are two main regulatory models operating in the water sector:

1. *The policing approach* – 'which checks scrupulously on infringements of standards and requires large resources of staff as inspectors and analysts'.
2. *The improvement approach* – 'which identifies what has to be done in order to maintain or improve standards and then secures enforceable undertakings to make sure that the promised action is taken' (Carney, 1992).

Carney claims that the policing (or *enforcement compliance*) model is popular with the media and politicians in general because of its emphasis on prosecutions. In contrast, the improvement (or *negotiated compliance*) approach sees discharges policing themselves by checking the standards and taking samples (see also Hunter and Waterman, 1992).

In practice the position is rather more subtle than this. Each of the two main water regulators would claim to be adopting a mixed regulatory style – being tough (policing) when appropriate, yet trying (often successfully) to develop a consensual and negotiative style of regulation consistent with the traditional British regulatory style and consistent with good administration (the improvement approach).

In many respects, the conflict is less about differing regulatory styles and more about differing regulatory *objectives*. Indeed, despite the view of some critics both inside and outside the industry, having two regulators with quite different objectives is positively desirable as it exposes issues to public scrutiny and debate. In essence, there is nearly always a conflict between environmental improvement and costs – whether in the water sector or in any other sphere – and a trade-off has to be reached in practice. The central question is how much improvement and at what cost? Following from this is the question, who pays? (That is, there are some complex welfare questions.) The differing stances of the NRA and OFWAT reflect the unavoidable conflict of goals. The fact that the two agencies are lead by two forceful characters who are not afraid of public debate has merely facilitated the opening up of the sector to greater public scrutiny and accountability.

Since their formation, the two agencies, as agencies normally do, have developed their own organisational styles and cultures – and their own constituencies of interests (Downs, 1967). Both Byatt and Lord Crickhowell have been quite clear in stating what they expected their agencies to achieve and have identified clearly those issues which divide them. For example, in its consultation paper the *Costs of Quality*, published in 1992, OFWAT pointed out that 'if the European Community and the Government approve further increases in standards, and the environmental regulators implement those standards in a way which imposes unexpected costs, bills could continue to rise significantly faster than the rate of inflation' (OFWAT, 1992a, p. 4). In itself, this was an unexceptional statement. However, OFWAT went on to warn that:

> Improvements in the quality of drinking water and the water environment are beneficial. But they cost money which many customers can ill afford. Our evidence of customer views, shows that, while they are concerned with water quality and the environment, they are also concerned about bills. *The issue is particularly acute when much of the cost is incurred in making high standards even higher – standards which, it is sometimes argued, are not always securely based on scientific evidence of the risks to health. Customers might ask whether the drive for higher quality should go quite so fast.* (ibid., p. 4, emphasis added)

A particularly interesting aspect of OFWAT's growing concern, both about the ever-increasing demands of European legislation and the possibility of over-zealous environmental regulation, has been the impact of cost increases on the poorer sections of society. This 'welfare' concern seems to have been developed largely at OFWAT's own initiative. In warning that charges could increase by more than 35 per cent if all projected new legislative measures were put in place (particularly the EC Urban

Waste Water Treatment Directive) it drew special attention to the fact that this 'could have quite severe consequences for customers on low incomes' (ibid., p. 5). At its most basic, OFWAT's 'organisational ideology' is quite straightforward:

> In an age of consumer choice, customers should be given options about the services they receive and have to pay for. Such choice is constrained by legal requirements when distributing water and impacts on the environment are concerned. As far as other aspects of service are concerned, however, *customers should be sovereign and given material on which they can make informed judgements about the quality of the service they want and the price they are prepared to pay.* (ibid., p. 6, emphasis added)

Though rather general philosophical statements of intent, they do indicate where the regulator stands. In practical terms, the costs of quality exercise meant that the companies were required to produce market plans, 'after consulting their customers'. The plans had to set out the strategic options facing each company. Customer preferences were to be central. Thus 'on the basis of research into customer preferences, and initial discussion with Customer Service Committees, the plans will set out the consequences of standards imposed on water quality and the levels of service which appear best to reflect customer preferences about the trade off between prices and quality' (ibid., p. 7). In a subsequent report *Paying for Quality. The Political Perspective* (OFWAT, 1993a), Byatt revealed part of the motivation behind his considerable concern with customers: 'I do not believe that, due to the constraints of privatisation, enough was done at the time the initial price limits were set to assess whether customers were willing to pay the price of substantial improvements in standards that were required of the companies'. Thus, Byatt has shown an unswerving determination to fulfil his statutory duties to protect the consumer alongside his duty to ensure the financial viability of the companies. This philosophy was evident from the outset when, in 1990, OFWAT published *Paying for Water*, when, in addition to circulating a questionnaire and leaflet via the bills to customers from their companies, it commissioned a survey by the Office of Population and Census Survey. This formed the basis of a consultation paper, *Paying for Water: the Way Ahead*, and later of *The Cost of Quantity and Paying for Quality* (see above).

It should not be thought, however, that OFWAT has been slavish to consumer interests. For example, in its consultation paper, *Paying for Growth* (OFWAT, 1993b), Byatt commented that present arrangements were scarcely satisfactory as it was 'neither economically nor environmentally justified to meet all possible demands for water when the customer is not charged for additional use' (ibid., p. i). (Currently only 5 per cent of revenue based on charges relates to consumption.) He warned that where provision for growth in demand was particularly expensive – for example where new reservoirs were needed to be built – 'companies should consider whether metering households on a compulsory basis, even for part of the area, is likely to lead to lower bills than developing the reservoirs'. (Thus, price should reflects costs and might be used to constrain demand.) Moreover, 'when the direct cost of additional water to the customer is zero some rationing may be preferable to ever rising bills' (ibid., p. iii).

The NRA, under Lord Crickhowell's leadership, has been equally clear in its regulatory philosophy. The NRA has been very anxious to resist any diminished standards or to see a significant slowing-down in the drive towards higher standards. As Lord Crickhowell has made clear, the NRA 'will always be robust in putting forward clear recommendations about what we believe is necessary' (Crickhowell, 1993a, p. 2.1). Indeed, as he noted, the Water Act 1989 has already led to a dramatic improvement in water quality (ibid., p. 2.2). Referring to the debate about the setting of new water quality objectives (the responsibility of the Secretary of State, not the NRA) he argued that 'far from their being any benefit in halting this process, there would be the disastrous consequences that we would have to proceed blindfold without any proper public debate or cost benefit analysis' (ibid., p. 2.2). The question of cost benefit analysis has, of course, been central to the debate about water quality. The NRA has not been afraid to debate this issue in robust terms. For example, Crickhowell has berated the industry for demanding cost estimates (via cost–benefit analysis) at the outset when an environmental improvement is suggested by the NRA. He has stressed that the true costs of a proposed environmental improvement can only be determined by a process of *consultation* (ibid., p. 2.5) (In fact the NRA had been subject to bitter criticism from the industry in 1990 for its report, *Discharge Consent Compliance: A Blueprint for the Future*, which contained no cost estimates). In a direct reference to Byatt's concern with the customer's interest, Lord Crickhowell has, quite rightly, pointed to an equally valid regulatory philosophy, adopted by the NRA – namely that there are wider interests in society than just the customer interest. Thus, referring to Byatt's view that the customer should have the last word, Lord Crickhowell argued that 'no self-respecting Regulator could accept that proposition *because there is a wider interest to be protected and the principle of sustainability to be upheld* (ibid., p. 2.5, emphasis added). Here we see some fundamental philosophic differences in regulatory approach emerging, with the NRA seeing 'the environment' as a collective good to be protected for future generations and Byatt possibly more concerned with individual goods. While not quite accepting the jibe 'what has the future generation done for me?' Byatt's concerns with consumer preference, whilst perfectly valid, do raise difficult questions about inter-generational justice of which Lord Crickhowell seems to be especially aware. Thus, Crickhowell (and the NRA) have a clear objective:

> In my view, the Regulator must always aim high. He must be ambitious, pressing people rather faster than they wished willingly to go. Government and Parliament can regulate the pace if he [sic] is too demanding. That is the policy that the NRA has always followed: that is the policy we intend to follow in the future. (ibid., p. 2.5)

The NRA is concerned, centrally, with externalities. Using a humorous example to tease Byatt in public – Lord Crickhowell cited the hypothetical example of externalities, as follows (quoting his interview on the BBC Panorama programme the previous evening):

> I asked people to imagine that we were still living at a time when it was the practice to empty chamber pots out of open windows and that Mr Byatt was hurrying down an alley somewhere in London and passed a house owned by a customer who thought it extravagant to install the new fangled water closets. I suspect that in that potentially unpleasant situation even Mr Byatt might think that the customer, i.e. the house owner with the chamber pot, did not necessarily come first. (Crickhowell, 1993b, pp. 2—3)

He went on to point out that 'Sustainability; the need to protect our precious environment; the ecology of our rivers and seas; the health of those who use and enjoy them are all as important as the customer, who in Mr. Byatt's terms, is the person who pays the water bill' (ibid., p. 3).

The substance of the differences between the NRA and OFWAT – reflecting their different statutory obligations and different concerns, as well as their different 'ideologies' – has, in practice, centred upon costs, cost estimates and possible rates of improvement in standards. Herein also lies the solution to their difficulties as these more detailed questions are susceptible to incremental bargaining – and ultimately to consensus-building mechanisms.

REGULATION AS A TWO-LEVEL GAME: ISSUE NETWORKS AND CONSENSUS BUILDING

Throughout this study, it will have been noted that it is often quite accurate to describe the political game using apparently contradictory images. Yet again this seems the case with the politics of regulation. On the one hand, there is open and public conflict between the two main regulators of the privatised industry in England and Wales – and conflict between the regulators and the regulated industry. On the other hand, there is a considerable degree of co-operation, co-operative problem-solving, and even consensual decision-making. In a variant of Putnam's concept of a two-level game (used to describe the behaviour of nation-states in international negotiations (Putnam, 1988) we can describe the regulatory process. In this game, there is public conflict over the differing goals of the various actors – essentially between the 'quadrapartite group' of DOE, NRA, OFWAT and WSA – accompanied and/or followed by the usual process of private bargaining in order to reach acceptable and workable outcomes. As in international negotiations, some of the key players are responding to, and to a degree articulating, the interests of their 'home' constituencies of groups. Each player, therefore, has particular obligations (often statutory) and objectives and can mobilise the support of its own network of groups and organisations. This is especially true for the NRA and OFWAT.

For example, in reviewing the trajectory of the increasingly public debate over the conflict between higher environmental and quality standards and the need for environmental improvement, Lord Crickhowell noted that:

> at the outset it was a debate largely conducted between the Water Industry, faced with a huge capital programme, and the Environmental Regulators, by which I mean the EC, the Government, and the NRA, all determined to halt the

deterioration that had been taking place in the quality of our rivers and ground water. Heavy supporting fire was brought down by the environmental campaigners with only a desultory, small-arms response from those who had to pay the bills. (Crickhowell, 1993a, p. 2.1)

Crucially, he went on to note that the mood was now changing as 'stimulated by the pain of recession others are entering the fray'. While criticising media reports of allegedly prohibitive costs facing the industry as well as the allegations by Greenpeace and Friends of the Earth (FOE), it is nevertheless clear that the NRA benefits from the vociferous environmental movement. Being able to point to the external pressure that one is under (even if it is ill informed) is often a very useful bargaining chip in the private negotiations which follow these public debates. The NRA have been irritated and embarrassed by the fact that FOE issued a press release in April 1993 giving the NRA a twenty-one day deadline concerning pollution from a particular chemical works in Castleford – Prosecute or We Will! ('Friends of the Earth Gives 21 Deadline to NRA', FOE press release 29 April 1993). Yet this kind of activity is not necessarily dysfunctional to the agency's goals. Similarly, FOE attacked the NRA for its river survey in 1994, arguing in its press release that the survey masked a trend to mediocrity and that top wildlife sites were not being protected (FOE press release, 13 April 1994). Yet, FOE was ready to spring to the NRA's defence in July 1994 when the Government restricted spending by water companies on certain improvement schemes for rivers and beaches, contrary to NRA's advice ('Rivers to Remain Polluted – NRA Chairman Publicly Despairs of Government Policy', FOE press release, 6 July 1994). Indeed, it quoted with approval the NRA's own press release in which Lord Crickhowell had confirmed that many important projects of local significance would be postponed until after the year 2000 as a result of the decision (NRA press release, 6 July 1994). Byatt and OFWAT have also come under fire from the environmentalists. For example, in its press release of 16 July 1993 ('Millions Supplied with Polluted Drinking Water – 'Customers' Champion Tries to Sell Them Short') FOE attacked Byatt for pressing the Secretary of State for the Environment to allow water companies more time to complete their investment programmes because customers allegedly could not afford the cost. Byatt (and the Government) were also criticised for the outcome of the Periodic Review (FOE press release, 28 July 1994, 'Ian Byatt Fails to Stop the Water Industry Gravy Train – The Environment and Water Customers Doomed to Pay the Price').

The ultimate threat of the environmentalist is, of course, legal action at the European level. As *The Financial Times* noted in July 1993:

In November 1992 the European Court of Justice (ECJ) ruled that the UK Government was guilty of breaching EC rules on drinking water quality because nitrate levels in 28 supply zones in England exceeded the permitted levels. In July 1993 it also ruled that Blackpool beaches were failing to meet EU environmental regulations. The British Government was not fined, but was ordered to pay costs. (15 July 1993)

The Court's important position in monitoring the implementation of EU legislation has not been lost on environmental groups, especially in the UK. For example, the 1992 ruling was precipitated by FOE's complaint that the UK Government was failing to fulfil its obligations (*The Financial Times*, 25 November 1992). Indeed, the British Government has complained that the UK's more vigorous interest groups have caused more legal actions than those in other countries (*The Financial Times*, 19 July 1993). FOE may be seen as the most critical of the environmental groups, of course. Often, groups such as the CPRE are seen as more balanced and, indeed, do not necessarily clash with OFWAT on all issues. For example, on water metering, the CPRE and OFWAT share the same basic position – namely that metering is a way of conserving scarce water resources.

The constant pressure from the environmental movement – both at the national and European levels – presents a major challenge to the Government and OFWAT. Both are currently trying to reduce the impact of environmental and quality improvements on costs. From the Government's perspective it can draw upon support from other Whitehall departments – such as the Treasury and the DTI. It can also expect (and receive) support from bodies such as the CBI which are just as concerned about the prospect of tighter European regulations, for example.

OFWAT's position, politically, is somewhat more difficult. Traditionally, consumers have not been well organised or vociferous. However, in the manner predicted by Downs (1967), OFWAT has set about creating and sustaining a viable constituency of groups and other organisations. It, too, now has its own network (or constellation) of groups which it can quote in the struggle to restrain charges in the face of demands for higher and higher standards. Though OFWAT has clear statutory obligations to the companies, it is politically important for it to be seen to be 'representing' an important constituency of interests. Thus, in addition to setting up the Consumer Service Committees (CSCs) for each of the privatised water companies, Byatt also established a CSC Chairman's Group in 1990 which met about six times a year. This evolved into the OFWAT National Customer Council (ONCC) in 1993. These are not 'sham' consultative bodies on the old nationalised industry model. For example, the chairmen of the CSCs were closely involved in the price setting process in the summer of 1993. They saw the confidential reports which OFWAT sent to the companies and saw the companies' representatives and attended the meetings with 'their' companies (Byatt 1994, p. 8). OFWAT also maintains close contact with other consumer bodies (that is, not just those which it created) – such as the National Consumers' Council and the Public Access Forum which represents the interests of customers disadvantaged by low income or poor health (ibid., p. 9). OFWAT also has contacts with the National Association of Citizen's Advice Bureaux and the Consumers' Association.

These bodies can be useful to OFWAT in its public stance on behalf of the consumer interest. For example the ONCC condemned the price increases suggested in the market plans published by the companies in 1993. The companies were claiming that bills would need to rise by approximately 6 per cent in each of the five years 1995 to 2000 to achieve environmental obligations and satisfy customers' views on levels of service. The ONCC claimed that this could produce annual water bills of £450 in some areas. It therefore, pledged itself to 'put pressure on the Director General of Water Services and the British Government to keep prices down and on the EC to limit obligations on companies which are drawing up bills faster than customers are willing to pay' (ONCC press release, 5 July 1993). It has specifically urged the Government to renegotiate the timetable for implementation of the Urban Waste Water Treatment Directive (ONCC press release, 13 July 1993). Pressure from other groups can also be useful to OFWAT. For example, the continued high political salience of water has led to wider participation from a more diverse range of groups – including organisations such the British Medical Association (BMA), Dr Barnado's Homes, and Surfers Against Sewage (SAS). The latter was formed in April 1990, and has been lobbying Westminster, Whitehall, both of the main regulators, NRA and OFWAT, and indeed the companies themselves, especially South West Water. It has also been active at the European level. The BMA has also published reports on pesticides and water disconnections: respectively calling on the Government to introduce greater monitoring of pesticides in drinking water (*Water Bulletin*, 19 October 1990, no. 431); and criticising the 143 per cent increase in disconnections since 1990–1.

   The involvement of this varied array of groups and organisations in the sector is central to the public game. In no sense could this collection of actors be described as a network in the strictest sense. Behind and beyond that game is a willingness on the part of the key stakeholders to consult and negotiate a way forward. Moreover, the Government is the ultimate arbiter in these conflicts. It can determine the extent of obligations and the pace of change albeit within the (very considerable) constraints of European legislation – for example in its role of deciding the statutory water quality objectives discussed above. Space does not permit a detailed analysis of regulatory consensus building. However, one spectacular example of conflict between the regulators – over the actual cost of meeting planned improvements in standards – illustrates perfectly the two-level game of work. Thus, in its paper, *Paying for Quality: The Political Perspective*, published in July 1993, OFWAT argued that 'the cost of cleaning up Britain's water has become unacceptable, and *it is up to the government* to reduce it by renegotiating or relaxing water quality standards' (OFWAT, 1993b, emphasis added). Byatt claimed that when Britain signed up for the 'waste water directive the cost was estimated to be approximately £2 bn it has now risen to £10 bn'. I don't believe that increases of that kind are what people want or what they are prepared to pay' (*The Financial Times*, 14 July 1993). The NRA rejected OFWAT's claims arguing that the OFWAT document 'exaggerated the problem and provided misleading analyses of the issues' (*The Financial Times*, 14 July 1993). Jan Pentreath, Chief Scientist at the NRA, believed that it is the Government's responsibility to ensure that environmental improvements flow from privatisation. 'When the industry was privatised Government said that we would get cleaner beaches and rivers. The public haven't got that short a memory' (*Water and Environmental Management*, September 1993). This public game eventually had to be settled in private. Thus, the quadrapartite group of DOE (and DWI) NRA, OFWAT and WSA

~~ventually had to resolve the question of cash estimates and did so by treating it as an essentially technical and bargainable matter. The conflict itself forced a close examination of the problem by those who have to run the industry. As Lord Crickhowell noted, one consequence of the vigorous public debate over costs was that 'much valuable new information has been revealed and increasingly we are finding common ground' (Crickhowell, 1993b).

A year earlier he had spoken vigorously against what he called OFWAT's exaggerated estimates about what the costs might be. Thus, at that time

> the NRA made it very clear that it was unhappy that initial consultation with the public, particularly that undertaken by water companies, was based on information that was partial and inaccurate and which included inflated cost estimates, double counting, and for a good deal of proposed expenditure that we believed would be wholly unnecessary. (ibid., p. 4)

The conflict was resolved in the traditional way – in private. Thus, Crickhowell reported that throughout the summer the NRA and the Drinking Water Inspectorate worked closely with OFWAT, DOE, and the WSA in clarifying requirements and obligations, and in seeking to get a much more accurate picture of real costs' (ibid., p. 4.5). In the event OFWAT reduced its cost estimates significantly from the initial projection of £10 bn. Following this exercise, work continued at a more detailed level, company by company, producing cost estimates that were broadly agreed by all participants. Effectively, the game shifted from the public to the private level, at which point some kind of policy community, on the old model, emerged, consisting of only four or five key actors.

A similar process takes place in the case of OFWAT's detailed regulation of the companies. Here, the obvious charge is of regulatory capture on the American utility model. Again, contrasting images can be presented. On the one hand, OFWAT has clearly been part of the process of 'regulatory creep' referred to earlier. It has rewritten the initial regulatory bargain which Byatt felt was too generous. Although the privatised companies have been very successful financially, they have been operating under a tightening regulatory environment devised by OFWAT. This has caused conflict between OFWAT and the industry [and between the NRA and the industry] but there is also a two-level game in operation. Thus, Byatt has placed great emphasis on detailed consultations with the companies in the first Periodic Review, the results of which were announced in July 1994. This consultative style (he is at pains to deny that it is a *negotiative* style) is a common feature of OFWAT's approach. For example, there was an intensive consultation exercise over OFWAT's paper, *The Cost of Capital*, published in 1991 – including detailed discussions with one of the new 'players' in the game, the City (Byatt, 1994, p. 3). Prior to the publication of its Periodic Review 'White Paper' in 1993 (*Setting Price Limits for Water and Sewerage Services*; *the framework and approach to the Periodic Review*), OFWAT had issued several Green Papers. Detailed discussions were held with each company prior to OFWAT's decisions on the Periodic Review. With few exceptions the Periodic Review, when published in July 1994, was greeted with an almost deafening consensus. While, Byatt 'repeatedly insisted that the price review process was anything but a negotiation' (*The Financial Times*, 29 July 1994), the evidence suggests otherwise. In almost every case the draft K factor distributed to the companies in May 1994, were revised upwards at the final announcement in July. Despite Byatt's claim, one water company finance director is reported in *The Financial Times* as saying 'everyone knows this is a negotiation' (*The Financial Times*, 29 September 1994). Generally Byatt received a bad press for the outcomes of his Periodic Review, the argument being that his approach to the companies had been too cosy and consensual, that is, he was accused of regulatory capture. For example, *The Sunday Times* (31 July 1994) argued:

> Byatt could, and should, have imposed tougher controls … Had he done so, he would have triggered a rash of appeals to the Monopolies and Mergers Commission instead of just one – by South West Water, whose exceptionally severe treatment by Byatt proves the generally lax rule applied to the other nine … Compared with BT and British Gas, both of which are having to cope with hefty cuts in real prices while funding significant capital spending, the water companies' price regime is generous in the extreme … Whichever way you look at it, apart from South West Water, the water companies have got off incredibly – and intolerably – lightly.

Even *The Financial Times* was grudging in its reception ('Watered Down Regulation') although it conceded that Byatt had done a tough and good job in tackling the size of the capital spending programme – several billion pounds below what the industry had demanded. In other respects, it was claimed, he had been too generous – especially in setting the annual price rise (*The Financial Times*, 29 July 1994). On the latter, OFWAT was also attacked by its own 'constituency' – the consumers. The reaction from the City and the industry was said to be one of satisfaction (ibid.). More mature reflection, however, suggested that Byatt may not have been quite so generous and 'captured' as his critics supposed. Moreover, as the companies are always anxious to gauge City reaction, they were hardly likely to cry 'stinking fish'! Thus, a few days after the Review was published, *The Financial Times* Lex Column was noting that initial enthusiasm was being tempered by the realisation that dividend growth of 4 per cent was not especially good in market terms – especially in view of the long-term regulatory risk (*The Financial Times*, 6 August 1994). It seems that the more cautious City analysts were worried by the possible consequences of the two-level game described above. While problems are ultimately processed in the second-level game, the parameters of that game are set elsewhere. As the utilities analyst for S. G. Warburg has observed, Byatt had secured a major victory in securing a 30 per cent reduction in the investment obligations of the companies (Dale, 1994, p. 4). (This was, in fact, a victory for Byatt's consumers. Without it, they would have faced much bigger price increases). Significantly, Dale identified 'regulatory risk' and 'political risk' as two of the main risks facing companies and their shareholders in future. As he noted, 'regulatory risk has always been investors' number one fear ...' (ibid., p. 6). Moreover, as he pointed out, 'all current projections are in any event at the mercy of the quality regulators – and particularly the European Commission' (ibid., p. 9). Even at the time of his observation, a new regulatory uncertainty was emerging – in the shape of the new Environmental Agency. Thus, in October 1994, the Government published plans for the new agency which would bring together HMIP, NRA and the local waste regulation authorities – essentially so that a more integrated approach to pollution control could be developed (DOE, 1994). Whatever the effects of the new agency, water regulation is likely to continue to exhibit a two-level game as discussed above. This, it should be said, is in sharp contrast to the old regulatory regime. As Lord Crickhowell has observed:

> In the old days when I was Secretary of State for Wales and shared responsibilities for the operations of water companies and their charges, decisions were taken which affected both the environment and the customers by cosy, or sometimes not so cosy, discussions behind closed doors. (Crickhowell, 1993b)

NOTES

1. However, it should be noted that the overwhelming majority of the NRA's staff were previously employed by the regional water authorities (RWAS). Thus, the transfer from one organisation to another, essentially saw many of these individuals change from self-regulators, to regulators of external organisations. In doing so, it is clear that they have created a new organisational culture and that they have not been 'captured' by their former colleagues.
2. The Welsh Secretary of State managed to secure a concession that any one shareholding in Welsh Water Plc would be restricted to 15 per cent in perpetuity, unless 75 per cent of the shareholders agreed otherwise.
3. In size terms the company is now the seventh-biggest water undertaking in England and Wales, 'leap-frogging Northumbrian Water, Wessex Water, and South West Water, among the privatised water service companies' (*Water Bulletin*, 18 January 1991, no. 442).
4. Its K factor is not to exceed 1.1 per cent which represents a fall of 9.9 per cent from its existing level of 11 per cent.
5. To date, there have been three other mergers in the statutory company sector. Eastbourne Water, Mid Sussex Water and West Kent Water merged to form South East Water. Newcastle and Gateshead, and Sunderland and South Shields merged into North East Water, and finally Bournemouth Water Company and West Hampshire Water became Bournemouth and West Hampshire Water Companies.
6. Byatt is a former Deputy Economic Adviser at the Treasury.
7. Wholesomeness is defined by standards laid out in the Regulations (the Water Supply [Water Quality] Regulations 1989).
   Water supplied for the domestic purposes of drinking, washing or cooking will be regarded as wholesome provided:
   > it meets the standards prescribed in the Regulations for the particular properties, elements, organisms or substances;
   > the hardness or alkalinity of water which has been softened or desalinated is not below the prescribed standard;
   > and it does not contain element, organism or substance, whether alone or in combination, at a concentration or value which would be detrimental to public health.
   The last requirement is a catch-all provision which reflects the concept of wholesomeness as developed over the years (DWI, 1991b, para. 1.4).

REFERENCES

Butler, E., Robinson, C., Kay, J., Gillick, D., Call, M., Veljanouvski, C., Booth, M. (1993), *But Who Will Regulate the Regulators?* (London: Adam Smith Institute).

Bowman, J. C. (1992), 'Improving the Quality of Our Water: The role of regulation by the National Rivers Authority', *Public Administration,* vol. 70, no. 4, pp. 565–75.

Breyer, S. (1979), 'Analyzing Regulatory Failure: Mismatches, less restrictive alternatives and reform', in A. I. Ogus and C. G. Veljanovski' (eds) (1984), *Reading in Economics and Law* (Oxford: Clarendon Press) pp. 234–40.

Byatt, I. (1994), 'The Periodic Review: An industry overview', paper presented to Centre for Regulated Industries Conference, 'The Water Industry Looking Forward From the Period Review', London, 11 October.

Carney, M. (1992), 'The Costs of Compliance with Ever Higher Quality Standards', in T. Gilland (ed.), *The Changing Water Business* (London, CRI) pp. 27–50.

Crickhowell, Lord (1993a) 'Regulation: Water and Pollution – the UK Water Quality Objectives', paper presented to *The Financial Times* conference, 'The European Water Industry', (London, *The Financial Times)* 15 and 16 March.

Crickhowell, Lord (1993b), 'Water Service Quality and Water Bills', paper presented to '*The Economist* Water Conference', London, 9 November.

Dale, B. (1994), 'The Investors' Judgement', paper presented to Centre for Regulated Industries Conference, 'The Water Industry Looking Forward from the Periodic Review', London, 11 October.

Department of the Environment (DOE) (1993), *Making Markets Work for the Environment* (London: HMSO).

DOE/Welsh Office (1991), Drinking Water 1990: *A Report by the Chief Inspector,* Drinking Water Inspectorate (London, HMSO).

Drinking Water Inspectorate (1991) Details to be supplied at proof stage.

Downs, A. (1967), *Inside Bureaucracy* (Boston: Little Brown and Company).

Graham, C. and Prosser, T. (1991), *Privatising Public Enterprises* (Oxford: Clarendon Press).

Hancher, L. and Moran, M. (1989) (eds), *Capitalism, Culture and Economic Regulation,* (Oxford: Clarendon Press).

Healey, M. G. (1993), 'Drinking Water Inspectorate's View of What Has Been Achieved and What Remains to be Done' (London: DWI).

Hunter, S. and Waterman, R. W. (1992), 'Determining an Agency's Regulatory Style: How does the EPA Water Office enforce the law?', *The Western Political Quarterly,* vol. 45, no. 2 (June), pp. 403–18.

Kinnersley, D. (1988), *Troubled Water: Rivers, Politics and Pollution* (London: Hilary Shipman).

Lawson, N. (1992), *The View From Number 11* (London: Bantan Press).

Littlechild, S. C. (1988), 'Economic Regulation of Privatised Water Authorities and Some Further Reflections', *Oxford Review of Economic Policy,* vol. 4, no. 2, pp. 40–68.

Monopolies and Mergers Commission (MMC) (1990a), *General Utilities Plc, The Colne Valley Water Company and the Rickmansworth Water Company: a Report on the Proposed Merger,* Cmnd 1029 (London: HMSO).

MMC (1990b), General Utilities Plc and the Mid–Kent Water Company: a Report on the Proposed Merger, Cmnd 1126 (London: HMSO).

MMC (1990c), *Southern Water Plc and Mid-Sussex Water Company: a Report on the Proposed Merger,* Cmnd 1126 (London: HMSO).

MMC (1992), *The Role of The Commission* (4th Edn) (London: HMSO).

National Consumer Council (NCC) (1989), *In the Absence of Competition* (London: HMSO).

National Rivers Authority (NRA) (1990), *Discharge Consent Complain Policy: A Blueprint for the Future,* Water Quality Series No. 1 (London: NRA).

NRA (1994)

O'Connell Davidson, J. (1993), *Privatisation and Employment Relations: The Case of the Water Industry* (London: Mansell).

OFWAT (1990), *Annual Report 1989* (London: HMSO).

OFWAT (1991), *Annual Report 1990* (London: HMSO).

OFWAT (1992a), *The Cost of Quality: A Strategic Assessment of the Prospects for Future Water Bills* (Birmingham: OFWAT).

OFWAT (1992b), *Issues Involved in Regulation of Privatised Water Utilities* (Text of speech delivered by Alan Booker, Deputy DG OFWAT, to the Institute for International Research, Malaysia, January.)

OFWAT (1993a), *Paying for Quality: the Political Perspective* (Birmingham: OFWAT).

OFWAT (1993b), *Paying for Growth: A Consultation Paper on the Framework for Relecting the Costs of Providing for Growth in Charges* (Birmingham: OFWAT).

Putnam, R. (1988), 'Diplomacy and Domestic Politics: the logic of two level games', *International Organisation*, vol. 42, no. 3, pp. 427–60.
The Treasury (1990), *Privatisations in the United Kingdom: Background Briefing* (London: HM Treasury)
Vickers, J. and Yarrow, G. (1990), 'Regulation of Privatised Firms in Britain', in J. J. Richardson (ed.), *Privatisation and Deregulation in Canada and Britain*, (Aldershot: Dartmouth).
Water Services Association (WSA) (1993), *Water Facts* (London: WSA).

APPENDIX 5.1: Inspection of water companies summary of main tasks of DWI.

TASK DESCRIPTION

1. *Sampling arrangements:*
    a) check general procedures in place to satisfy sampling requirements
    b) check delineation of water supply zones
    c) check selection of sampling points
    d) check proposed sampling frequencies
    e) inspect sampling manual or other relevant documentation
    f) check training and supervision of staff

2. *Analytical arrangements:*
    a) check general procedures in place to satisfy analytic requirements
    b) check methods of adequate performance
    c) inspect internal and external AQC systems
    d) check training and supervision of staff

3. *Compliance assessments:*
    a) check correct sampling frequencies used
    b) scrutinise analytical results against standards or conditions attached to authorisations
    c) check action taken where infringements occur
    d) inspect public record
    e) check audit trails: from sampling programme to public register; from public register back to sampling programme

4. *Improvement programmes:*
    a) where complete, check that work is satisfactory and that water now complies
    b) where not complete, monitor progress and chase all schemes behind schedule
    c) scrutinise schemes in detail

5. *Water treatment:*
    a) check general procedures in place to satisfy treatment requirements
    b) check that appropriate treatment is being applied
    c) check that approved products and processes are used
    d) check that appropriate steps are being taken to reduce risk of water becoming unwholesome after supply, that is progress of lead surveys and investigations

6

Organisational Responses to the Market-place

CHANGING ORGANISATIONAL CULTURES IN PUBLIC UTILITIES:
PRIVATISATION AS A 'CULTURAL TRAIN WRECK'?

Public utilities such as water supply and sewage disposal are difficult to classify in terms of a traditional public/private distinction. Indeed, whether public or private they are inevitably subject to pressures which other organisations can often avoid. Public regulation – discussed in Chapter 5 – is a central feature of the environment of public utilities throughout the world. Yet utilities are also subject to the broad shifts in organisational and managerial fashions that have affected public and private organisations throughout the developed world over the past decade and a half. Thus, the 'marketisation' of the public sector either via privatisation or via public sector management reforms – especially of the public utilities – has been one of the main characteristics of the 1980s and 1990s.

This trend has been very marked in Britain, of course, because of the comprehensive (almost universal) programme of privatisation. Even so, these trends, which are often seen as part of a wave of reforms specific to public sector management, are also quite similar to trends taking place in the private sector. The kinds of economic and resourcing pressures that have arisen in the public sector are also very familiar in private sector organisations. For example, the 'contracting out' of public service has its parallels in the private sector – especially in multi-national and multi-functional firms. Similarly, the increased pressure for monitoring and evaluation, and the pressures to become more competitive and market orientated are phenomena which cross public and private sector boundaries and national boundaries alike. The policy and managerial fashions – and even the changing language used within organisations – are so strong that they tend to sweep through all organisations at roughly the same time. Moreover, there is now much cross-sectoral learning via conferences and journals. Hence, to take a current example, it is now common for all public services to be more focused on their 'customers' and to adopt values which were once the exclusive concern of private sector market organisations. The public utilities, of course, have had to make a much bigger adjustment to accommodate these 'new managerial fashions' than have many private sector organisations.

(Although one wonders if the changes which have taken place in say, the Rover Group are any less remarkable?)

It should not be argued, however, that the utilities were total strangers to market forces. They were often in competition with each other. More importantly, one of the central features of public utilities has been the attempt to create incentives for managerial efficiency via the regulatory process, reflecting the near monopoly position of many utilities. The 'trick' for public regulators is to know what efficiency gains are actually *possible* in the absence of market competition. Usually, there is a marked imbalance in expertise between regulators and regulatees, resulting in the under-estimation of what can be achieved by an organisation such as a public utility. As one observer has suggested, 'commissions can generally observe a firm's actual costs, for instance, but they cannot directly observe the level of management effort or the quality of managers' decision' (Schmalense, 1986, pp. vii–2). (Financial markets have to cope with the same problem, of course. As the utility analyst for S. G. Warburg has commented, even some years after the privatisation of water, investors still have to try to anticipate risk by identifying the 'men' from the 'boys' amongst management in the water industry (Dale, 1994).) At its core, the regulatory process is about trying to change organisational behaviour via a change in organisational culture. Generally, the record in achieving this key objective has been poor. As Strasser and Kohler suggest:

> Traditional utility regulation has been largely unsuccessful in motivating im-proved company performance. Traditional regulation creates a number of incentives for inefficient operation, and controls efficiency only crudely; some counterbalance is needed. When regulators have tried to use performance incentives, in rare cases, the results have been terrible. The goal of incentive plans should be to motivate better utility management performance. (1989, p. 168)

As seen in earlier chapters, the water sector in England and Wales was subject to regulation when in the public sector, but this was a mixture of rather 'light' public regulation and a good deal of self-regulation – almost literally the private manage-ment of public business. In part, this was because the British regulatory style is both non-adversarial and has a tendency to favour self-regulation. It was also because it was always assumed that public sector values and norms were a kind of guarantee of good organisational behaviour. The water industry – like local government, the nationalised industries, and the civil service – was thought to be 'governed' by the public service ethic. Yet it was public regulation that provided the 'spark' for the dramatic change introduced by privatisation – namely the prospect of tougher 'rate of return' regulation. In so far as there had been public 'control' of the industry (alongside actual public *ownership*) it had begun to bring about a gradual shift in the nature of organisational cultures and organisational behaviour. Undoubtedly, change had begun to take place, often via the introduction of 'change champions' (such as Roy Watts at Thames) with previous experience of the 'ramping up' of organisations in other sectors, as well as via legislative developments for example, the Water Act 1983.

This had also been happening in other parts of the public sector. For example, at British Airways (from which Watts had been recruited) there had been two broad categories of organisational change. 'First was a radical slimdown of the overall size of the company, both in terms of manpower and flight operation. Second was the setting up of profit consciousness, through organisational reshuffling, from top to bottom' (Shibata, 1994, p. 6). Key to the process was the setting-up of profit centres and the introduction of management by objectives, originating from the BA Chairman's private sector experience (ibid., p. 10). This was later followed by a market-orientated structure and a corporate image campaign.

Shibata suggests that these approaches have been common across sectors and countries. Citing Stoetzer's notion of the elimination of 'managerial discretionary behaviours' (Stoetzer, 1990, p. 127), he argues that these 'behaviours' accumulate over time and become deeply rooted in the organisations concerned. Often, new managers are brought in to institute radical reforms, for example, at British Airways, Pan Am and NTT (Shibata 1994, p. 78). Similarly, Pitt has argued that Ian Vallance, at British Telecom, played a key role in what Pitt terms the 'ramping up' of BT (Pitt, 1990). Pitt concluded that 'BT's efforts at intensive organisational change aimed at giving it a "crackerjack" image have closely paralleled the experience of AT&T which has, since divestiture, experienced what one commentator has described as a "cultural train wreck"' (ibid., p. 61).

Pitt's focus on the effects of severe external shocks to organisational culture is a useful pointer to the concern, here, with the post-privatisation phase in water. The implication of his study of BT is that for a major change in public policy to succeed it also needs to bring about a change in *organisational culture*. In practical terms, the success or failure of public policy can be measured by the extent to which 'managerial discretionary behaviour' is changed. It may also be about changing the 'discretionary behaviours' of ordinary workers in the organisation too. In this sense the implementation process is about changing the way people think and behave within organisations or, indeed, about changing the personnel if existing staff are unable or unwilling to adopt new values and behavioural norms. The change in the water industry involves a shift from being 'community' and 'service' orientated organisations (perhaps the overriding characteristic of the industry under local government) towards a more market or investor orientated, profit orientated, and 'customer orientated' culture – the equivalent of AT&T's 'cultural train wreck'. For example, the Chairman and Chief Executive of Welsh Water have likened their approach to managing the company to a 'crusade' designed to bring a free market culture into a rigid monopoly (*The Times*, 15 October 1994). In so far as water privatisation in England and Wales finally developed a 'coherent rationale', it was surely about shifting the industry towards a customer orientated and profit-centred organisational culture. Without us necessarily *accepting* the pro-privatisation rationale, it has been clearly argued by Glynn that 'by harnessing the profit motive, privatisation is capable of encouraging greater technical efficiency, lower unit costs and more innovative methods' (1992, p. 8.2). A major feature of this regime is, of course, *risk* – a phenomenon absent under the old system of public ownership. As Glynn suggests, businesses face 'the risks arising from power management or from changes in the economic climate in the medium term period – described as at least five years after privatisation' (ibid., p. 8.3). Glynn suggests further that the pressure from shareholders and the need to operate in competitive capital markets which private sector organisations have to operate under, *appears* particularly apposite for the water industry. The need to take note of the judgement of City investors has perhaps been even more important to the industry than the need to recognise its customers.

Some caution should, however, be adopted in suggesting that changes in organisational culture or behaviour always have to be *enforced* in some way – either directly by regulation itself, or via the threat of take-over or by market failure. It should be recalled that a large part of the momentum for the privatisation of water (as in other publicly owned industries) came from the managers of the industry themselves, that is, there was a high degree of self-motivation for change. Thus, one of the conditions necessary for successful implementation of public policy was already present before privatisation got underway. There was a good correlation between the basic objectives of policy-makers and the objectives of those who would be in charge of policy implementation. A typical example of this attitudinal change was provided by Bill Harper, Deputy Chairman of Thames Water, who has been in the industry under both public and private ownership. Speaking in 1992, he stated that:

> As far as I am concerned, I want as far as possible to avoid the regulated industry stereotype. In terms of drinking water quality I find analogies with any food producer who is regulated. That is not a special thing. In terms of discharges we are analogous to any other waste disposer. Other parts of the waste disposal industry do not see themselves to be regulated industries. The bit that is special about us is price. I think we have got to find the means of handling that as a business which has got a price regulation not a regulated industry. I do not like that tab, it fits us into a stereotype which I do not find attractive. So try and avoid a regulation stereotype. Retain initiative and responsibility. (1992)

Not only did privatisation unleash these new (and possible unrealistic) attitudes, it also provided some inbuilt and very effective *incentives* for the key managers in the industry to 'ramp up' their organisations in line with the new values. They were offered attractive share option deals, for example. Thus, in addition to generous salaries (by existing public sector standards), their share options have, in the event, produced quite spectacular gains reflecting their organisation's success in the market-place. They have received rewards consistent with the very successful shift of their organisations from a fairly boring and unexciting 'backwater' of the public service to a key position in any safe portfolio of shareholdings. (Indeed, if one were to devise just one indicator of change in the water industry, over the period 1945 to

1994, one could do worse than select the centrality of the industry, alongside other private utilities, in almost any investors' guide today. Had this been suggested to those running the industry in the 1950s and 1960s, it would have been regarded as ludicrous.) For example, John Bellak as Chief Executive of Severn Trent RWA was earning £49,000 prior to privatisation. Yet on leaving the privatised company earlier than intended in 1994 he received compensation of £511,000 (£404,000 in lieu of salary and £107,000 for pension contributions). This was in addition to his previous year's salary of £230,000 and the £226,000 he had earned in 1993 from his shares (*The Guardian*, 28 July 1994). The salary rises of the chairmen of the privatised water companies have attracted significant public criticism. For example, Sir Desmond Pitcher, North West Water's Chairman, received a £100,000 salary increase which took his earnings to £338,000 in 1993 (*The Guardian*, 19 July 1994). Though much criticised in the press, and by the Opposition parties and consumers, these remuneration packages are undoubtedly very effective incentives for changing 'managerial discretionary behaviours' and for managers to force through policies necessary to bring about a fundamental change in organisational culture and organisational behaviour – such as centralisation of policy-making, de-manning and the adoption of modern business practices.

In practice, the implementation phase of water privatisation has been characterised by two key features – the new and much tougher regulatory framework described in the preceding chapter (itself a central feature in the degree of risk faced by the industry) and an acceleration of changes in organisational culture within the privatised companies as they adjust to life in the market-place. In combination, these two factors have had an enormous impact on the industry – hence our reference to privatisation as a cultural train wreck. These factors are interacting in the broader context of change in utility management in Britain. Despite the many changes, however, the utilities have retained some of their unique features. For example, the privatised water companies still retain a significant degree of what Bozeman termed 'publicness'. The paradox is that they are now subject to a greater (and more effective) degree of public regulation and to a much higher degree of issue salience than under public ownership. For investors, as Dale suggests, these are risks that need to be taken account of in assessing the industry as an investment opportunity (Dale, 1994, p. 9). There is also the added risk of the impact a change in government might have on the regulatory system. As Kahn notes, 'the exposure of public utility executives to public scrutiny and criticism, their desire to be associated with growing and progressive companies, to enjoy the approbation that comes from giving a good service, and to avoid unpopular rate increases, are reinforced by the presence of regulation' (Kahn, 1971, p. 1,001). Although written in 1971, Kahn's analysis of the organisational environment of utilities would be recognised instantly by any water company executive in Britain today! All of these features are present – the executives are exposed to an unprecedented level of public criticism, they see their central objective as heading successful, expanding and progressive international companies, they seek the approbation from improved level of services at acceptable costs to the consumer, and they are certainly subject to an unprecedented level of regulation. This subtle and complex amalgam of exogenous and endogenous factors is discussed below.

THE RAMPING-UP OF THE WATER COMPANIES

It is exceedingly difficult to introduce direct competition into the water industry, for obvious technical reasons. However, there is a significant degree of surrogate competition in the sense that there is a high degree of awareness – by both the regulators and the companies – of the notion of comparative performance. This inevitably leads to a considerable degree of organisational copying – and not just between water companies, but between the privatised utilities generally. Indeed, the privatised water companies have often modelled themselves on other utilities. Thus, many of the features now to be found in the privatised water companies are also to be found in British Gas, British Telecom and the regional electricity companies. The process has been common to all of the privatised utilities and they have all been going through a process of rapid organisational and cultural change. This 'ramping-up' process has a common theme, namely that they are all, despite their 'public-ness', becoming (as intended) much more like private firms. As he argues in the case of British Telecom, the message for staff has been that 'bureaucracy is no longer in residence' (Pitt, 1990, p. 6).

There are many indicators of this fundamental shift. One very obvious (and superficial) sign of change is in the annual reports of the water companies. Today they are even more glossy and professional than was typical under the last few years of public ownership. Typically, the *financial performance* of the organisation is the primary focus of the reporting process. For example, the 1994 Annual Report of Anglian Water has, on page 1, details of group turnover 1992/4, group profits before tax 1992/4, and group investment expenditure 1992/4. 'Financial highlights' are central – thus, for example, it reported turnover up by 18 per cent, profits up by 3.7 per cent (in a recession). The report itself is replete with the goals (and language) of any private sector company – particularly in terms of making it a customer-focused organisation. It announced the implementation of changes following a strategic review that would result in 'a radical shift from a hierarchical structure to an integrated process based organisation' (Anglian, 1994, p. 8). Interestingly, in terms of the focus of this chapter, it warned that '*the process will involve a substantial change in company culture as well as in structure*' (ibid., p. 8, emphasis added). Similarly Northumbrian Water Group emphasised that it too 'has in the past year concentrated much effort on re-examining and re-shaping our business and our approach to our customers' (Northumbrian, 1994, p. 2). The Board was carrying out 'new philosophies and practices' deep into its companies. Again the 'customer' focus was prominent. (It is difficult to find the word 'customer' in regular use prior to privatisation.) Thus, the company had hired the International Institute for Management Development (IIMD) to help develop a new vision of the group's future. At the heart of this vision 'is the need for all of us within Northumbrian

Water to focus our effort ever more intensely on the needs and desires of our customers'. Part of this effort involved the setting of 'aggressive operating efficiency targets' (ibid., p. 7). Every privatised water company has gone through this process of reorientating the organisation to a customer focus. In Northumbria's case this involved a 'customer focus programme' (developed with IIMD) which all employees will attend during 1995.

It would be churlish to doubt the quite genuine motivations of both managers and employees in these companies in trying to become more consumer friendly. Yet, it is also the case that, as suggested in the previous chapter, *regulation* is always present in the industry. As North West Water pointed out, its own 'positive initiatives' to refocus the company 'have improved customer service performance as measured by the Director General's standards for responding to billing queries, written complaints and interruptions to supply. *This is an area, largely due to our specific circumstances at privatisation, where we have been below industry average standards and we are devoting significant attention to rectifying this position*' (North West Water, 1994, p. 10, emphasis added). Thus, even in the absence of direct competition, the use of industry standards by the regulator can encourage changes in organisational behaviour.

Commonly, more effort has been put into the more efficient management of the direct interface with customers. For example, Severn Trent has developed telephone call software management specifically designed to improve customer service. Under the system, a single local rate number connects customers, wherever they are, to a central enquiry office – Birmingham. Advanced call identification systems are used to identify the location of the call, which is then routed to a customer liaison officer dedicated to calls from that area (Severn Trent, 1994, p. 3). Similarly, Thames' new customer centre at Swindon became fully operational in July 1993, combing both billing and operation enquiries (Thames, 1993, p. 5). Yorkshire, too, has implemented ambitious targets for call response rates and has received OFWAT's 'good' rating for its responses to the one million billing contacts (Yorkshire, 1993).

The new focus on customer care can be attributed to three factors – a genuine shift in attitudes on the part of those running the organisation, the high issue salience of water and pressure from the regulator, OFWAT. For example, Southern Water, in its 1994 Annual Report was anxious to point out that it had 'performed particularly well' according to OFWAT and that its overall performance in those aspects of standard of service which OFWAT monitored on a comparative basis was the best among the ten water and sewerage undertakers. These areas, where direct comparison between companies was possible were: mains water pressure, supply interruptions and speed of response to billing enquiries and written complaints (Southern Water, 1994, p. 13). From the outset, OFWAT has been very keen to set up procedures and measures of the effectiveness and efficiency of the services which the companies are supplying to their customers. For example, in July 1990 it contracted Focus Software Consultants to develop a complaints database at OFWAT headquarters in Birmingham and in the ten Consumer Service Committees which had been set up by the Director General in 1990. The name finally adopted for software was Watercare (Water Complaints

TABLE 6.1: Customer complaints.

Company	Number of connections (to the nearest 1,000) 1993–4	Number of complaints received 1993–4	Rate per 10,000 connections 1993–4	Number of complaints received 1992–3	Rate per 10,000 connections 1992–3
Water and sewerage companies					
Anglian Water Services Ltd	2,318,000	920	4.0	987	4.3
Dwr Cymru Cyfyngedig (Welsh Water)	1,267,000	1,248	9.9	1,093	8.7
North West Water Ltd	2,864,000	885	3.1	1,084	3.8
Northumbrian Water Ltd	1,152,000	279	2.4	273	2.4
Severn Trent Water Ltd	3,520,000	1,133	3.2	1,666	4.7
South West Water Services Ltd	672,000	1,154	17.2	1,190	17.8
Southern Water Services Ltd	1,661,000	701	4.2	568	3.4
Thames Water Utilities Ltd	4,969,000	3,168	6.4	2,831	5.7
Wessex Water Services Ltd	1,018,000	532	5.2	645	6.4
Yorkshire Water Services Ltd	2,003,000	1,910	9.5	1,708	8.6
Water only companies					
Bournemouth and West Hampshire Water Plcs	177,000	71	4.0	54	3.2
Bristol Water Plc	428,000	246	5.7	422	9.6
Cambridge Water Company	108,000	61	5.6	100	9.3
Chester Waterworks Company	44,000	11	2.5	12	2.8
Cholderton & District Water Company Ltd	1,000	0	0.0	2	*
East Surrey Water Plc	133,000	103	7.7	121	9.2
Essex Water Plc	590,000	287	4.9	288	5.1
Folkestone and Dover Water Services Ltd	69,000	31	4.5	20	3.0
Hartlepools Water Company	38,000	14	3.7	9	2.4
Mid Kent Water Plc	213,000	142	6.7	118	5.5
Mid Southern Water Plc	269,000	112	4.2	108	4.1
North East Water Plc	560,000	281	5.0	351	6.1
North Surrey Water Ltd	191,000	42	2.2	41	2.2
Portsmouth Water Plc	280,000	62	2.2	72	2.6
South East Water Ltd	270,000	283	10.5	246	9.6
South Staffordshire Water Plc	504,000	195	3.9	313	6.2
Suffolk Water Plc	114,000	71	6.2	60	5.6
Sutton District Water Plc	117,000	41	3.5	53	4.5
Tendring Hundred Water Services Ltd	63,000	53	8.4	48	7.6
Three Valleys Water Plc	953,000	209	2.2	267	2.8
Wrexham and East Denbighshire Water Company	61,000	31	5.1	21	3.4
York Waterworks Plc	74,000	26	3.5	21	2.9
TOTAL	26,701,000	14,302	5.4	14,792	5.6

NOTES: The number of connections has been taken from the additional information supplied with each company's principal statement for 1994–5. For the water and sewerage companies, the figure is the total number of properties connected for both water and sewerage, plus the number connected for water only and the number for sewerage only.
*Cholderton is an exceptionally small company.
SOURCE: OFWAT, 1993, p. 22.

Actioned and Resolved Expeditiously). Each CSC now has a free standing computer for Watercare. Complaints nationally, broken down region by region, are provided regularly to OFWAT's management. By March 1992 the number of complaints held on the central computer had reached 16,213 (actually not high for an industry supplying a population of over 56 million). The substantial increase in both absolute and percentage terms from the pre-privatisation situation probably reflects the different perceptions of the industry's customers after privatisation. This large database facilitates a detailed analysis of complaints issues and trends and the development of customer care policies. It is also used in the Periodic Review process (OFWAT, 1992, p. 19). In its Annual Report, OFWAT publishes comparative complaints data (see Table 6.1).

The complaints data reported by OFWAT are very detailed indeed – far more than any other private sector company (other than fellow utilities) would publish. The danger, of course, is that the heavy emphasis on facilitating and monitoring customer complaints becomes a self-fulfilling prophecy, exacerbated by the continued high political salience of water. In many ways the very fact of privatisation (and the controversy over the salaries of senior managers) has focused attention on the performance of the companies. It is no surprise, therefore, that there has been a steady rise in the number of complaints. For example, the 1992 OFWAT Report notes that customer complaints rose sharply during the year, including a peak of 1,637 complaints in April 1991, coinciding with the delivery of the new water bills and delivery of the OFWAT 'Paying for Water' leaflet and questionnaire (OFWAT 1992, p. 20). As OFWAT itself conceded, 'the increase in complaints was to be expected as public awareness grew of the existence of a body to help in resolving customer complaints. *There is no evidence to link the increase to a corresponding decline in the standards of service provided by companies*' (ibid., p. 22, emphasis added). Much of the increase in complaints is likely to be an artefact of the new complaints structure and the fact that water charges have increased in both level and in transparency. Thus, it is not at all surprising that the proportion of complaints about charges rose from 29 per cent in 1990/1 to 38 per cent in 1991/2. Moreover, OFWAT itself can sometimes be the direct cause of a change in level of complaints. For example, it admitted that it was 'the Director General's determination in December 1991 of South West Water's application for an interim adjustment of the K factor and the dispatch of bills for 1992/3 which resulted in a very large increase in complaints about charges to the South West CSC (ibid., p. 23).

The pressure from OFWAT for the companies to be increasingly customer responsive is continuous and cannot be ignored. Indeed, in 1991, OFWAT commissioned its own MORI survey of customers (later to feature in a dispute with the NRA Chairman Lord Crickhowell who referred, somewhat disparagingly to 'Mr Byatt's customers'). The primary objective of the survey was to identify the key issues from the customers' perspective and the standards of service they expected – and to assess the willingness of customers to pay for a higher quality of service. As suggested in Chapter 5, this issue has emerged as central to the dispute between the NRA and OFWAT – with the companies as some kind of 'pig in the middle'. The regulatory pressure for the intensification of the new customer orientation – surely the key feature of marketisation – continued with the inclusion of the utilities in the Citizen's Charter in March 1993. With the passage of the Competition and Services (Utilities) Act in March 1992 OFWAT's powers were strengthened. For example, the companies now have to have a procedure for handling complaints which has been approved by the DG; the DG's powers to make binding decisions in disputes have been extended and the DG can specify how the companies should inform their customers about the company's performance (OFWAT, 1991, p. 29).

The 'customer as king or queen' ideology is central to OFWAT's concern once it has fulfilled its statutory duty to ensure that the companies carry out their functions properly and can finance them. It has placed particular emphasis on the ability of the customer to pay for improvements. Specifically, the companies have been encouraged to draw up their business plans 'in a way which allows for growth in demand which customers are prepared to pay for' (OFWAT, 1993, p. i). The justification for this regulatory pressure is, of course, that the water industry is atypical of private industries. As OFWAT has pointed out, 'in most industries, increases in demand can be expected through competitive pressures to lead to additional supplies, not higher prices. This does not happen under current arrangements in the water industry' (ibid., p. i).

There is, of course, competition in capital markets rather than in product markets, as the DG has pointed out (Byatt 1994). This presents OFWAT with some difficulties, however, as it requires a degree of confidentiality and a lack of transparency in the regulatory process. Indeed, Byatt has admitted that, if the water companies revealed too much information, it could make life difficult for them in raising capital. There are also difficulties for OFWAT in terms of the use of comparisons. For some comparators – such as the cost of implementing EU directives – cost comparisons are appropriate – beyond that, the difficult issue of the sensitivity of capital markets becomes an issue.

The central question in terms of the focus of this chapter – changes in organisational culture and organisational behaviour – is whether OFWAT's regulatory focus on the consumer and the NRA's focus on the environment leaves the companies sufficient scope to develop new behavioural patterns of their own. As Alan Booker, Deputy Director General of OFWAT, has conceded 'providing they [the companies] operate within the framework set by the public interest, companies must be given scope for using and developing business skills and exercising their business judgement' (1992, p. 15).

An important indicator of whether the privatised companies have been able to develop behavioural characteristics common to other private sector companies – notwithstanding the complex regulatory framework under which the industry operates – is such behaviour as rationalisations, mergers and diversification. There is some evidence that these developments are, indeed, taking place. The scope for rationalisations and mergers is limited by regulation. For example, if a case is referred to the Monopolies and Mergers Commission it must have due regard to the effect that any mergers or acquisitions might have on the DG's ability to make comparisons between companies. As the number of water companies is already small, further concentration could weaken the potential for comparison to act as a surrogate for competition. Rationalisations and mergers have taken place – for example between Mid Sussex, West Kent and Eastbourne water companies, and also between Sunderland and South Shields Water Plc and Newcastle and Gateshead Plc (both controlled by Lyonnaise UK, a French company). Diversification has, however, become more common – facilitated by the fact that the ten privatised companies were set up as holding companies on privatisation. Thus, the particular form of privatisation has encouraged diversification measures, with companies keen to diversify into non-regulated areas of activity as a means of increasing their profits. However, OFWAT has been keen to ensure that diversification has not put at risk the main functions of the holding companies. In its view, diversification 'should not interfere with the ability of the appointed company to finance its function' (OFWAT 1992, p. 55). This concern led OFWAT, in June 1991, to secure a modification of the conditions of appointment of the appointed companies. As a result, each company board (which normally includes a member of the Plc board) now has to produce an annual certification to the effect that there will be sufficient financial and management resources available to enable the appointed company properly to perform its functions for the next year (ibid., p. 51). Also, cross-subsidy between companies is now prohibited. Moreover, OFWAT's concerns regarding diversification are shared by City investors. Thus, in his review of the categories of risk facing investors in the industry, Dale specifically identifies 'diversification risk' as one category of risk which has grown over the industry's first five years in the private sector (Dale, 1994, p. 8).

Commonly, the privatised water companies report diversification measures as a key part of their business strategies. This has been part of a twin-track strategy which they have developed for coping with having to operate in a highly regulated market in a highly politicised environment. The central strategy has been to meet the various regulatory targets – in terms of environmental and cost standards – and to produce efficiency gains that allow the development of a profitable company and an acceptable return to investors. The second 'track' has been to build up other, unregulated, activities in order to escape the constraints of regulation. For example, Anglian, in its 1994 report, commented that 'we propose to continue to concentrate on the regulated business by containing operating costs through the rigorous pursuit of efficiency initiatives and at the same time build up our unregulated activities' (1994, p. 6). However, it did not see its unregulated activities as 'true diversification' 'Anglian Water International and Anglian Water Processes both reinforce and feed off our expertise in operating and designing clean water and waste water systems' (ibid., p. 17). Similarly, Northumbrian Water Plc reports that 'substantial progress has been made in the development of the other business activities, though the operating service companies have still to convert this progress into profit (Northumbrian, 1994, p. 19). It reported that the proportion of turnover derived from outside the 'appointed business' rose from 24 per cent to 30 per cent largely reflecting the growth of the Entec consulting business (ibid., p. 19).

Diversification has been a common feature of all of the privatised utilities in Britain. As Ferner and Colling point out, 'privatisation and the ending of political control have provided both the opportunities and the incentives for companies to diversify out of their "core" utility activities into new areas: the question of "what business are we in?" can again be placed on the management strategy agenda' (Ferner and Colling, 1993, p. 132). Indeed, they cite Welsh Water Plc's purchase of a stake in one of its major customers, South Wales Electricity, as a typical example of this more general phenomenon.

OFWAT has expressed concern that diversification by the privatised companies has, in general, not been very successful (OFWAT, 1992, pp 55–6) – a view apparently shared by the City investors. As with companies traditionally in the private sector, diversification presents risks as well as opportunities. For example, Thames Water Plc has admitted that the 'excellent performance' in the utilities division has been offset by adverse factors in its other divisions where markets have not fully recovered from recession (Thames, 1994, p. 3). Indeed the annual accounts for 1994 include £35 m. for exceptional items, for losses on old contracts in Egypt and for the restructuring of some of its companies. Nevertheless, the chairman could still claim that 'since privatisation we have quickly established ourselves as a major international company, but one focused clearly on water and waste water services' (ibid., p. 3). In terms of turnover, the non-regulated water business at Thames (organised into three principal divisions) is quite significant when compared with the turnover of the utility operations (approx. £872 m. for the latter in 1994 compared with approx. £271 m. for the non-regulated business). The Thames Water Group of companies now serves domestic, municipal, industrial and commercial customers in the UK and throughout the world and is structured as follows: Water and Wastewater Utility Operations, carrying out the regulated businesses of supplying drinking water and the collecting and treating of waste water; Products and Services, developing, manufacturing and installing products for industrial customers and water utility operators overseas – for example, the company is an international leader in membrane technology for the food, beverage and pharmaceutical industries; Environmental Services, providing UK utility operators and commercial and industrial customers with specialist underground and maintenance services; International Operations and Process Contracting, providing engineering and contracting skills to municipal and private water utility operators and customers world-wide for the construction and design of new treatment plants (Thames, 1994, p. 10). For the industry as a whole, however, diversification has, so far, not been a success. As Dale notes, diversification was grasped eagerly by both the industry and its investors following the 'freedom bestowed by privatisation' (Dale, 1994, p. 10). However, as he notes, those investors who were more sceptical of the benefits of diversification have been proved right. They, apparently, harboured doubts about the ability of management teams with limited private sector experience to be successful when moving into higher risk commercial markets. The more extreme sceptics argued that all they were getting for their equity premiums was diversification risk! (ibid., p. 10). As he comments:

To date, the extremists have it: when you compound margin erosion due to recessionary pressures with substantial interest payable on acquisition cost and additional overhead charges, and throw in write-offs against non-performing contracts and ventures which didn't quite work out, the sum total is a net earnings deficit of £100 million over the last two years for the ten principle water plc. (ibid., p. 10)

The moves towards diversification – essentially an attempt to develop the organisations as businesses outside the regulatory constraints imposed by the privatisation settlement – should not be seen as the *overriding* feature of the behaviour of the companies after privatisation. As suggested above, diversification has had quite mixed results. The financial success of the companies has depended upon two key factors relating to their core businesses – delivering the massive post-privatisation investment programme and achieving sufficient efficiency gains within the regulatory framework to generate profits which are acceptable to investors. Every privatised water company has been involved in a major investment programme to deal with the backlog of under-investment under public ownership and to meet both existing and new environmental and quality standards. Thames is not untypical, having invested £367 m. in 1993/4. Similarly, North West Water has invested over £2 bn since 1989 – including an investment of £150 m. for an interceptor tunnel and waste water treatment plant on Lancashire's Fylde coast, designed to improve the quality of discharges to bathing waters between Blackpool and Fleetwood (see Chapter 8) (North West, 1994, p. 8). Decisions such as this, though made much of in public relations terms were, of course, *regulation* driven – not responses to the 'market-place' as such. Thus, as North West Plc admitted in its publicity for its £500 m. investment programme to clean up the bathing waters of North West England (its so-called Sea Change programme featuring environmental campaigner, David Bellamy), 'at present only 13 of the regions 33 bathing waters achieve European Union standards' (ibid., p. 9). In total, the water companies will have spent approximately £28 bn in investment by the year 2000 causing (up to 1994) an average annual rise in water charges of 5 per cent in excess of inflation. (See Table 6.2 for total capital expenditure 1985/6 to 1992/3.)

In 1989 the average household waste and sewerage bill was £120 (£145 at 1992/3 prices) and had risen to £170 by 1992/3, and to £185 by 1994 – representing approximately 1 per cent of household income (See Table 6.3).

OFWAT has estimated that approximately £30 of the increase is due to higher drinking water and environmental quality standards; £5 for improved standards of service to customers and £10 to provide for new resources to meet the growth in demand (OFWAT, 1992). The WSA has estimated that some 42 per cent of the new investment is so that the industry can meet improved drinking water quality standards.

Responding to regulation is, of course, not inconsistent with successful market behaviour. The test of the companies' ability to generate profits in the context of a highly regulated business environment is the market itself. As David Kinnersley has argued, the rise in share prices since the flotation of water shares in 1989 to mid

TABLE 6.2: Total capital expenditure 1985/6 to 1992/3 (£m).

	85/6	86/7	87/8	88/9	89/90	90/1	91/2	92/3
Anglian	106.0	123.0	140.7	141.3	192.0	221.6	293.4	326.7
Dwr Cymru	54.4	61.7	67.8	89.8	105.3	160.0	189.7	201.0
Northumbrian	39.3	36.9	39.4	41.4	65.9	98.4	104.5	110.0
North West	163.0	184.3	201.6	216.9	269.4	408.0	511.5	489.5
Severn Trent	119.8	149.3	159.7	206.9	262.2	394.7	577.5	536.6
Southern	62.6	65.6	71.2	89.8	125.5	132.6	162.1	114.7
South West	36.1	37.2	46.7	51.6	80.2	120.0	174.7	205.0
Thames	108.8	127.1	169.8	184.5	265.7	418.0	424.7	400.4
Wessex	49.1	59.4	72.8	74.5	100.0	96.6	137.8	130.2
Yorkshire	94.6	126.7	142.5	146.5	188.2	250.2	290.2	303.1
TOTAL	833.7	971.2	1,112.2	1,243.2	1,654.4	2,300.1	2,866.1	3,040.2
Water supply companies	75.4	77.7	88.2	99.8	111.3	196.0	261.6	220.0
NRA	–	–	–	112.0	131.0	74.6	67.4	59.5
Scotland	93.5	102.9	98.6	110.6	127.4	144.5	171.1	224.3[1]
Northern Ireland	25.2	25.8	25.3	25.2	27.7	33.0	37.1	47.6
UK	1,027.6	1,177.6	1,424.3	1,590.8	2,051.8	2,748.2	3,403.3	3,591.6

NOTE: 1. Estimate.
SOURCE: *Waterfacts*, 1993, p. 35.

1993 indicates that organisations which were previously thought to be hierarchical, bureaucratic and averse to change, have been reasonably successful in the market-place. Thus, he argues that *The Financial Times* (100) Index had risen 22 per cent while the shares in the six most successful privatised water companies had risen between 85% and 135%' (Kinnersley, 1994, p. 179). Dale, as an investment analyst, is, however, more cautious. He points out that the sector as a whole has managed only 5 to 6 per cent growth in earnings in each of the years up to 1994 (Dale, 1994, p. 5). Whatever the arguments relating to the investment rating of the privatised companies (assessments very from the rather cautious, such as Dale, to the more optimistic, such as *The Financial Times*), it is clear that the privatised companies have been rather successful, to date, in moving from the public sector to a market environment. Cultural train wreck or not, they have, quite clearly, been very adaptive and successful organisations, notwithstanding the continued public and political criticism of their achievements. Apart from the basic functions that they perform, they are unrecognisable from the old structure which characterised the industry prior to privatisation.

In the future, their ability to thrive in the market-place will depend on their ability to continue to deliver efficiency gains within the 'regulatory bargain' under which they operate. One might argue that this could become more difficult over time. All of the privatised utilities have achieved significant efficiency gains after

TABLE 6.3: Average household bills for unmeasured water and sewerage, 1993–4.

Company	% increase 1989/90– 90/91	% increase 1990/91– 91/92	% increase 1991/92– 92/93	% increase 1992/93– 93/94	Level for 1993–94 £
WATER					
Anglian Water Service Ltd	22.3	19.7	13.4	9.0	116
Bournemouth and West Hampshire Water Cos[1]	19.6	23.2	13.5	11.5	85
Bristol Water Plc	7.2	15.5	11.6	9.5	86
Cambridge Water Company	19.1	26.5	13.4	6.3	92
Chester Waterworks Company	11.5	18.4	6.3	4.4	105
Cholderton and District Water Company Ltd	10.0	19.0	9.1	9.0	111
Dwr Cymru Cyfyngedig	18.3	16.2	9.4	8.2	123
East Surrey Water Plc	34.0	25.8	5.3	6.1	141
Essex Water Plc	16.0	13.1	9.9	8.6	91
Folkestone and Dover Water Services Ltd	17.5	18.4	11.3	7.7	92
Hartlepools Water Company	15.9	14.9	9.9	8.0	71
Mid Kent Water Plc	25.1	12.9	6.4	4.1	114
Mid Southern Water Plc	21.8	21.9	11.3	8.5	102
North East Water Plc	7.4	29.9	3.5	7.9	84
North Surrey Water Ltd	15.6	23.2	12.3	12.4	79
North West Water Ltd	12.7	14.8	8.6	9.0	79
Northumbrian Water Ltd	8.3	17.2	10.6	9.8	80
Portsmouth Water Plc	12.6	14.5	8.1	10.3	65
Severn Trent Water Ltd	14.9	14.0	9.2	7.8	73
South East Water Ltd[2]	29.1	27.0	12.6	3.9	155
South Staffordshire Water Plc	12.5	14.4	8.9	5.7	69
South West Water Services Ltd	12.9	16.6	12.9	13.4	106
Southern Water Services Ltd	12.2	15.6	9.3	7.1	77
Suffolk Water Plc	31.9	17.0	18.2	15.8	105
Sutton District Water Plc	20.3	22.8	13.7	10.0	99
Tendring Hundred Water Services Ltd	30.1	31.2	17.1	18.3	134
Thames Water Utilities Ltd	16.0	12.9	5.5	6.8	75
Three Valleys Water Services Plc[3]	16.2	17.5	10.2	4.4	86
Wessex Water Services Ltd	12.6	17.1	8.7	9.5	95
Wrexham and East Denbighshire Water Co.	22.7	17.8	13.4	7.8	124
York Waterworks Plc	16.3	13.1	7.2	6.4	80
Yorkshire Water Services Ltd	11.4	14.8	6.3	9.1	94
SEWERAGE					
Anglian Water Services Ltd	7.3	12.5	9.3	9.0	132
Dwr Cymru Cyfyngedig	9.7	16 3	9.4	10.1	109
North West Water Ltd	12.5	14.5	9.7	8.4	90
Northumbrian Water Ltd	19 5	16.5	10.3	9.3	92
Severn Trent Water Ltd	12.9	14.7	9.5	8 4	91
South West Water Services Ltd	12.2	17.1	23.0	19.1	160
Southern Water Services Ltd	10.3	18.4	9 6	7.6	114
Thames Water Utilities Ltd	10.3	16.2	11.3	9.1	77
Wessex Water Services Ltd	11.2	13.0	7.9	9.3	114
Yorkshire Water Services Ltd	9.8	13.1	6.7	6.8	84

AVERAGE UNMEASURED HOUSEHOLD BILLS, 1993–4		AVERAGE MEASURED HOUSEHOLD BILLS, 1993–4	
Water	£88	Water	£98
Sewerage	£97	Sewerage	£106
TOTAL	£185	TOTAL	£203

NOTES
1. Bournemouth and West Hampshire Water Companies comprise Bournemouth and District Water Plc and West Hampshire Water Plc.
2. South-East Water Limited comprises Eastbourne Water Plc, Mid Sussex Water Plc and West Kent Water Plc.
3. Three Valleys Water Services Plc comprises Lee Valley Water Ltd, Colne Valley Water Ltd and Rickmansworth Water Ltd.
SOURCE: OFWAT 1992, p. 37

privatisation as they attacked the old public sector practices and agreements. Thus, a common feature has been changes in working practices and de-manning.

For example, O'Connell Davidson found a 'bifurcated pattern' of employment operating in her case-study of a privatised water company – given the fictitious name 'Albion Water'. She found 'two types of employment ... 'standard. direct employment', i.e. full-time permanent employment', and contract labour (1993, p. 142). Since privatisation the company has further commercialised its relationship with its direct employees, for example, by contracting out ancillary services such as vehicle maintenance. More significantly, however, has been Albion's decision to reduce 'its manning levels by 2% per annum' and its decision 'to restructure the Building and Maintenance Services (now the Building Maintenance Unit [BMU]) along the lines of the compulsory competitive tendering model imposed upon local authority Direct Labour Organisations' (ibid., pp. 147–8). Thus, 'rather than allocating an operation budget to this unit, Albion distributed the maintenance budget amongst the various departments which used building and maintenance services' (ibid., p. 148). Consequently, departmental managers put all maintenance work out to tender and the BMU had to submit its tender with at least three other (external) organisations for Albion Water contracts. The BMU were required 'to give fixed price quotes, ... to show a return of 5% on capital employed ... (and) a probationary period of one year' to meet its targets and since 1988 the unit has been required to win external as well as in-house contracts (ibid., pp. 148–9).

The water industry has seen a significant decline in manpower since the early 1980s – long before privatisation (see Table 6.4). The pressure for further reductions is likely to continue. As Yorkshire has indicated, for example, the company 'faces regulatory challenges to increase efficiency through technology and outsourcing. These will inevitably mean substantial job reductions' (Yorkshire, 1994, p. 11). Similarly, Anglian has reported that 'there have to be job losses over the next two or three years ... overall we expect there to be 900 fewer jobs' (Anglian, 1994, p. 10). The effects of the 1994 Periodic Review, introducing a K factor of inflation + 1.4 per cent (instead of inflation + 5 per cent), mean that 'company management will have to work hard in order to maintain any earnings momentum at all' (Dale, 1994, p. 5).

Some five years after privatisation and with the 1994 Periodic Review complete, the water industry might be able to envisage a stable future as a secure traditional utility. Conflicts will continue, of course, particularly as there is little sign of the regulatory capture so common in the US, for example. Thus, regulatory creep, rather than regulatory capture, is likely to remain an important feature of the industry's business environment. However, the water industry appears to exhibit the general features of British business identified by Wilson – namely a political culture less hostile to government 'interference' and with regulators enjoying considerable authority. As he argues, 'regulations may be ironically less irritating when the authority of the regulation is more secure and he or she is more able to achieve a friendly yet authoritative relationship with the regulated' (Wilson, 1984, p. 225).

TABLE 6.4: Manpower in the water industry.

	Full-time equivalent employees at 31 March											
	1981	1982	1983	1984	1985	1986	1987	1988	1989	1991	1992	1993
Anglian	6,744	6,700	6,560	5,826	5,549	5,264	5,184	5,102	5,068	3,629	3,927	3,970
Dwr Cymru	5,736	5,677	5,424	5,179	4,709	4,746	4,845	4,618	4,406	3,455	3,505	3,437
Northumbrian	2,309	2,151	2,077	1,919	1,759	1,636	1,523	1,459	1,463	1,193	1,222	1,317
North West	9,120	8,782	8,629	8,278	8,166	8,055	8,134	7,936	7,766	6,839	5,928	5,393
Severn Trent	10,886	10,502	10,182	9,720	9,269	8,908	8,493	8,174	7,890	7,054	7,456	7,070
Southern	4,101	3,948	3,720	3,494	3,336	3,183	3,160	3,162	3,185	2,259	2,226	2,428
South West	2,450	2,276	2,255	2,194	2,023	2,008	2,003	1,958	1,938	1,855	2,084	2,144
Thames	11,945	11,753	11,227	10,321	9,089	8,896	9,152	9,210	9,321	7,400	7,218	6,974
Wessex	2,398	2,291	2,266	2,182	2,050	1,994	1,925	1,891	1,907	1,755	1,821	1,871
Yorkshire	6,522	6,506	6,021	6,052	5,835	5,472	5,254	4,981	4,941	4,074	4,031	3,813
WSCS	62,211	60,586	58,361	55,165	51,785	50,162	49,673	48,491	47,885	39,513	39,418	38,417
Water supply cos	8,641	8,369	8,190	8,010	7,821	7,340	7,101	6,865	6,768	7,000	7,101	6,356
NRA[1]										6,805	7,591	8,195
Scotland	6,318	6,226	6,121	6,144	6,129	6,155	6,182	6,194	6,094	6,229	6,614	6,608
Northern Ireland	2,892	2,708	2,605	2,524	2,518	2,510	2,605	2,552	2,507	2,598	2,543	2,442
UK	80,062	77,889	75,277	71,843	68,253	66,167	65,561	64,102	63,254	62,145	63,267	62,018

NOTE: 1. The NRA was set up in 1989 and most of the staff transferred from the water authorities.
SOURCE: *Waterfacts*, 1993, p. 39.

The 1994 Periodic Review suggests that this type of relationship has, indeed, been achieved in the water sector – at least between the present DG and the industry. Moreover, as will be suggested in our concluding chapter, there are some signs that the years of policy turbulence in water may be over in that the key players – the DOE, OFWAT, NRA and the WSA – are beginning to exhibit the characteristics of a stable policy community. In that sense, a phase in organisational life may be coming where organisations 're-freeze' following a period of rapid change in order to achieve a degree of stability in the new system (See Sofer, 1972, p. 295 quoting Lewin). However, as Sofer warns, assessing organisational change is not an easy task – if only because 'organisational change is a social process, not a once and for all act' (ibid., p. 314). External challenges can derail apparently successful reform movements. Water may be no exception, especially in the context of an increasingly Europeanised policy environment, where key decisions will continue to be made by policy actors distant from the day-to-day running of a privatised water company. It is this unstable and unpredictable policy environment that is examined in the next chapter.

REFERENCES

Anglian Water Plc, *Annual Report 1994*.
Booker, A. (1992), *Issues Involved in Regulation of Privatised Utilities*. Speech delivered to the Institute of International Research, Malaysia, Symposium on 'Financing Water Utilities' (Birmingham: OFWAT).
Bozeman, B. (1987), *All Organisations are Public* (San Francisco: Jossey-Bass).
Byatt, Ian (1994), *'The Periodic Review': An Industry Overview'*, paper presented to Centre for the Study of Regulated Industries Seminar, London, 11 October.
Dale, B. (1994), 'The Investors' Judgement', paper presented to Centre for Regulated Industries Conference, 'The Water Industry – Looking Forward from the Periodic Review', London, 11 October.
Ferner, A. and Colling, T. (1993), 'Privatization of the British Utilities: Regulation, decentralization and industrial relations', in T. Clarke and C. Pitells (ed.), *The Political Economy of Privatization* (London: Routledge).
Glynn, D. (1992), 'Trends in the Economic Regulation of the Water Industry', paper presented to *The Financial Times* Conference on the European Water Industry, London, 10 and 11 March.
Harper, W. (1992), 'Business Excellence: Everybody wins', in T. Gilland (ed.), *The Changing Water Business* (London: CRI), pp. 62–72.
Kahn, A. (1971), *The Economics of Regulation: Principles and Institutions* (New York: John Wiley).
Kinnersley, D. (1994), *Coming Clean: The Politics of Water and the Environment* (London: Penguin).
Northumbrian Water Plc, *Annual Report 1994*.
North West Water Plc, *Annual Report 1994*.
O'Connell Davidson, J. (1993), *Privatisation and the Employment Relations: The Case of the Water Industry* (London: Mansell).
OFWAT (1992), *Annual Report 1991*.
OFWAT (1993), 'Paying for Growth', Consultation paper on the framework for reflecting the costs of providing for growth in charges (Birmingham: OFWAT).
Pitt, D. (1990), 'An Essentially Contestable Organisation: British Telecom and the Privatisation Debate', in J. Richardson (ed.), *Privatisation and Deregulation in Canada and Britain* (Aldershot: Dartmouth).
Schmalense, R. (1986), Paper presented to National Economic Research Associates Inc., Electric Utility Conference, 'Surviving an Era of Changing Regulation', Arizona, 12–15 February.
Severn Trent Water Plc, *Annual Report 1994*.
Shibata, K. (1994), *Privatisation of British Airways: Its Management and Politics 1982–87*, Working Paper EPU No. 93/9 (Florence: European University Institute).
Sofer, C. (1972), *Organizations in Theory and Practice* (London: Heinemann Educational Books).
Southern Water Plc, *Annual Report 1994*.
Stoetzer, M. W. (1990), 'Efficiency and Prices in the European Air Transport Market: Some further

evidence', in G. Majone (ed.), *Deregulation or Reregulation? Regulatory Reform in Europe and the United States* (London: Frances Pinter).

Strasser, K. A. and Kohler, M. F. (1989), *Regulating Utilities With Management Incentives* (New York: Quorum Books and Greenwood Press).

Thames Water Plc, *Annual Report 1993*.

Thames Water Plc, *Annual Report 1994*.

Wilson, G. K. (1984), 'Social Regulation and Explanations of Regulatory Failure', *Political Studies*, vol. 32, pp. 203–25.

Yorkshire Water Plc, *Annual Report 1993, 1994*.

7

The Europeanisation of Water Policy

In assessing the impact of the European Union on water policy in Britain one needs to note that the sector has been subject to other exogenous changes as outlined in previous chapters – particularly the effects of privatisation and the institution of a completely new regulatory regime. In addition, these 'shocks' to the sector have taken place in the context of a major shift in the *political salience* of water policy over time. It is, therefore, somewhat difficult to isolate EU factors and to assess their impact, if only because so much change has been taking place since privatisation in 1989. As has been argued, the whole sector has been undergoing a series of both incremental and radical changes – legislative, institutional and cultural. In particular, the move towards a privately owned system in England and Wales had implications for the way in which Britain is currently responding to EU water policy. This is because the network of actors involved at the national level is now more complex and less consensual, and because privatisation exposed the difficult question of how to finance improvements much more clearly than in most other EU states. To some degree, the challenge of Europeanisation – familiar in other policy areas (Kassim and Menon, 1995) – has arrived in the water sector alongside the destabilisation and erosion of hitherto relatively stable policy communities. As one official in a national agency put it to us, 'the ever increasing number of EU directives is one of the major challenges facing the industry'.

Although it will be argued that Britain's history and traditions of environmental management have made it a difficult European partner in the water sector, it should be noted that many of the financial and economic issues currently causing controversy in Britain are beginning to emerge in other EU states (for example Germany after reunification). It can be argued that Britain's position in terms of policy bargaining at the EU level could well improve over time as her partners face up to the costs of meeting EU legislative requirements.

Many of Britain's difficulties in coping with the Europeanisation of water policy are attributed both to Britain's general position in resisting a federal European Union and the massive investment programme (now underway) commonly attributed solely to 'Brussels'. Indeed, it might be argued that had it not been for the strict financial regime instituted in Britain throughout the 1970s and 1980s (which, as we have argued, itself played a key role as the 'spark' for privatisation), Britain would be no more uncomfortable with EU water policy than say, Germany, France, Holland or Denmark. It was the funding policies pursued under public ownership which caused the severe backlog of investment in water supply and sewage treatment infrastructure – not *an overburdening European 'superstate'*.

The Government has argued that 'compliance with European directives has played a major part in deciding the composition of the substantial investment programmes of some £30 bn which the water companies have put in since privatisation' (Maclean, 1993, p. 8.1). While industry spokespersons have also emphasised the cost effects of European directives, they also recognise that Britain's infrastructure investment record is not good by European standards. For example, the Director of the WSA (Janet Langdon) has argued that the 'cost of water has been increasing since the 1980s due to two factors – catching up on the lack of investment in water infrastructure since the second world war and the quality standards required by the EC Directive and by customers' (Langdon, 1993, p. 5.2).

Moreover, it cannot simply be argued that Britain had been subject to an *impositional* policy style by the European Community in the past. Much of the policy framework now in place was agreed by unanimity and not under qualified majority voting. Not for the first time, Britain finds itself objecting to the costs of implementing policies to which it agreed some years ago. In part, therefore, current difficulties are due to lack of foresight by Britain at the policy formulation and policy decision phases of the European policy process. Prior to privatisation, Britain had been gradually sliding down the European 'league table' in terms of environmental and water quality indicators and investment just as it had in many other sectors quite unrelated to water policy – such as education and training, and even infant mortality rates.

The question of water charges has emerged since privatisation as the overriding issue in much of the public debate. Yet in *comparative* terms, Britain is in the process of catching up prices commonly charged for water elsewhere in Europe. Low investment in the past produced low prices. In 1992 the special 'Water Tariffs' Working Group of the Standing Committee of the International Water Supply Association (IWSA) found that British water prices were relatively low by international standards.

If laying the blame for increased water charges at the EU's door is to be credible, it requires a sustained argument that raising environmental and drinking water standards and the renewal of old infrastructure is unnecessary, or that it would not have been required if Britain was not a member of the EU.

One needs to be cautious, therefore, in assuming 'cause and effect' when evaluating the impact of Brussels. The WSA (1991 p. 3) has conceded that 'most (of the investment) is needed to make up for past under-investment'. Much of the action now being taken might well have happened in any case. Even so, it appears that the general effect of European legislation has been to force the pace of infrastructure

TABLE 7.1: International comparison of drinking water prices.[1]

Country/city	Annual charge (ECU)	Country/city	Annual charge (ECU)	Country/city	Annual charge (ECU)
Austria		Germany		Malaysia	
Linz	98	Frankfurt	255	Kuala Lumpur	25
Salzburg	152	Gelsenwasser	300	Netherlands	
Vienna	165	Hamburg	245	Amsterdam	130–60
Belgium		Munich	162	The Hague	180
Antwerp	104	Stuttgart	275	Utrecht	87
Brussels	228	Hungary		Spain	
Liege	143	Budapest	33	Madrid	129
Denmark		Miskolc	111	Barcelona	138
Aarhus	111	Pecs	133	Seville	79
Copenhagen	92	Italy		Alicante	71
Odense	100	Bologna	75	Murcia	150
Finland		Milan	20	Switzerland	
Helsinki	144	Naples	95	Berne	97
Tampere	156	Rome	41	Geneva	326
France		Turin	38	Zurich	251
Banlieue/Paris	225	Japan		United Kingdom[2]	
Lyon	234	Nagoya	63	Bristol	103 (189)
Marseille	185	Osaka	39	Cardiff	149 (264)
Nice	232	Sapporo	87	London	94 (136)
Paris	111	Tokyo	69	Manchester	95 (199)
Germany		Yokohama	63	Newcastle Upon Tyne	100 (210)
Berlin	154	Luxembourg			
Dusseldorf	240	Luxembourg	206		

NOTES:
1. Comparison of annual water charges for a family of two adults and two children living in a house and consuming 200³/years (expressed in ECUS as at 8 November 1991).
2. Data for the UK are unmetered with metered in parentheses.
SOURCE: *Journal of Water SRT-Aqua*, 1992, vol. 41, no. 6, p. 360.

investment in Britain. As Haigh (1994, pp. 4.5–7) argues, the Bathing Water Directive, for example, has 'had a considerable impact in the UK. It has led to the commitment of substantially greater expenditure on sewage treatment and disposal than would otherwise have occurred'.

Thus, Britain is possibly an extreme, if not unique, case of price increases resulting from an amalgam of endogenous (that is, decayed Victorian infrastructure) and exogenous (that is, EU directive) changes. Within this complex amalgam, the EU is undoubtedly now the main source of exogenous change. It provides the main legislative framework – and source of future legislative change – under which the water industry operates.

POLICY THEORY, POLICY INSTRUMENTS AND RELUCTANT COMPLIANCE?

EU water policy is in that class of cases where Britain is often at odds with its European partners unlike, say, EU competition policy or aviation policy, Britain does not play a leading role in driving policy forward. Indeed, water shares many of the characteristics of EU social policy where Britain is seen as a 'laggard'. The general picture is of the UK reaching a *reluctant* compromise on some policy issues and occasionally of more serious difficulties leading to cases being brought against the UK in the European Court of Justice (ECJ). With regard to European water policy, rather than being a *policy innovator*, Britain has tended to be a *policy resistor*.

Nigel Haigh has captured the essence of Britain's 'problem' with the EU. He quotes the Report of a Royal Commission on Sewage Disposal in 1912, as follows:

> A chemical standard can be applied in any one of two ways – either to the contaminating discharge by itself or to the stream which has received the discharge.

As he (1992, p. 3.1) argues '*the choice between the two types of standard quoted above has been the cause of a long running dispute between Britain and other Member States over water pollution*' (ibid., p. 3.1, emphasis added).

Essentially, the dispute is about whether emission or environmental quality standards are the most appropriate policy instruments for controlling pollution. However, as Haigh (ibid., p. 3.7) goes on to argue, 'to characterise the difficulties between the EU and the UK simply in these terms would be misleading', not only because in practice the UK has a mixture of policy instruments in place, but also because '(the) catalogue of available tools for controlling pollution shows that the Community has used them all'. Britain's difficulties have been only partly due to differences in what Haigh terms 'pollution theory'. One theory (which has been advanced by Britain) is that 'emission standards need be no more stringent than required to meet … quality objectives. The emission standards will therefore quite logically vary from place to place' (ibid., p. 3.8). The opposing theory, reflected in the German concept of *Vorsorgeprinzip* (that is, the principle of anticipation and foresight) is 'that the point of emission is the logical point to set up controls and they should be as stringent as available technology permits' (ibid., p. 3.9). However, of equal importance in the disputes between Britain and the other member states are questions of administrative convenience and economic competition (ibid., p. 3.9). In practice there has been a considerable degree of bargaining, usually leading to greater flexibility and longer periods for compliance as a result of Britain's lobbying efforts.

The hydrological conditions discussed in Chapter 1 are directly relevant here. The fact that Britain is an island with fast flowing rivers presents it with policy options not available to some of its continental European partners. Much of the British argument has been, quite plausibly, that physical conditions are quite different in Britain and that it is economically irrational to adopt policy instruments specifically designed to meet quite different (continental European) conditions. Just as the punishment should fit the crime, the policy instrument should fit the *actual* problem.

While Haigh is correct to emphasise the mixed nature of policy instruments (in terms of the dichotomy between emission and quality standards), at both the European and British level, Britain has been consistently cautious in terms of the ways in which it believes the EU should behave – almost irrespective of the particular policy instruments under debate. In a sense, the 'centre of gravity' of Britain's approach has been rather different from its European partners – which cannot fail to leave the impression of Britain as the 'reluctant partner'. Almost any speech by British ministers or officials is characterised by certain key caveats and phrases. For example, at *The Financial Times* conference on the European water industry in March 1993, David Maclean, Minister of State for Environment and Countryside, while conceding that the improvements resulting from the massive investment programme were needed, nevertheless argued that 'in fixing standards we must have regard to what is practically achievable by all states within a realistic timescale. Achievability must include whether society, particularly consumers, can bear the cost' (Maclean, 1993, p. 8.1).

Illustrating the importance which the Government places on consumers' rights he warned that consumers were now taking a keen interest in what their charges cover and were asking for increases in their bills to be justified 'in terms of value for money as well as on medical and scientific grounds'. There was no point in pursuing 'scientific perfection' without recognising that the consumer and/or taxpayer did not have a bottomless purse. It was 'essential that all concerned *including the Commission* are fully briefed on the costs of meeting any proposed standards' (ibid., p. 8.2, emphasis added). A second very important theme raised by the minister was the question of the role and use of scientific research and evidence. The Government was concerned that legislation should be based upon good science yet was also concerned that scientific knowledge might also be the drawing force of some kind of regulatory escalator (Richardson, 1994).

The important question of the *level* at which decisions should be made has also been a central feature in the British Government's broad approach. There has been a steady twin-track European lobbying strategy, the second aim of which involves pressure either to 'repatriate' certain policy decisions or to maximise the degree of flexibility allowed to member states in the implementation of European water legislation. The repatriation/flexibility strategy might be seen as a fall-back position in

Britain's Euro-water strategy. If the first option – of successfully influencing the formulation and re-formulation of European water policy – was not delivering the hoped for policy pay-off, then a sensible fall-back position is to press for greater flexibility for member states in implementing whatever European water laws are passed in the future. The central weakness of this strategy is that it has some potentially severe cross-sectoral consequences. While Britain may seek greater national autonomy in water (and other environmental legislation), it is clearly less than happy if the French, for example, seek a similar degree of flexibility in subsidising Air France. Nevertheless, British environmental ministers are left with little option if they wish to reduce or slow down the cost effects of European water legislation. Referring specifically to Article 3.3 of the Treaty on European Union, the minister argued that the new emphasis on subsidiarity was one of the most significant of the recent developments. Essentially, the Community should 'exercise a certain degree of humility in taking a view about what can be better done at the Community rather than the national level' (Maclean, 1993, p. 8.1). For example, the minister had a specific concern about the Public Procurement Directives (including the Utilities Directive) and the use of mandatory European standards for contracts over a prescribed threshold. In a rather revealing passage he argued that:

> the objective of opening up a single market in Europe and EFTA countries is not to achieve a total uniformity in practice and products across all members states … As long as products meet the essential requirements of the Construction Products Directive, *due account must also be taken of different geographic and climatic conditions, ways of life and the technical traditions of each state.* (ibid., p. 8.2, emphasis added)

An increased emphasis on the need for effective European level *monitoring and enforcement* is also apparent in Britain's European water strategy. With considerable justification, the British Government has been pressing for improved monitoring of what is *actually* happening in all of the member states. It believes that part of the explanation of Britain's poor reputation at home in the water sector is due to more effective and open systems of measurement and monitoring of environmental and water quality standards. As the then Chairman of the Water Services Association argued, 'outside the UK there is often relatively little information on the actual implementation of water directives and little to match the level of detailed information available on the thousand or so water catchment zones designated in the UK' (Courtney, 1992, p. 4.2). His views are shared by the British Government which, in its memorandum to the Director General of Water Services (DGWS) published in October 1993, argued that Britain's monitoring and record keeping 'are among the best and most publicly available in Europe' (DOE, 1993, p. 5). Linked to this view has been Britain's pressure for the setting up of the European Environmental Agency, and its pressure for a much more rigorous 'effectiveness auditing' system.

Thus, Britain is unlucky to be painted as the 'dirty man of Europe'. (For example, it seems unlikely that any country that uses surface water to any extent complied with the Surface Water Directive). The Minister for the Environment and the Countryside, David Trippier, pointed out in 1992 that although Britain had by then been taken to the ECJ twice for non-compliance with environmental legislation, the Commission had taken over 100 cases to the ECJ against other member states for similar offences (Trippier, 1992, p. 1.1). While continuing to emphasise that responsibility for enforcing Community legislation should remain with individual members states, he argued that 'the Commission should seek to ensure that every member state has not only legislation in place transposing Community Directives, but also regulatory bodies with the necessary duties, expertise and resources to ensure full compliance' (ibid., p. 1.1). The British Government had, therefore, put forward the concept of an 'audit inspectorate' to operate at Community level on similar lines to the fisheries and veterinary areas.

In the absence of a generally accepted and universally applied monitoring and measurement system, the British government is going to remain trapped on the classic 'indicator problem'. Because data are available, its critics will always be able to point to a 'problem' to be solved (Stringer and Richardson, 1980). If 'the problem' is not measured (or if the measurements are not made public as in some member states) essentially 'it' has been defined away and governments will avoid the obloquy from environmental groups.

Finally, the British Government's ultimate fall-back position is identical to that adopted by all polluting, water supply and waste disposal industries alike – to press for more implementation time, thus spreading the cost (and the incidence of charges) over a longer period of time. For example, the Government has calculated that if the investment required for the Urban Waste Water Directive between 1995 and 2000 were rephased over a ten-year period (that is, that the requirement for 1995 to 2000 was halved) price limits between the later dates might be reduced by about 1.5 per cent on average (DOE, 1993, p. 10).

It might be predicted that the more that Britain can shift the policy debate to these questions (as it is trying to do) the more it is likely to exercise influence over policy re-formulation and policy innovation – especially now, in times of economic difficulties within the EU as a whole. Thus, there may be a degree of policy theory convergence – both in terms of a continuation of a mixed policy instruments approach and in terms of cross-national policy learning (Rose, 1993). In this process, rational technical argument plays a significant role and can 'dampen' cross-national differences in policy style (Richardson, 1982; 1994). Haigh cites a specific example of this process at work. Britain has finally agreed to abandon its complete opposition to uniform emission standards (even for the most dangerous substances) at the North Sea Conference in 1987. This reversal followed a 1986 House of Lords Report which in turn had taken up proposals launched earlier by Haigh himself, as an influential 'policy watcher'. Moreover, Britain has moved to adopt a general system of integrated pollution control with the passage of the Environmental Protection Act 1990 – an approach in advance of OECD recommendations. Thus, Britain is not always the policy resistor (or laggard).

At the EU level, water policy developed quite early, the first major proposals being adopted in 1973–5. The sector is now subject to a wide range of EU directives and regulations covering areas such as: drinking water, waste water, water use, discharge of dangerous substances, controls over industry and products, sewage sludge disposal and public procurement of works and supplies. Exposure or product standards for drinking water were added in 1980. It is, however, in the discussions over EC proposals to limit the discharge of dangerous substances into water that the fundamental differences between the British and continental approaches were most evident. The Commission proposed to limit pollution of the most dangerous substances by emission limit values, whereas the UK sought a policy of quality objectives that would allow varying emission standards. A compromise was reached whereby both limit values and quality objectives were allowed, with member states (in practice only the UK) free to adopt quality objectives provided they could satisfy the Commission through an agreed monitoring procedure that quality objectives were being attained (Haigh, 1992, pp. 4.2–1).

Space does not permit other than a brief summary of some of the more salient legislation and the effect of this legislation in the UK. (However, for an excellent and up-to-date review of the impact of EC water legislation in the UK, and the UK's political response, see Haigh, 1994).

Surface Water for Drinking

The Water Act 1989 provided the opportunity for EC law to be brought formally within UK law. Considerable upgrading of treatment plants has taken place, though Haigh concludes that (as suggested above) it might be a mistake to attribute this to EC law, as many of the improvements would have been programmed anyway. 'The most that can be said is that the Directive has drawn attention to some deficiencies and may have hastened improvements' (Haigh, 1992, pp. 4.3–4).

Drinking Water

Passage of the Drinking Water Directive proved problematic. Britain was particularly concerned about regulations on lead, because of the special problem faced in Britain and the potential difficulty in complying. The compromise that resulted increased the degree of flexibility and extended the period of compliance needed to comply with the various parameters. The UK was the only government to suggest that the nitrate parameter – now more widely recognised as problematic – would present difficulties (ibid., pp. 4.4–4). Although the UK has, under the Water Act 1989, made formal provision for the implementation of the directive, it has still caused problems. In 1992 the ECJ ruled that the UK Government was guilty of breaching EC rules on drinking water quality because nitrate levels in twenty-eight supply zones in England exceeded the permitted levels. This ruling was precipitated by FOE's complaint that the UK Government was failing to fulfil its obligations (*The Financial Times*, 25 November 1992).

Haigh concludes as follows:

The Directive has therefore had a considerable impact on legislation and practice in the UK. It has led to greater public scrutiny of water supplies, for it has
been necessary for water undertakers to apply for derogations and delays and
this has clearly exposed problem areas. The Directive has resulted for the first
time in the setting of detailed statutory quality standards for drinking water,
and ensured that consumer and environmental interests were not overlooked in
the privatization of the UK water industry. In particular, it has ensured that
water supply companies' undertakings to improve the quality of those supplies
of drinking water below EC standards were made more rigorous than they
otherwise might have been. (ibid., pp. 404–10)

The Drinking Water Directive has, undoubtedly presented the water industry in
Britain with a very serious exogenous 'shock' – causing both compliance problems
and forcing the belated introduction of massive investment programmes. It has also
played a disproportionate role in Britain's (possibly unreasonably) bad reputation in
the sector.

Bathing Water

This directive has also proved very problematic for the UK – if not farcical at times.
'Along with the problems over the Drinking Water Directive, the UK's non-compliance with the Bathing Water Directive has been a politically salient issue. In short,
the main conclusion of a long and difficult saga is that the UK has often been in breach
of the Directive and has been subject to a series of Commission actions to force
compliance. The UK's difficulties provided a classic example of the dictum that: He
(or indeed She) who implements decides! Britain decided that in designating bathing
beaches in compliance with the directive, bathing waters with fewer than 500 people
in the water at any one time should not be identified, that any stretch with more than
1,500 people in the water per mile should be identified and that those with between
750 and 1,500 per mile were open to negotiation! Blackpool was assessed at between
750 and 1,500 and by agreement between the water authority (as it then was) and the
district council, was not identified. The total exercise resulted in only twenty-seven
bathing waters being communicated to the Commission in 1979 compared with
8,000 in the rest of the EC, thirty-nine of which were in landlocked Luxembourg
(ibid., pp. 4.5–5). Since then there has been a gradual improvement in Britain's
record – not surprising in view of the very high level of adverse publicity following
the earlier poor results. For example, in July 1993 Britain was praised by the European Commission for tackling pollution at coastal beaches after years of being
dubbed the 'dirty man of Europe' (*Water Bulletin*, 2 July 1993). However, it should
be noted that the 3 per cent improvement on the previous year (raising the success
rate of beaches tested from 76 per cent to 79 per cent) involved only 455 of Britain's
beaches – and still left over 20 per cent failing EC standards. In July 1993 the Court
also ruled that Blackpool beaches were failing to meet EU environmental regulations.
The British Government was not fined, but was ordered to pay costs (*The Financial
Times*, 15 July 1993). However, it is also worth noting that in 1993 the Court took

action against every member state except Denmark over their failure to comply fully with the Bathing Water Directive.

Caution should be used, therefore, in seeing Britain as the *only* member state having difficulties. For example, in August 1993 the Consumers' Association complained that Mediterranean beaches, including one which has been awarded the prestigious Blue Flag, were contaminated with sewage. The association considered that official figures released by the EC could not be trusted and that the reporting procedure was 'farcical' because it relied on data supplied by governments *(Water Bulletin*, 6 August 1994). In its 1994 report the Association reported that although Britain came close to bottom of the most recent Euro-bathing water statistics (beating only Germany) its position was probably better than it looked because not all the league table results were reliable. For example, half the countries – France, Germany, Greece, Italy and the Netherlands – failed to test all of the beaches often enough to make the results valid. Others – Italy and Greece – admitted to EC officials that they ignored the results of tests after rainfall! *(Water Bulletin*, 17 June 1994).

Even so, faced with an Article 169 letter from the Commission, the British Government has had to make very substantial changes to the investment programme (for example, in November 1989 a £1.4 bn long sea outfall programme was announced with a further £1.5 bn programme announced in March 1990).

Urban Waste Water Treatment Directive

The Urban Waste Water Treatment Directive has proved problematic for many EC states. Essentially, the Directive is designed to improve the treatment of domestic sewage, industrial waste water and rainwater run-off, so-called urban or municipal waste water. There are vast differences in degrees of treatment between the member states. Britain's response is interesting in two respects. Yet again the UK is being drawn into line, sooner or later, although with varying degrees of reservation. Also, the EC/EU is not the only source of exogenous pressure on the UK. (Some of the directives discussed above were influenced by the OECD and by the WHO, see Richardson, 1994.) In this case pressure from the North Sea littoral states was also important, alongside the pressure from the EC and from domestic public opinion (Haigh, 1992, pp. 4.6–5). As Haigh argues, these pressures produced a major 'U' turn in UK policy – it agreed to secondary treatment of sewage prior to discharge into the sea, despite its earlier position that the disposal of crude sewage at sea caused no *lasting* environmental damage. The UK also announced the ending of the dumping of sewage sludge at sea, necessitating the future construction of expensive (and possibly environmentally damaging) incineration plants on land (ibid., pp. 4–6).

DOMESTIC CONFLICT AND THE CONTINUED EUROPEANISATION OF THE UK WATER POLICY PROCESS

As Stephen George (1990, p.1) has suggested, Britain has been regarded as an awkward partner since it joined the EC in 1973. This is especially true in the field of water policy, yet it would be quite wrong to see Britain as unique. There is little doubt that some of the problems which Britain has faced in complying with EU law are being replicated elsewhere in the Union. It has also not been alone in pressing for more flexibility and longer lead-times for the implementation of EU policy. Domestic pressure – and the willingness of (domestic) pressure groups and individuals to see the EU as an alternative policy-making area (Mazey and Richardson, 1992) – have undoubtedly reinforced the pressures from the EC and, via 'whistle blowing', have been the cause of specific EU actions against the UK.

The domestic pressures are, however, developing a new degree of complexity. Until fairly recently, such pressure upon the British Government was mainly uni-directional – the media and public perception was of 'good EC, bad British Government'. Two domestic changes are taking place that might lead to a modification of this simple view. First, as would be predicted by interest group theory, countervailing action is emerging from those groups who are disadvantaged by the new policy settlement. For example, the CBI, in its response to OFWAT's paper on meeting the costs of continual environmental improvement in water, has pointed out that the driving force for higher levels of expenditure in the water industry is the standards set in legislation *(CBI News*, October 1993). More generally the CBI has attacked the European Commission's proposals to impose stricter liability on business to pay for pollution damage. Even *bankers* are joining the lobby against this proposal, fearing that they will be liable for pollution costs incurred by their borrowers *(The Financial Times*, 3 September 1993). More hopefully (from the British Government's perspective) the *scientific* debate is becoming more pluralistic. The expert scientific community is clearly not monolithic. For example, in July 1994 a Dutch microbiologist told a House of Lords Select Committee that the methodologies laid down for the proposed updates of the Bathing Water Directive were neither practicable nor did they reflect advances in scientific thinking *(Water Bulletin*, 29 July 1994).

Secondly, as discussed in Chapter 5, OFWAT has emerged as an institutionalised countervailing power to the hitherto powerful lobby of environmentalists and the NRA. OFWAT's broad stance is not inconsistent with the Government's broad Euro-strategy, outlined earlier.

For example, the DGWS, Ian Byatt, has argued that what matters to customers and citizens (not the same), is not the work done (the inputs), but the results achieved (the outputs). 'Such outputs should, moreover, emanate from what the customers want and are ready to pay for – not what the producers – or regulators, *including the European Commission* – say they ought to have' (Byatt, 1993, p. 4.1, emphasis added). Thus, the independent OFWAT National Customer Council (ONCC) condemned the price increases planned by the water companies in their 1993 market plans. The companies claimed that bills would need to rise by approximately 6 per cent above the rate of inflation in each of the five years between 1995 and 2000 to achieve environmental obligations and satisfy customers' views on levels of service. This, the ONCC claimed, could produce annual water bills of £450 in some areas. It therefore, pledged itself to 'put pressure on the Director General of Water Services and the British Government to keep prices down, and on the EC to limit obligations on companies which are drawing up bills faster than customers are willing to pay' (ONCC, 5 July 1993). It specifically urged the Government to renegotiate the timetable for implementation of the Urban Waste Water Treatment Directive 'which is the major factor behind huge increases in bills forecast for the next ten years' (ONCC, 13 July 1993). The problem was quite simple. The cost to Britain of implementing the waste water directive was originally estimated to be £2 bn. At the time, the Government, the industry and OFWAT suggested that it was near £10 bn (subsequently considerably revised downwards), most of which would have to be passed on to consumers.

In contrast, the chairman of the NRA, Lord Crickhowell, has been anxious not to see a reduction in the pressure for improved standards – either from the EU or from the DOE in its capacity as the body responsible for setting national water quality objectives. In particular, Lord Crickhowell has attacked Byatt on numerous occasions for his 'exaggerated' estimates of likely costs. (In fact, OFWAT subsequently reduced its estimates as a result of consultations with NRA and others as suggested in Chapter 5.) In a counter move to avoid the accusation that the NRA had been 'captured' by environmentalists, it commissioned its own survey of water customers ('a ... survey of Mr Byatt's customers' as Crickhowell put it!) which showed high support for quality and environmental issues and, indeed, for EC legislation with 91 per cent of respondents feeling that EC agreements were 'a good thing' (Crickhowell, November 1993). Referring specifically to the possibility of Britain securing an easement of EC environmental obligations he expressed doubts. He pointed out that the Government had stated quite clearly that 'there must always be satisfactory implementation of the requirements of community legislation while they remain in place', and he also reminded his audience 'that while they remain in place the NRA will carry out its duty to monitor and enforce those obligations, using its scientific and professional skills in a realistic but not excessive way ' (ibid.). On the Government's belief (expressed in its paper, *Water Charges – The Quality Framework*) that some modification of the waste water directive was desirable, he remained doubtful 'that Brussels or our European colleagues are much inclined to make substantial changes' (ibid.). However, there are significant signs that the Commission may be adopting a more consensual policy style under the Fifth Action Programme, including trying to assess the charges and advantages of implementing policies (Garvey, 1993, p. 1.3). For example, in February 1994, the Commission announced a call for tenders for a contract to assess the financial and economic costs of a reduction in the current lead standard in the Drinking Water Directive. The 1990 Directive had a modest target for lead and in the 1989 UK drinking water regulations the parameters were stiffened ahead of EU parameters. The new initiative from the EU (responding to new WHO guidelines) could have a major impact in the UK. Potentially, the costs of a lowering of the EU standard for lead from the current 50 Mg/l to the revised WHO guideline of 10 Mg/l would be enormous – probably £8.5 bn for England and Wales according to a WRC estimate in 1992 *(Water Bulletin*, 25 February 1994).

CONCLUSIONS

To what extent does the emergence of a slightly more cautious and cost conscious approach by the Commission represent a major opportunity for Britain? It is applying pressure to the Commission to reconsider and delay the directives on water quality, particularly for a review of sewage treatment, following the EU's agreement to review the Drinking Water Directive and to cost its proposals fully. One of the Government's difficulties is that any retreat by the EU will provoke an environmental backlash both at the UK and EU levels. At the EU level, environmentalists are undoubtedly a more effective lobby than at the UK level (Mazey and Richardson, 1992). Indeed, the British Government has complained that the UK's more vigorous interest groups have precipitated more legal actions than those in other countries (*The Financial Times*, 19 July 1993).

Moreover, as suggested earlier, Britain's EU partners sometimes have very different arrangements for the water sector, especially in terms of its funding. Thus, as Neil Summerton, Head of the Water Directorate at the DOE, recently observed, the old British system (prior to water privatisation) of making decisions in smoke-filled rooms in the Treasury is still the norm in most other parts of Europe. Elsewhere in Europe:

> water charges are a matter of political determination – often by municipalities rather than central governments. Some countries continue to subsidise price from tax revenues in a variety of ways. Others cross-subsidise between consumers in different places rather as we do. In principle, the situation for them, as for us, has however been crucially changed by the existence of the urban waste water treatment directive. That imposes a stiff timetable for improvement and therefore for investment to achieve it. Everywhere this measure is proving more expensive than was assumed when it was negotiated, with some notable price effects. But the different funding system means that there is no need for other governments to admit this yet. (Summerton, 1993)

He has captured perfectly the situation facing Britain and the potential for it to influence its European partners:

> Pace is the main issue. It is already clear that many of our partners are finding the timetable in the (waste water) directive an immense burden which is not surprising as they have poor systems, in some cases poorer than ours. It is clear that some of our partners are going to find the existing timetable impossible financially as well as practically. (ibid.)

Thus, there may be a window of opportunity for Britain to reverse its ill fortune in the field of EU water policy, simply because its partners are also in financial difficulties. This will present opportunities to form *ad hoc* coalitions on specific issues – such as the successful Anglo–French demand to exempt sewage sludge incineration from the Hazardous Waste Incinerator Directive, agreed in July 1993. In the longer run, however, the British Government, if it is to avoid the difficulties of the past, must achieve at least four things. First, it will need to come more into line with the continental style of environmental regulation, as in other policy areas. Secondly, it will need to succeed in its campaign to secure elsewhere in Europe something like the British approach to monitoring and enforcement. Failure to do so will leave Britain exposed to a 'double disbenefit' – weak influence over policy formulation yet a tradition of taking implementation relatively seriously. Thirdly, it will need to secure a means of influencing the EU agenda setting process – particularly the process by which scientific ideas are translated into public policy via the activities of epistemic communities (Richardson, 1994). Fourthly, it will need to address the equally difficult task of ensuring that the Europeanisation of British water policy networks – which is now developing quite rapidly – (Maloney and Richardson, 1994) does not leave the Government isolated from the European policy process. None of these tasks is likely to prove easy. The current (1994) balance sheet shows some gains and some losses in this overall strategy. Clearly, there is a sense in which the British argument about costs and benefits is being won at an intellectual level. Gone are the days when the Commission really could ignore costs. Some (relatively minor) Euro-regulations have even been removed. Moreover, as a senior Commission official has pointed out, the Commission's style and approach to legislation has changed over the last few years reflecting 'a considerable change in attitude in how the Community's policy is to be realised. It provides greater flexibility for member States to take action which is appropriate for a particular situation' (Garvey, 1993, p. 1.2). Nevertheless, for Britain to become a really powerful actor in the formulation of EU water policy will require some difficult adjustments of culture and tradition on the part of the Department of the Environment (DOE) and the industry. Essentially, the British have maintained a 'policy style' (both in terms of content of policies and policy formulation) which is often quite different from 'continental' traditions. As in the field of social policy (Mazey, 1994), it will be difficult for Britain to convince its partners that it is they who are out of step. For Britain to increase its influence over the formulation of European-level water policy will require a fundamental change in its approach to pollution control and environmental management.

Finally, cost pressures – in France, Germany, Italy and elsewhere – are becoming much more apparent, although it would be wrong for Britain to assume a necessary linkage between rising costs to consumers and rising opposition to European legislation. On the debit side, there is still no sign of a major or meta-policy shift at the level of the EU. For example, Ionnis Paleokrassas, the EU Environment Commissioner, has vigorously defended EU environmental legislation (particularly the controversial Urban Waste Water Treatment Directive) against UK criticism, pointing out that the directive was agreed unanimously in 1991 *(Water Bulletin, 23 July 1994)*. Specifically referring to British appeals to reduce strict pesticide limits, the Commissioner warned that the problems to be addressed were very real and that deferring action would mean that 'our difficulties become greater' *(Water Bulletin, 8 October 1993)*. Thus, 'Europeanisation' is certain to continue to present a strong challenge to Britain and it seems safe to predict that a continuation of the erosion of national autonomy will result.

REFERENCES

Achtienribbe, G., Horner, V., Papp, E., Wiederkehr, Z. (1992), 'International comparison of drinking-water prices', Journal of Water SRT – Aqua, vol. 41, no. 6, pp. 360–3.

Byatt, I. (1993), 'Economic Regulation – the Way Ahead', paper presented to *The Financial Times* Conference on 'The European Water Industry', 15 and 16 March.

Courtney, W. (1992), 'Prospects for the UK Water Industry', paper presented to *The Financial Times* Conference on 'The European Water Industry', 10 and 11 March.

Crickhowell, Lord (1993), 'Water Service Quality and Water Bills', paper presented to *The Economist* Conference on Water Policy, 9 November.

Department of the Environment (DOE) (1993), *Water Charges: The Quality Framework* (London: DOE).

Garvey, T. (1993), 'Regulation: Water Pollution – Water Policy in the European Community', paper presented to *The Financial Times* Conference on 'The European Water Industry', 15 and 16 March.

George, S. (1990), *An Awkward Partner: Britain in the European Community* (Oxford: Oxford University Press).

Haigh, N. (1992 and 1994), *Manual of Environmental Policy: the EC and Britain* (London: Longman).

Kassim, H. and Menon, A. (eds) (1995), *The EU and National and Industrial Policy* (London: Routledge).

Langdon, J. (1993), 'The Cost of Drinking Water and the Customer', paper presented to *The Financial Times* Conference on 'The European Water Industry', 15 and 16 March.

Maclean, D. (1993), 'Keynote Address', paper presented to *The Financial Times* Conference on 'The European Water Industry', 15 and 16 March.

Maloney, W. and Richardson, J. (1994), 'Water Policy in England and Wales: Policy communities under pressure', *Environmental Politics*, vol. 3, no. 4 pp. 111–39.

Mazey, S. (1992), 'The Adjustment of the British Administration to the European Challenge', paper presented to Conference on Administrative Modernisation in Western Europe, University of Perugia, Italy, July .

Mazey, S. (19943), 'The Development of EC Equality Policies: Bureaucratic expansion on behalf of women?', paper presented to Conference on National Policy-Making and the EC, Oxford, 14 and 15 January.

Mazey, S. and Richardson, J. (eds), (1993), *Lobbying in the EC* (Oxford: Oxford University Press).

Mazey, S. and Richardson, J. (1992), 'British Pressure Groups and the Challenge of Brussels', *Parliamentary Affairs*, vol. 45, no. 1, pp. 92–127.

OFWAT National Customer Council (ONCC) (1993), 'New National Council Calls on Government to Halt Water Price Rises', *Press Release*, 5 July.

ONCC (1993), 'Water Consumer Body Urges Government to Re-Negotiate Sewage Treatment Directive', *Press Release*, 12 July.

Richardson, J. (ed.) (1982), *Policy Styles in Western Europe* (London: Allen and Unwin).

Richardson, J. (1995), 'Actor-Based Models of National and EU Policy-Making: Policy networks, epistemic communities and advocacy coalitions', in A. Menon and H. Kassim, *The EU and National Industrial Policy* (London: Routledge).

Richardson, J. (1994), 'EU Water Policy-Making: Uncertain agendas, shifting networks and complex coalitions', *Environmental Politics*, vol. 3, no. 4. pp. 140–68.

Richardson, J., Maloney, W. and Rüdig, W. (1992), 'The Dynamics of Policy Change: Lobbying and water privatisation', *Public Administration*, vol. 70, no. 2, pp. 157-75.

Rose, R. (1993), *Lesson-drawing in Public Policy: A Guide to Learning across Time and Space*, (New York: Chatham House).

Royal Commission on Sewage Disposal (1912), Eighth Report, Cmnd 6464.

Stringer, J. and Richardson, J. (1980), 'Managing the Political Agenda: Problem definition and policy-making in Britain', *Parliamentary Affairs*, Winter, pp. 23–39.

Summerton, N. (1993), 'Water: Paying for Quality', paper presented to *The Economist* Conference on Water Policy, 9 November.

Trippier, D. (1992), 'Opening Address', paper presented to *The Financial Times* Conference on 'The European Water Industry', 10 and 11 March.

Water Services Association (WSA) (1991), *Water – Two Years On* (London: WSA).

8

Episodic Policy-making:
Policy Communities under Pressure?

Most areas of public policy in Britain have been subject to very considerable change in the 1980s and 1990s. Policy turbulence has been more common than policy stability (Richardson, 1994a). The causes of these changes can be categorised as follows. First, growing financial and economic pressures have forced policy-makers to re-examine existing policies and existing rules of the game. Secondly, a new ideological climate developed, starting in 1976 but accelerating after the election of Mrs Thatcher's first Conservative Government in 1979. Thirdly, the Europeanisation of both policies and the policy process presented an enormous challenge to British policy-makers. Each of these factors represented a major source of exogenous change to existing policy networks. In the water sector, the outcome of this amalgam of factors (and others) has been a radical change from what existed before. Moreover, few of these changes in water policy can be attributed purely to the behaviour or characteristics of the existing policy network as such. Put simply, much of the policy change had its causes external to the *policy network* as such. The water sector has also been caught up in the resurgence of environmental concern to the high levels first witnessed in the 1970s. This strong interest – what Gregory (1971) had earlier called the 'halo effect' for environmental policy – has been exacerbated by the transfer of the water industry from the public to the private sector, enormously raising the political salience of 'water'.

Consequently, since the early 1970s, water policy in England and Wales has been transformed from an area of extremely low to extremely high political salience. This change has seen the introduction of radical new policy ideas, the involvement of new actors hitherto not involved in either the formation or implementation of water policy, and the creation of new regulatory institutions. Existing policy networks (be they policy communities or issue networks) have been subject to considerable stress, the magnitude of which forces a reconsideration of the analysis of British water policy solely in terms of policy networks.

This major shift in the political context of the sector makes a single characterisation of politics of water policy difficult. One important effect of the increased political

TABLE 8.1: Range of consultation in water regulation

UK government and legislature	UK statutory bodies and other authorities	Water industry	Industry associatons	UK interest groups	UK academics and hidden persuaders	EC institutions
DoE	Association of County Councils	Water Services Association	British Agrochemicals Association	British Trust for Conservation Volunteers	Centre for Env and Medicine	Commission and the EC
MAFF	Commission for the New Towns	Water Companies Association	British Carpet Manufacturers' Association	British Trust for Ornithology	Institute of Biology	European Parliament Econ and Soc. Committee
DTI	Clyde River Purification Board	Inland Waterways Association	British Foundry Association	Council for the Protection of Rural England	University of Dundee	
FCO	Council for Nature Protection	Campagnie Général des Eaux	British Leather	Country Landowners'	Wye College	UK Embassy
Dept of Energy	Countryside Commission		CBI	Farmers Union of Wales	University of East Anglia	
Scottish Office	Inst. of Environmental Health Officers	Federation	Engineering Employers Federation	National Farmers' Union	Royal Agricultural College	
Welsh Office	English Nature	Institution of Water and Environmental Management	Friends of the Earth	Kleinwort Benson		
Royal Commission on Environ. Pollution	Scottish National Heritage		Glaxo Chemicals	Greenpeace	Securities	
MoD					Nat West Securities	
Parliamentary Env Group				Green Alliance	Smith New Court Securities	
Agriculture Select Committee				London Wild Life Trust	Middlesex Polytechnic Centre	
				Geographical Association	Centre for Research into Env Health	
				Women's Environ. Network		
				WWF		
				YHA		
TOTAL 48	76	11	105	147	40	6

salience of water is that participation opportunities have increased and new actors have entered the process, although often as 'sporadic interventionists' (Dowse and Hughes, 1977). For example, surfers played no part in water policy in the 1950s, 1960s and 1970s, yet sporadically 'intrude' into the policy process via high profile media campaigns highlighting the dumping of raw sewage into the seas in which they surf. Less dramatic interventions are secured by long-established groups which were previously 'confined' to their own sectors – such as the poor, homeless and disabled. Many of these have begun to impinge on the policy process in some way, often assisted by one of the new regulators. It appears that the hitherto well-defined boundaries of the sector have begun to erode, questioning previous notions about the sectorisation and segmentation of policy-making in Britain. Participation within the sector is now more complex and less predictable and water policy is characterised by numerous cross-sectoral linkages. The number of policy actors who might participate in some aspect of water policy is now potentially in the hundreds rather than the tens. For example, the scope of organisations consulted when the DOE was conducting its exercise as part of the Government's deregulation programme in 1993 was extremely broad – ranging from the WSA to the Metal Finishing Association (See Appendix 8.1). Even this list did not include many organisations who have specialised interests in water policy – such as the Industrial Water Society, the Filtration Society, numerous research establishments, and dozens, if not hundreds of sectoral trade associations. The CPRE was (accidentally) 'excluded' from the original list. (The eventual response rate was approximately 50 per cent, although some fifty additional organisations wrote in, once they gained knowledge of the consultation document.) Indeed, on one occasion the DOE received over 800 responses to one of its consultation documents on water. The practicalities of these kinds of exercises, where the potential population of 'interests' is huge, demand a more 'customised' approach to consultation. As one regulatory official told us, referring to the agency's consultation lists:

> they are certainly not definitive, and we try to tailor each consultation, so that any one consultation list will be made up of selections from these lists, and the addition, if necessary, of some other organisations. The lists are of course continually being updated, thus I know what I am sending you is inevitably going to be already out of date. (Private communication, 29 July 1994)

The classification was itself illuminating as the consultation list was divided into seven sub-categories – (i) UK Government and legislature; (ii) UK statutory bodies and other authorities; (iii) the water industry; (iv) industry associations and industry; (v) UK interest groups; (vi) UK academics and other hidden persuaders (vii) European Community institutions. In total, several hundred organisation were involved – far too numerous to list here. For example, the 'industry associations and industry' category included 105 organisations representing industries which were either consumers or polluters of water (or both). The UK interest groups category was even larger and more diverse, and included 147 organisations. The range of organisation in each category is indicated in Table 8.1.

CHANGING THE CORE ACTORS IN THE WATER POLICY PROCESS:
WINNERS, LOSERS AND EXOGENOUS CHANGE

As has been seen, technocrats in Britain have been some of the most successful interest groups. Their insider status has allowed them privileged access to the Government through their membership of tightly drawn policy communities, which has enabled them to develop and maintain their influential position in many policy sectors. Indeed, as Dunleavy has argued, they constitute a professional community which is 'likely to have major and direct implications for the substantive content of public policies' (Dunleavy, 1981, p. 8). By defining issues as technical and apolitical, political salience is reduced – and the cosy *milieu* of decision-making within closed policy-making arrangements remains stable and unthreatened. Policy-making is endogenous to the 'community' or 'network'. Professional power was also enhanced by the relatively strong sectorisation characteristic of most policy-making in Britain in the 1970s and 1980s (Richardson and Jordan, 1979). If a sector became relatively self-governing it could insulate itself from other potentially relevant policy areas and action, and this could facilitate the development of a stable 'exchange relationship' between fellow policy-making professionals. These processes were all operating in the water sector prior to the 1974 reorganisation in England and Wales and prior to the changes now (1995) taking place in Scotland. Thus, water policy had been tucked away from public debate and was largely the result of 'intramural' policy-making by water professionals. It seemed to conform, rather closely, to the 'policy community' model first developed in Britain by Richardson and Jordan in the late 1970s – just as Mrs Thatcher came to power and the British policy process began to change.

The beginnings of the long reform process in water did not necessarily challenge this professional power. During the 1973–4 reorganisation, the continuation of engineering dominance was ensured by the application of two recruiting principles, 'passing on the torch' and 'ring fence' (Parker and Penning-Rowsell, 1980, p. 48). Indeed, the Water Act 1973 which created the new regional water authorites (RWAS) and began the demise of local authority involvement, was largely shaped by the inputs of the professions (Jordan et al. 1977). Moreover, the Ogden and Paterson Reports (on management structures in England and Wales, and Scotland), reinforced the calls for a technically and managerially efficient industry through their advocacy of corporate management principles. In the early period of reform, institutional change reinforced rather than challenged professional power. The managers of the water industry in Britain perceived themselves to be politically neutral, and were 'wedded to an ideology grounded in positivism ... which stresses "facts" over political "prejudices" and expertise over personal values' (Saunders, 1983, p. 34). In holding these views, they merely reflected broadly based public sector values at that time. It was, therefore, accurate to characterise the water policy process as a relatively closed policy-making arrangement, akin to a professionalised network or a policy community. Network characteristics appeared to be important variables in the policy change process. The 1973 Act had a technical imperative at its roots – the integration of water supply and sewage disposal functions to meet anticipated water supply difficulties, using the integrated river basin concept as its policy *rationale*. The major policy change in setting up the RWAs is, however, more an example of endogenous rather than exogenous change. Indeed, Richardson and Jordan argued that it was a good example of policy community politics in that change occurred only when an internal consensus emerged among water professionals about its necessity, and about what shape change should take (Richardson and Jordan, 1979).

However, the stable, private and professionalised world began to change in 1974 with the implementation of the Water Act 1973. The fact that the engineering profession's dominance began to be challenged is rather ironic given that the changes introduced in 1974 were largely technically driven. As is discussed below, it was exogenous developments which eventually had the greatest impact on their position – namely the changing (and worsening) financial environment in the economy as a whole.

Moreover, a closer examination of the effects of the 1973 act – certainly a meta-policy change in terms of the sector as whole – challenges the notion that policy communities prevent radical policy change, or indeed, that they are always characterised by consensus. Thus local authority interests, though clearly members of the existing policy community, were major losers in the reform process, partly because they were preoccupied with what they saw as *the* major challenge to their position – the reorganisation of local government. In practice, as seen, the 1973 Act created a RWA membership dichotomised along two lines of legitimation, each rooted in competing ideologies – *technical* and *electoral*. Within this arrangement, the domination by professionals, whose legitimacy derived from their technical competencies, sat somewhat incongruously with local authority nominees whose legitimacy derived from popular election. Fashions and ideologies were changing – 'managerialism and efficiency' were 'in' and traditional notions of accountability, representation and democracy were 'out'. This broad shift had consequences for the structure of power within existing policy communities in that it affected the legitimacy and status of members of the community. In the end, local authorities were there because of (by then) outdated notions of legitimacy. Moreover, the state, in the shape of the Conservative Government, was keen to exercise *its* authority over who was 'inside' and who was 'outside' the policy sector, provided other key actors in the sector were enthusiastic. Being able to mobilise legislative majorities, the state, therefore, had some rather special powers over other actors.

Water professionals, in contrast, still retained their legitimacy, albeit not for much longer. Hence the only real losers in 1973–4 were the local authorities. They had been moved from running the water industry, to playing an ineffectual role in the new institutional structure. In terms of network analysis, a member of the core policy community had been pushed to the periphery (and, as was described in Chapter 2, was eventually excluded altogether under the Water Act 1983). As original key members of the 'network', they neither agreed to this change in status and position, nor were they able to stop it. Like turkeys facing Christmas, it happened whether they liked it or not! Neither was this a simple case of an impositional policy style by *government*, as the original reform proposals were more or less generated from within the industry. Essentially, the water professionals seized an opportunity for change and were able to mobilise the necessary governmental backing to push the reforms through against a rather ineffective (and heavily distracted) local authority resistance. By 1983, the Government was able to deal decisively with the issue of democratic accountability by removing any pretence of a democratic basis. In so far as changes in policy networks were taking place, they were designed to restrict participation still further. The policy process was becoming more closed rather than more open. The policy community was still very much in place, but one of its members had been shown the door. 'Business as usual' was still, apparently, the private management of public business. The 1983 Act was designed to let the water authorities get on with policy implementation. In practice, government became increasingly concerned with financing and also it under-estimated exactly how much policy had been transferred to Brussels.

In fact, subtle but important changes were taking place and the Water Act 1983 also impacted on the shape of policy networks in other ways. For example, the abolition of the National Water Council led RWAS to liaise directly with the Department of the Environment (DOE). Consultation and negotiation occurred directly between DOE officials, chairmen of the RWAS and ministers. In practice, much of the interaction concerned ceilings for RWA borrowing and the setting of RWA water charges. Once agreement was reached over the total financial package, the RWAS had the power to distribute the resources as they wished. The relationship can be described as one where the RWAS determined their own objectives within the strict financial frame-work laid down by the Government. Saunders summarised the relationship as follows:

> the RWAS make policy while the government controls the purse strings, and while this certainly does not indicate autonomy, nor does it suggest subordi-nation. Important policy decisions are taken at the regional level by the chairmen and his senior officers, and it is for this reason that private sector groups with an interest in water find it more than worthwhile to try to cultivate relations with them. (Saunders, 1984, p. 9)

The implication here is of some kind of 'layered system of policy communities' with wider participation only at the regional level and only for certain types of issue. As was suggested in Chapter 2, the 'relative autonomy' view has been subsequently confirmed to us by the chairman of one of the (subsequently) privatised RWAS, Sir Gordon Jones of Yorkshire Water Plc. He said that Government interference was low and that the authorities were 'left on a fairly loose rein subject to severe financial constraints'. The caveat 'subject to severe financial constraints' is a significant one. It again suggests, as Smith has argued, that state autonomy can be as important as network characteristics in determining policy (Smith, 1993). Thus, the beginnings of a second major change to affect water networks is evident – which *eventually* caused seismic shifts in the sector as a whole. As elsewhere in the public sector at this time, financing began to come to the fore as an issue of concern. Public sector finances were increasingly under pressure after 1976 under the Labour Government, a trend which accelerated rapidly after the election of the Conservatives in 1979. The increasing governmental preoccupation with financing may have contributed to a decline in the Government's own expertise in the sector, as one of the effects of a general trend to reduce the size of the central bureaucracy. Thus, two possibly conflicting trends emerged. First, the increasing pressure from government regarding the financing of the industry, that is a rather more *dirigiste* style – suggesting at least elements of a state autonomy model and, secondly, a decline in government's interest in and capacity to 'interfere' in the details of the sector, so long as the financing was kept under control – suggesting an intensification of the 'private management of public business' model.

At the same time, the organisational culture of the RWAs was changing – at least at the senior management levels. The organisational culture and ethos of the industry changed markedly after 1983 as most of the RWAs began to think of themselves as 'businesses'. These broad cultural changes (described more fully in Chapter 6) were as much exogenous as they were endogenous. Members of the water policy sector were as affected by these new cultural forces as were actors in other sectors – such as universities and the health service. The water sector had to respond in its own way, but it was a common enough task in the 1980s (Richardson, 1994a). In the case of water, (and in others such as British Telecom and British Steel) some interests were able to exploit and benefit from these value changes – although exploiting the new values often needed a new type of professional, not necessarily the engineer or local government accountant.

The trend towards a more business orientated approach – and the emergence of new types of professional to 'ramp up' organisations in this way – still left the uncomfortable question of accountability. This was not quite as easy to dispose of as had been the local authority interests in 1983. The important political symbol of 'accountability', therefore, did not end with the disenfranchisement of directly elected local representatives. The consumer consultative councils, established in each RWA, and the regional recreation conservation committees (RRCCs) had the potential to involve quite a wide range of groups as some kind of 'stakeholders' in the policy sector. However, as suggested, these bodies were rather symbolic. 'Core insiders' (Maloney et al., 1994) continued to exercise influence, and power, through the traditional routes – informal and regular contact with the regional headquarters of the water authorities and directly with the Government – rather than through the official consultative structures.

The operation of a privileged or weighted access system was also a consequence of existing behavioural norms. It was not possible to consult every conceivable interest. In any case, *intensity* of interest is always an important factor in influencing participation, especially as the focus of policy change moves towards the implementation phase. Here the old notion of 'core' groups is useful. In most policy areas there is usually a core of actors whose interests are vitally affected by a particular policy or by the actual ways in which a chosen policy instrument is to be implemented.

These actors are likely to devote more time and resources to participation, are more likely to see continuous participation as cost effective, having more knowledge as a result, and arguably having more to win or lose.

Yet, their very preoccupation with detailed implementation can blind them to exogenous factors which may have very considerable importance. Between 1974 and 1983 reforms were being implemented by these 'core actors', while contextual and exogenous changes regarding managerial styles and financial constraints were beginning to have a more profound effect on the distribution of power within existing networks – the balance between the professions was beginning to change. Almost without the 'old' water professionals realising it, a new agenda was being set and new values were being introduced. These long-term changes culminated in the arrival and processing of the privatisation issue. It was this event which proved to be an enormous shock to existing policy networks. Thus, although water privatisation itself had its specific origins within one very small part of the water policy community, its eventual form presented an enormous shock and challenge to the existing policy process. Eventually, it changed the whole structure of the policy network itself – producing, as was suggested in Chapter 6, some kind of 'cultural train wreck'.

As suggested in Chapter 2, the pre-privatisation history of the industry had seen a process of major institutional restructuring, particularly the rationalisation of the publicly owned industry, into ten regional water authorities. The period up to privatisation was, perhaps, a period of 'coping' but at the expense of meeting discharge standards and suppressing the voice of those concerned with river management. The industry had also begun to develop a more 'managerial' culture in common with other public sector organisations at the time. Thus, in one sense, the eventual decision to privatise may not have been quite as radical as it initially appears, in that both structurally and attitudinally, the industry had changed in a direction which at least facilitated, if not provoked, privatisation. As is often the case in the reform process, a 'spark' is needed to provoke change and to mobilise 'change champions' within the sector. In the case of water, it was a specific event derived from the broad contextual changes in the industry's financing. (See Chapters 3 and 4 for a full discussion of the privatisation process.) This 'spark' lead the Conservatives to execute a complete 'U' turn on water policy, over a period of two years, suggesting that the Government, too, was not in complete control of events, or of the long reform process.

POLITICAL SALIENCE AND THE INFLUENCE OF POLICY NETWORKS ON POLICY: FROM BACKWATER TO GOLDFISH BOWL?

Certainly, the reality of the politics of water since privatisation is quite different from the pre-privatisation situation. There is now much greater conflict within the sector than was ever the case under public ownership, the range of organisations involved is undoubtedly greater, the power to decide the main lines of policy is increasingly in Brussels rather than in Whitehall or Westminster and the policy network as a whole is more open and vulnerable to external influences than at any time in its previous history. Moreover, the 'state' has not gone away, either. In broad terms, the shift has been from a sector in which a fairly coherent network linking recognisable policy communities could be identified, to a sector where its boundaries are indistinct, the agenda setting process is unpredictable and decisions emerge from a rather loose extended issue network of actors constrained by the complex national regulatory structures and subject to considerable extra-territorial influences. This produces a very different kind of politics.

Why has this rather unstable and unpredictable situation arisen? Several answers seem plausible. Privatisation itself has had unintended and profound consequences for all existing actors. As an example of policy change it was a leap in the dark for all concerned. Though clearly facilitated by the succession of changes which had taken place within the industry since the mid 1940s, it was a break with the past and, naturally, brought with it lots of uncertainties. One obvious change was that privatisation was controversial and brought the industry more fully into the political spotlight – raising water consumers' expectations. When sewage disposal and water supply were a local government service paid out of general or local taxes (property rates) then a particular set of public perceptions and attitudes followed: legitimacy was high and expectations were relatively low. Providing the service via profit maximising private companies produces a rather different set of perceptions and expectations which manifest themselves in at least four ways: (i) general consumer bodies such as the National Consumers' Council have begun to articulate consumer interest in water policy; (ii) the industry's own consumer bodies see themselves in a different and more pro-active light; (iii) individual consumers appear to be more demanding in their relations with the companies, and (iv) as a consequence of the above, all actors appear to be more conscious of the consumer interest and of its potential to cause 'trouble'. The last point is of special significance in the changing nature of policy networks. In a very real sense consumers now 'participate' in a way which never used to be the case. They occupy what Dudley terms an 'empty seat' during policy discussions (Dudley, 1994) and their potential political reactions have to be anticipated. The recent events in Scotland are a case in point. Following the publication, in November 1992, of the Scottish Office's consultation paper – *Water and Sewerage Services in Scotland: investing for our future* – the Government received some 4,069 responses from individuals! This exceeded the number of responses to its consultation on the reform of local government (3,317) and indeed, to the original privatisation proposals in England and Wales. Even the Scottish Conservatives opposed privatisation.

A second new factor is that environmental interests have continued to play a significant role in influencing the policy agenda at the national level and, especially, at the European level. To some degree, they are directly involved as participants in the consultative process and, increasingly, in the legal process. For example, Friends of the Earth (FOE) has begun reporting breaches of the Drinking Water Directives to the European Commission and has challenged the UK interpretation of values for such parameters as nitrates. The main resource of such groups is, of course, publicity and their position as some sort of 'surrogate' public opinion. However, resorting to

legal processes is a relatively new strategy for British interest groups and is similar
to that adopted in the USA. Thus, the constant pressure from the environmentalists is
very much a key feature of the sector in the 1990s. These groups are also becoming
more technically orientated and are seeking to challenge water professionals on equal
terms. For example, Greenpeace's activity prompted the Department of the Environment (DOE) to commission studies of organic pollutants in water which showed
that, in the Mersey estuary and Liverpool bay, many chemicals exceeded values
recommended by WHO (Ends, September 1991, p. 21). Groups such as Friends of the
Earth (FOE), Greenpeace, the Council for the Protection of Rural England (CPRE), the
Royal Society for the Protection of Birds (RSPB) and the Royal Society for Nature
Conservation (RSNC) which manage to play a significant role in the agenda setting
process, are now regularly included in the consultation process, and can, at least, be
termed 'peripheral insider groups' (Maloney, et al., 1994).

Environmentalists also 'participate' indirectly by presenting a constant threat to
those water policy-makers who may be said still to constitute the 'core' policy
community. Environmentalists are 'present' in most deliberations and can, to a
considerable degree, invoke the law of anticipated reactions. Simply by being 'out
there' they exercise influence on those who participate intensely (and full time) in
the water policy (and regulatory) process(es). Thus, an important qualification to the
utility of network analysis is that focusing on actual, regular and observable participation can mislead the observer into neglecting some broad contextual factors.
Today, water policy is made in the context of high political salience, including influences from the Labour Party, anxious to exploit any post-privatisation implementation problems. Making policy in a goldfish bowl is a more accurate analogy than the
old description of water policy as the private management of public business. The
irony is that a privatised industry which was literally intended to be the private
management of what used to be public business, is now much more 'public' than
under public ownership.

A third reason for a more open and less predictable style of policy-making and
implementation is the existence of the new regulatory structure, discussed in Chapter
5. This complex and more open regulatory structure for England and Wales has been
of enormous significance. Almost literally, the 'politics of water' became regulatory
politics after privatisation. Moreover, the central feature of this new regulatory politics has been the tendency for regulatory conflict to cause water issues to expand
rather than for the resort to regulatory politics to cause a narowing of issues. It has
facilitated the opening-up of the sector to an extremely wide-ranging debate, and has
exposed to public scrutiny quite genuine (and perfectly natural and unavoidable)
conflicting goals of national policy. Yet, again, contrasting images of reality are
possible. On the one hand there was an emergence of an almost unique degree of
conflict *between* regulators in the sector, with an associated interest group politics.
On the other hand, the traditional British regulatory style of bargaining and consensus
is also present, as the key stakeholders in the implementation process recognise that
successful implementation demands co-operation. Without it, issue salience would

increase still further, reducing everyone's power. Conflict and disconsensus amongst the rival 'regulatory communities' there may be, but there is also a logic of collective action, with all sorts of incentives for playing co-operative games.

A fourth factor leading to significant changes in the politics of water is the diminished role of the sponsoring department – the Department of the Environment. This is not to suggest that the department is an unimportant actor. However, quite clearly, it has lost a significant amount of its former leverage – both to the two independent regulators as well as to the European Commission and to fellow members states. The water sector is perhaps the best (or worst depending on one's views on Europe) example of the erosion of national autonomy. Whatever role the DOE (and to some degree the Scottish Office) retains as a partner in the *European* policy process, power has undoubtedly shifted to Brussels. *All* national actors have been weakened and the Government is no exception. To some degree, of course, this collective weakening also leads to greater incentives for collective national action in that both the Government and non-governmental actors have much to gain by trying to develop a common European strategy. In that sense, the European threat may help to bind some members of the policy network together. However, there are counter-trends, as individual members of the network develop cross-national links which may be at odds with national loyalties. Even though this study illustrates aspects of state power, the Government has lost some of its ability to steer and control the sector and may have become a weaker player.

The cumulative effect of these changes has been to create new opportunities for a more extended form of participation in the water policy process. For example, the Department of Social Security is beginning to exhibit some limited participation because of the welfare implications of rising water charges needed to pay for environmental improvements. Also, the Treasury may be re-entering the sector because of its general concern with the costs of regulation – particularly of European regulation. For example, in November 1993 the Chancellor of the Exchequer, Kenneth Clarke, called for a delay in the implementation of the Urban Waste Water Treatment Directive on the grounds that the costs of compliance within the current time limits had risen substantially and were 'unacceptable' (*The Financial Times*, 23 November 1993).

In terms of extra-Whitehall politics, those groups representing the poor, the disadvantaged and the disabled, have begun to claim some rather limited *stakeholder status* in the sector just as the environmentalists achieved stakeholder status some time ago. Similarly, City investors now have a very real stake in the industry and certainly secure the attention of the industry's managers.

It would be stretching the English language to use the term 'network' to describe this disparate group of actors and potential actors. The linkages between them are weak or non-existent and there may on occasion even be a lack of mutual awareness. In practice, no one in the water sector has a *definitive* consultation list – not even the DOE. Each division of the DOE (and of the NRA and OFWAT) has rather separate consultation lists reflecting that division's sub-sectoral special interests. It is at this detailed technical level that notions of policy community may still seem more applicable as a description of the actor population.

The temptation to exclude the esoteric and part-time participants and to concentrate on full-time 'core' participants is risky, especially in terms of agenda setting – and hence in terms of the exercise of power and the origins of policy change. This may be especially true for scientific research organisations whose findings can be translated into public issues at some stage particularly via the 'megaphone effect' of environmental groups (see Richardson, 1994b). For example, as one practitioner has commented in relation to oestrogen substances in water, 'the recent television programmes on oestrogen substances have made public questions being raised by research workers. Whether this will become a real water quality issue or not will depend on the outcome of further research' (Fawell, 1994, p. 2). Because of the high political salience of water, and the new openness of the sector, what may have remained esoteric in the 1960s is less likely to remain so in the 1990s. As a member of OFWAT has commented:

> People are very concerned by health issues and public opinion is hardening against environmental pollution, both atmospheric and water. There are arguments to the effect that on some issues public concern is exaggerated, but public opinion is understandably risk averse, and the burden of proof must always be on those who claim that a particular level of pollution is safe. (Howarth, 1994)

The central difficulty for any researcher is to distinguish between, on the one hand, rather loose participation in consultation which is so general as to be 'sham' and, on the other, effective influence over either agenda setting or the details of policy-making. At what stage does the action move from open consultation to a smoke-filled room with only the few that 'matter' present? As Jordan noted in his study of the reform of the engineering profession, large numbers of consultees can mask the fact that the crucial decision can eventually be made by a handful of key players (Jordan, 1993). Here, the level of analysis is of paramount importance. What level of decisions are being discussed? Much of the 'stuff' of politics is the politics of detail – indeed, it is the preoccupation of most interest groups, particularly of the professions. Thus, at the level of technical detail, it may be possible to continue to characterise water policy in England and Wales, and Scotland, in terms of traditional policy communities. At this level, much of the actor behaviour relates to detailed implementation. Thus, a typical example is the one-day symposium on 'Odour Control and Prevention in the Water Industry' organised by the Institute of Water and Environmental Management in 1994. All of the speakers were water professionals from the industry and its associated consultancy sector. None of the issues was likely to attract media, public or parliamentary attention, and the nature of the symposium was typically esoteric. These gatherings probably group together the relevant policy community for these technical, but sub-sectoral, issues. Even so, they are also held against a backdrop of potential public concern and have the potential to mobilise a broader network of actors.

The notion that quite small issues have a big issue potential is an important one. Policy-makers in water can never be sure which problems can be expanded into public issues or what groups and organisations will be drawn into the policy process as a result. In one case, for example, the Watercress Association became particularly active in response to certain proposals. Yet, on any reputational study of water policy-making over the past twenty years it would not merit a mention! For many groups, 'the devil is in the detail'. Even minor changes in the regulatory environment or in the details of implementation can provoke significant – if sporadic – levels of participation from a potentially vast array of actors. Again, this suggests some caution in claiming that there is something out there called the 'water policy network'.

IMPLEMENTING PRIVATISATION: A STABLE 'EPISODE' OR A POLICY MESS?

Certain key issues have arisen in the post-privatisation era, particularly related to the regulatory game. These have led to a considerable degree of policy (and policy network) instability. The most central issue is the cost and pace of investment required to bring the system up to European and national standards. Related to this are the mechanisms for distributing the costs of that process and the incidence of those costs. And, of course, (as was suggested in Chapter 5) a more fundamental issue is the question of environmental risk and the costs of meeting that risk. How far does one go in eliminating potential (sometimes purely hypothetical) risks? To return to the concept of a water policy community or 'core' group of actors who have to deal with these central problems on a day-to-day basis in England and Wales, the following would be included on anyone's list.

1. The 'sponsoring' department – the Department of the Environment.
2. The Office of Water Services – OFWAT.
3. The National Rivers Authority – NRA.
4. The Water Services Association – WSA.

In addition, some observers would say that any in a 'reputational' survey would also include the DTI and the CBI which, though they may not participate on such a regular basis as the so-called 'quadripartite group', are forces to be reckoned with. In order to capture the essence of the 'new politics of water', it is useful to review the central position of these four key actors. First, the lead department, the DOE. In a real sense, the DOE was potentially the biggest loser under the new arrangements – because the public sector of which it had been formally in charge, is now a private industry controlled by independent (and so far, uncaptured) regulatory agencies. Indeed, one could say that a central intention of privatisation was deliberately to distance the department from policy-making. In a sense, water was potentially an example of the withdrawal of the state from a well-established policy community. In practice, this retreat has been limited, for two reasons. The state is very much part of the EU policy process. Britain is currently one of the most active of the national governments within the EU in trying both to amend existing EU legislation on water and to slow down the reform process. It is also necessary for the state to move back into the policy area (in addition to the natural tendencies of bureaucracies to want to expand their policy space) because of the public interest in the sector and because OFWAT has specifically requested the Government's involvement. Thus, the senior civil servant in change of water policy at the DOE has remarked that 'the economic regulator of the water industry has been anxious to have the help of Ministers in clarifying an important aspect of the framework within which he and the water industry has to operate' (Summerton, 1993).

In its 1993 paper *Water Charges: the quality framework*, the Government stated its position. The basic thrust was a continued commitment to improved standards, and therefore increased investment, but a caution in pushing the pace of reform too far or too fast, with plenty of references to the need to take costs into account, where this was legally possible. Crucially, however, the Europeanisation issue was identified as the key variable and illustrates the inherent weakness of the DOE. For costs to be contained 'to levels which people and Ministers would consider tolerable', action to change or rephase European legislation was necessary. Adopting a cautious approach to the prospects of achieving this, Summerton, Head of the Water Directorate at the DOE, warned that the task should not be under-estimated 'particularly in view of the constitutional changes which result from the introduction of the Maastricht changes'. In other words, this was a clear message that Her Majesty's Government might have great difficulties as a member of that other policy community – the Council of Ministers.

OFWAT has gradually emerged – ahead of the Government in some ways – as the champion of the 'restrain costs' argument. Thus, in a series of papers and statements, OFWAT has been raising the stakes in the debate over environmental and quality improvements versus costs to consumers. In a now much quoted passage, the Director of OFWAT, Ian Byatt, has argued that there is a general concern about price increases for water consumers, especially for customers on lower incomes. Thus:

> There is a world of difference between a necessary, once for all, adjustment in the price of something and an unending escalation in prices. The first will inevitably be accompanied by some protests, but, when complete, will often be accepted. The second would be intolerable. The escalator has, at some stage, to be stopped. Unless this is tackled through the current regulatory arrangements, public dissatisfaction will grow, putting pressures on government for change … The escalator started with the combination of privatisation and the decision rapidly to meet new objectives for the quality of drinking water and waste water. It is now in danger of being driven ever upwards by new obligations added to existing obligations with little regard for costs or either willingness or ability to pay. (Byatt, 1993)

As suggested, this increasingly robust line on the cost effects of the escalator has brought OFWAT into open conflict with the NRA. The environmental case has been put equally robustly by the NRA's Chairman, Lord Crickhowell, who said that he makes 'no apologies for the vigorous way that I have sometimes openly disagreed with Mr Byatt. He for, his part, has provoked controversy and has been right to do so' (Crickhowell, 1993a). These disputes between Byatt and Lord Crickhowell provided an important insight into the strengths and limitations of the policy community /network approach. Thus, the conflict between two of the key participants was bitter and public – no consensus, no agreement on values, no agreement on quantitative measures even – yet the key players ended up working closely together in order to reach an agreed cost analysis. Amid conflict, there was a recognition that there were still mutual advantages in co-operating via private discussions. But this was not as simple as the private management of public business. To say that, in the end, key actors get together in private in order to settle issues is important – but not earth shattering!

The industry, represented by the Water Services Association (WSA) and the Water Companies' Assocation was, of course, in the middle of this controversy. In one scenario, the pressure for higher standards should be no worry to the industry, indeed it is to the advantage of an industry which cannot really expand its market significantly. Basically, higher standards raise the value of the product. This is true, however, only if the industry secures a comfortable cost-pass-through agreement from OFWAT in order for industry to meet its statutory obligations – the so-called RPI + K factor. The potential for a cosy regulator/industry relationship is obvious. In practice, it has not materialised. Indeed, open conflict between OFWAT and the industry is sometimes apparent. Thus, the classic regulatory issue – to secure efficiency gains from a monopoly supplier – has proved so controversial that members of what one might expect to be a model policy community have been swapping arguments in the national press. The politics of the sector has 'escaped' into the public domain, indicating that the core actors have been unable to re-establish an effective policy community for the bigger issues.

The moves by the Conservative Government to reform the Scottish system in 1993–4 have, of course, produced exactly the same result. The sheer threat of privatisation, as was suggested above, transformed what was probably *the* most boring policy area in Scotland into a major political controversy – arguably more controversial than the poll tax in Scotland. (Surely no government in modern times can have been quite so adept at making trouble for itself – ignoring Denis Healey's message that when one is in a hole one should stop digging!)

THE POLICY CHANGE PROCESS: ORDERLY PLANNING OR JUST 'PLAIN DUMB LUCK'?

How, then, can the politics of water be best characterised? Inevitably, multiple images are needed. As has been demonstrated, the story has been one of the destabilisation of an existing and stable policy community based upon the role and power of professions. Once this policy community had been opened up, the system has passed through various episodic stages, as outlined in this case-study. At times, policy communities have been important and at times the process has been more characteristic of open issue networks on the Heclo model. At other times, neither model has been appropriate – for example during the period of 'internalised' policy-making by Ridley. At yet other times – recently in Scotland, for example the situation is best described as simply a policy mess.

Moreover, conflict rather than consensus has often been a feature of the policy process – and continues to be so in England and Wales, and in Scotland. This is in part due to institutional factors, particularly the regulatory structure, but also because new actors have become involved in the sector on a more or less permanent basis. Thus, a wider set of interest has to be 'accommodated'. And, of course, the Euro-peanisation of the sector has been enormously important, with a major shift in the locus of power from London and Edinburgh to Brussels. Policy-making at this new level draws in a very large number of actors and has seen the formation of a variety of complex and shifting 'advocacy coalitions' in which British interests are but one factor (Richardson, 1995). Thus, earlier characterisations of the water policy process (Jordan et al., 1977) need to be recast in order to take account of its *episodic* nature. There is much more to the analysis of British water policy than simply an analysis of policy network behaviour. Indeed, to some extent, existing policy networks have been the *product* of policy change rather than its *creator*. In effect, the politics of water policy has shifted from *the private management of public business* to the *public management of private business*.

This raises the central question of the origins of policy change. This study has, of course, shown that there is not a simple answer. Clearly, policy change can and does occur. But its origins are exceedingly complex and varied. This study began with a brief discussion of the policy problem – the need to address possible water shortages. It was suggested that there was a 'logical' (in a scientific and technical sense) solution available to policy-makers – namely integrated river basin management, IRBM. The ultimate *origin* of change was, therefore, within the natural environment – rain-fall, topography, hydrology – combined with the effects of industrialisation, urbani-sation and economic growth. Change did not occur because there was a water policy community or network – that community or network had to decide exactly how change would be implemented. This process was, of course, a political process and the fact that there was a community of actors in existence was an important feature of the processing of the problem. Yet other forces were at work – for example, finan-cial pressures from outside the sector, new policy ideas such as privatisation and the shifting balance of power between professions caused by broader shifts in values. All of these forced the existing policy communities and networks into a *reactive* model – hence the suggestion that the policy communities were as much a victim of policy change as they were its creator. In total, exogenous shocks were, over time, probably more important as a source of policy change than were policy network characteris-tics. Policy outcomes emerged from a process of mediation between the sector and its external world – and policy communities and networks were obviously important in this process. However, these communities and networks do not explain policy change. Neither can change be explained by resort to notions of state power. The state has at times been a strong and, at times, a very weak actor in the sector. Thus, some new model is needed which can take account of the role of ideas and knowledge, the role of events, and the ways that policy actors mediate the interaction of these factors.

The evidence from this study suggests that an approach similar to John Kingdon's pioneering work might best capture the complexities and uncertainties of the policy process. Thus, Kingdon argued that something is known about how issues get decided, but much less is known about how they got to be issues in the first place (Kingdon, 1984, p. vii). He posed a series of questions, following from this observation: How do subjects come to officials' attention? How are the alternatives from which they choose generated? How is the government agenda set? Why does an idea's time come when it does? (ibid., p. vii). It is hoped that this empirical study of the development of water policy in Britain over the past fifty years has in part answered some of those questions. As his own analysis suggested, describing the players in the game is insufficient – it is necessary to know more about the game itself. The concern, here, has been with that 'game' as well as with identifying the players. In this analysis of the game, Kingdon's own conclusion is echoed – it is a combination of three kinds of processes – problems, policies and politics (ibid., p. 17). The discussion began with an analysis of the *problem in the water sector* – shortage of supply. It then concerned the gradual accumulation of knowledge perspectives among *specialists*. And, finally, a large proportion of this study has been devoted to the *political process* which has mediated and manipulated these other processes. The overall picture is not one of 'plain dumb luck' but is certainly somewhat 'free form ... with problems, proposals, and politics floating in and out, joined by fortuitous events or by the appearance on the scene of a skilful entrepreneur who assembles the previous disjointed pieces' (ibid., p. 19). The policy sector has lurched along in episodic fashion – periods of stability interspersed with periods of major change. If this picture is correct, then the search for any *one* model of the policy process is as likely to be as complex and unpredictable as the policy process itself!

REFERENCES

Byatt, I. (1993), 'Economic Regulation: The way ahead', paper presented to *The Economist* Conference on Water Policy, London, 9 November.

Crickhowell, Lord (1993), 'Regulation: Water and Pollution – UK Water Quality Objectives', paper presented to *The Financial Times* Conference on 'The European Water Industry', London, 15 and 16 March.

DOE (1994), *Water Deregulation* (London: DOE).

Dowse, R. and Hughes, J. (1977), 'Sporadic Interventionists', *Political Studies*, vol. 25, pp. 84–92.

Dudley, G. (1994), 'The Next Steps Agencies, Political Salience and the Arm's Length Principle: Barbara Castle at the Ministry of Transport 1965–68', *Public Administration*, vol. 72, pp. 217–38.

Dunleavey, P. (1981), 'Professions and Policy Change: Notes towards a model of ideological corporatism', *Public Administrative Bulletin*, no. 33, pp. 3–16.

Gregory, R. (1971), *The Price of Amenity* (London: Macmillan).

Howarth, D. (1994), 'Implications for the Customer', paper presented to IWEM seminar, Churchill College, Cambridge, 15 March.

Fawell, John (1994), 'Water Quality Issues', paper presented to IWEM seminar, Churchill College, Cambridge, 15 March.

Jordan, G. (1993), *Engineers and Professional Self-Regulation: From the Finniston Committee to the Engineering Council* (Oxford: Clarendon Press).

Jordan, G., Richardson J. and Kimber, R. (1977), 'Outside Committees and Policy-Making: The Central Advisory Water Committee', *Public Administration Bulletin*, vol. 24, pp. 41–58.

Kingdon, J. W. (1984), *Agendas, Alternatives and Public Policies* (Boston: Little, Brown and Company).

Maloney, W. A., Jordan, G. and McLaughlin, A. M. (1994), 'Interest Groups and Public Policy: The insider/outsider model revisited', *Journal of Public Policy*, vol. 14, no. 1, pp. 17–38.

Parker, D. and Penning-Rowsell, E. (1980), *Water Planning in Britain* (London: George Allen and Unwin).

Rhodes, R. A. W. (1988), *Beyond Westminster and Whitehall* (London: Unwin Hyman).

Richardson, J. (1994a), 'Doing Less by Doing More: British Government 1979–93', *West European Politics*, vol. 17, no. 4, pp. 178–97.

Richardson, J. (1994b), 'EU Water Policy-Making: Uncertain agendas, shifting networks and complex coalitions', *Environmental Politics*, vol. 4, no. 4, pp. 141–68.

Richardson, J. (1995), 'Actor Based Models of National and EU Policy-making: Policy networks, epistemic communities and advocacy coalitions', in A. Menon and H. Kassim (eds), *The EU and National and Industrial Policy* (London: Routledge).

Richardson, J. and Jordan, A. G. (1979), *Governing Under Pressure: The Policy Process in a Post-Parliamentary Democracy* (Oxford: Martin Robertson).

Saunders, P. (1983), *The 'Regional State': A Review of the Literature and Agenda for Research*, Working Paper 35, Urban and Regional Studies (Sussex: University of Sussex).

Saunders, P. (1984), *We Can't Afford Democracy Too Much: Findings from a Study of Regional State Institutions in South-East England*, Working Paper 43, Urban and Regional Studies (Sussex: University of Sussex).

Scottish Office (1993), *Water and Sewerage Services in Scotland: Investing for Our Future* (Edinburgh: HMSO).

Smith, M. (1993), *Pressure, Power and Policy: State Autonomy and Policy Networks in Britain and the United States* (London: Harvester Wheatsheaf).

Summerton, N. (1993), 'Water: Paying For Quality', paper presented to *The Economist* Conference on Water Policy, London, 9 November.

APPENDIX 8.1: DOE water deregulation list of consultees in England and Wales.

All Water Companies
Association of County Councils
Association of District Councils
Association of Independent Business
Association of Metropolitan Authorities
British Agrochemicals Association
British Association of Chemical Specialists
British Ceramic Manufacturers Federation
British Chemical Engineering Contractors Association
British Clothing Industry Association
British Coal
British Colour Makers Association
British Dam Society
British Ecological Society
British Gas Plc
British Leather Confederation
British Nuclear Fuels Inc
British Paper and Board Industry Federation
British Petroleum
British Waterways Board
British Wood Preservers Association
Building Research Establishment
Chemical Industries Association
China Clay Association
Ciba Geigy Plc
Confederation of British Industry
Confederation of British Wool and Textile Manufacturers
Council of the Isles of Scilly
Country Landowners Association
Countryside Council for Wales
Electronic Components Industry Federation
English Nature
Environmental Control Consultancy Service
Fertilizer Manufacturers Association
Fibre Building Board Organisation
Fire Extinguishing Trades Association
Friends of the Earth
Greenpeace
Health and Safety Executive
Her Majesty's Inspectorate of Pollution

Institute for European Environmental Policy
ICI Laboratory
Institution of Civil Engineers
Institution of Water and Environmental Management
Lighting Industry Federation
London Boroughs Association
Metal Finishing Association
Motor Manufacturers Association
National Association of the Launderette Industry
National Farmers Union
National Federation of Self-Employed and Small Businesses
National Rivers Authority
North Sea Working Group
Packaging and Industrial Films Association
Paintmakers Association of Great Britain
Photographic Waste Management
Road Haulage Association
Royal Commission on Environmental Pollution
Royal Society for Nature Conservation
Royal Society for the Protection of Birds
States of Guernsey Water Board
Telecommunication Engineering and Manufacturing Association
Textile Finishers Association
The British Photographic Association
The Jersey New Waterworks Company Ltd
UK Nirex Ltd
UK Petroleum Industry Association Ltd
Union of Independent Companies
United Kingdom Agricultural Supply Trade Association Ltd
Water Companies Association
Water Research Centre Plc
Water Services Association
World Wide Fund for Nature
Assembly of Welsh Counties
Council of Welsh Districts
Farmers' Union of Wales

SOURCE: DOE, 1994.

Index

Note: 'n.' after a page reference indicates the number of a note on that page.